What Your Colleagues Are Saying . . .

"Lent and Voigt's *Disciplinary Literacy in Action* is an invigorating tonic for all educators interested in improving instruction and learning. By highlighting the intersectionality of disciplinary learning, literacy acquisition, and professional learning, the authors provide readers with a critical framework to improve instruction that serves as a foundation to prepare students for college, career, and citizenship. Peppered with visual and narrative examples of effective and efficient learning environments, the text can easily be employed to support the professional learning experiences of pre-service, novice, and experienced teachers."

—Enrique A. Puig
Director of the Morgridge International Reading Center
and President-Elect of the Florida Literacy Association

"Disciplinary literacy, argue Lent and Voigt, is a process rather than a product. You don't check disciplinary literacy off your to-do list—you engage in it daily, pursuing its paths toward the long-term flourishing of all of our kids. If there is more important work than this, I can't think of what it is. I can't imagine a better or more capable guide for the deep and practical exploration of this work than *Disciplinary Literacy in Action*. Each page shines with wisdom and research, and every chapter is rooted in what actually goes on in schools. I expect that teachers, teams, and administrators will turn this into a well-worn text."

—Dave Stuart Jr.
Author of *These 6 Things: How to Focus
Your Teaching on What Matters Most*

"*Disciplinary Literacy in Action* is a must-have resource for all middle and high schools. Rich with suggestions, this how-to guide for implementing disciplinary literacy immerses the reader in teacher experiences that paint a picture of how transformative this approach can be. With their call to action that 'it is no longer enough for students to memorize material and call it learning,' this book offers guidance on how to sustain a disciplinary literacy culture within an entire school and district. The authors deliver an open invitation to teachers to engage students in content learning as experts do."

—Kim Tackaberry
Designer of Professional Learning,
Calgary Regional Consortium

"Much of the professional literature has focused on *what* disciplinary literacy entails; this valuable contribution explores *how* it can be implemented in complex school settings. Lent and Voigt articulate a fresh examination of disciplinary literacy through the lens of professional learning communities. They bring an experienced and savvy perspective to the promises and pitfalls of PLCs and especially appreciated are the teacher voices interspersed throughout the discussion that illuminate collective inquiry and meaningful collaboration in action. This book is a welcome resource that will resonate with teachers and school literacy leaders."

—Doug Buehl
Author of *Developing Readers in the Academic Disciplines*

"This book can serve as manual for individuals and school teams who want to gain even more traction and build a culture of literacy learning and leadership. Learning from hours onsite with leaders, teachers, and students who have developed communities of literacy learning, Lent and Voigt share moves that can serve as an apprenticeship for practitioners."

—Lynn Angus Ramos
English Language Arts Curriculum and Instruction Coordinator
DeKalb County School District

"This book provides a balanced, timely, and instructive approach to solving complex problems of practice related to disciplinary literacy. The authors harnesses the power of collaborative dialogue, problem solving, and reflection and provide authentic, discipline-specific guidance to teachers and leaders about the skills required in reading, writing, and thinking in all content areas."

—Vicky Zygouris-Coe
Professor of Education
University of Central Florida

"*Disciplinary Literacy in Action* by ReLeah Cossett Lent and Marsha McCracken Voigt offers both practical advice and keen insights about how to engage learners in authentic and meaningful ways across the disciplines. The authors answer the critical question: How do we ensure our students develop the necessary literacy tools to be successful in discipline-specific ways? With the clarity of real examples, readers will find themselves inspired by a blueprint to ensure all students are well prepared for a world that awaits them."

—Judy Wallis
Literacy Consultant, Author,
and Former Language Arts Director

Disciplinary Literacy
in Action

Dedication

From ReLeah

To Amy Anderson, an unforgettable literacy leader (1967–2017).

From Marsha

To my dad, the storyteller, and my mom, the reader,
for sparking in me a lifelong love of literacy and learning.

Disciplinary Literacy in Action

HOW TO CREATE AND SUSTAIN A SCHOOL-WIDE CULTURE OF DEEP READING, WRITING, AND THINKING

RELEAH COSSETT LENT

MARSHA MCCRACKEN VOIGT

resources.corwin.com/lent-voigtDLinAction

FOR INFORMATION:

Corwin

A SAGE Company

2455 Teller Road

Thousand Oaks, California 91320

(800) 233-9936

www.corwin.com

SAGE Publications Ltd.

1 Oliver's Yard

55 City Road

London EC1Y 1SP

United Kingdom

SAGE Publications India Pvt. Ltd.

B 1/I 1 Mohan Cooperative Industrial Area

Mathura Road, New Delhi 110 044

India

SAGE Publications Asia-Pacific Pte. Ltd.

3 Church Street

#10-04 Samsung Hub

Singapore 049483

Publisher: Lisa Luedeke

Senior Acquisitions Editor: Tori Bachman

Editorial Development Manager: Julie Nemer

Editorial Assistant: Sharon Wu

Production Editor: Amy Schroller

Copy Editor: Deanna Noga

Typesetter: C&M Digitals (P) Ltd.

Proofreader: Lawrence W. Baker

Indexer: Jean Casalegno

Cover and Interior Designer: Rose Storey

Marketing Manager: Brian Grimm

Printed in the United States of America

Library of Congress Cataloging-in-Publication Data

Names: Lent, ReLeah Cossett, author. | Voigt, Marsha, author.

Title: Disciplinary literacy in action : how to create and sustain a school-wide culture of deep reading, writing, and thinking / ReLeah Cossett Lent, ReLeah Lent Educational Consulting, Marsha Voigt.

Description: Thousand Oaks, California : Corwin, a SAGE Company, [2019] | Includes bibliographical references and index.

Identifiers: LCCN 2018022979 | ISBN 9781544317472 (pbk. : alk. paper)

Subjects: LCSH: Language arts—Correlation with content subjects.

Classification: LCC LB1576 .L444 2019 | DDC 372.6—dc23
LC record available at https://lccn.loc.gov/2018022979

This book is printed on acid-free paper.

21 22 10 9 8 7 6 5 4

CONTENTS

Visit the companion website at
resources.corwin.com/lent-voigtDLinAction
for downloadable resources.

LIST OF FIGURES

ACKNOWLEDGMENTS

The book you hold in your hands came about from the efforts of a community of students, teachers, coaches, and administrators who generously shared their expertise and ideas. We incorporated their recommendations, took photos of them in action, and collected student work samples. From California to Florida, Illinois to Texas, South Carolina to Montana, Georgia to Colorado, and all across Alberta, Canada, we asked, we listened, and we learned.

Thank you to the teachers and administrators in Barrington, Illinois, with whom we worked for over four years—and especially to our own professional learning community from Barrington High School: Janet Anderson, Kathleen Duffy, Caroline Milne, and Nick Yeager, teachers you will meet early in this book. We also thank the students, teachers, and principals of Lakeside Middle and Lake Center Middle Schools in California who kindly provided classroom examples in all content areas. A shout-out goes as well to Armando Teves and the faculty at Western Island College, Alberta, who pitched in at the last minute to fill in missing pieces. Union County, South Carolina, one of the first districts to jump headlong into disciplinary literacy, provided assistance as we revised our appendix lists, and we are grateful for its contribution.

As for the Corwin staff, they are simply the best. Lisa Luedeke, the amazing publisher of the literacy line at Corwin, helped shape this book from the very beginning—and our own wonderful editor, Tori Bachman, moved it on into production with gentle prodding and insightful advice. We so appreciate Sharon Wu, senior editorial assistant, for her guidance (and calm presence) during our scary photo crisis as well as the talented production team: Amy Schroller, Jane Martinez, Deanna Noga, Lawrence W. Baker, Jean Casalegno, and Rose Storey. A special thanks goes to Lynn Angus-Ramos, whose comments during an early review of the manuscript as well as during a final read helped us make important revisions.

And a very special hug to our husbands, who founded a sort of lonely hearts club since their wives spent every spare minute immersed in their own disciplinary literacy world, one that, despite their best intentions, they became a part of as well.

Publisher's Acknowledgments

Corwin gratefully acknowledges the contributions of the following reviewers:

Lynn Angus Ramos
English Language Arts Curriculum
    Coordinator
DeKalb County School District
Decatur, GA

Melanie Spence
K–12 Curriculum Coordinator/
    Assistant Principal; Education
    Consultant
Sloan-Hendrix School District
Imboden, AK

Kim Tackaberry
Designer of Professional
    Learning/Educator
Calgary Regional Consortium
Alberta, Canada

Judy Wallis
Literacy Consultant
Sugar Land, TX

ABOUT THE AUTHORS

An international consultant, **ReLeah Cossett Lent** was a secondary teacher before becoming a founding member of a statewide literacy project at the University of Central Florida. The author of eleven professional books—including *This Is Disciplinary Literacy: Reading, Writing, Thinking and Doing . . . Content Area by Content Area*—and past chair of the National Council of Teachers of English's (NCTE) standing Committee Against Censorship, she is also the recipient of the American Library Association's Intellectual Freedom Award, NCTE's Intellectual Freedom Award, the PEN First Amendment Award, and state education awards from Florida and Wisconsin.

Marsha McCracken Voigt has thirty years of experience as a diagnostician and teacher, working with kindergarten through college-age students who struggled with literacy. She now focuses on professional development and serves as a consultant and literacy coach. In their article, "Growing Leaders From Within," she and ReLeah describe their first year of working together to facilitate a truly collaborative literacy learning community.

INTRODUCTION

In education we often come full circle and then go round again. Sometimes, the only things that change are the edu-acronyms that spin a language all their own: RTI, NCLB, AYP, RTT, CCSS, DI, and ESSA, for instance. It can be dizzying. This phenomenon often makes teachers (and many administrators) reluctant to fully engage in "one more thing" that may be viable only for the duration of a political season. Some of those new "things" appear to have been envisioned in places far removed from the classroom, but other times they spark positive change that leads to deeper learning. In both cases, educators often feel frustrated and overwhelmed as they scurry to meet deadlines or comply with mandates that come too fast and too often.

Two such initiatives that have generated widespread change in schools across much of the world, both of which were based on solid research and good intentions, form the foundation of this book: literacy initiatives and professional learning communities (PLCs).

We first look at how a preoccupation with content reading led to the misstep of identifying "every teacher" as "a teacher of reading" and, eventually, "every teacher" as a "teacher of writing" as well. All teachers, especially in middle and high school, were teachers of content, for sure, but asking them to become reading teachers led to frustration and resistance while they struggled to keep their subject front and center.

Then, we look at PLCs, a staple in most schools, if in name only. Instead of harnessing the power of professional learning, these communities, often more committee-like than community-like, frequently functioned mechanically through checklists and predetermined tasks. As districts rolled out plans to implement new literacy initiatives, common sense was often sacrificed to belief in the PLC silver bullet and, as we all know, there are no silver bullets, especially in a field that deals with the messy, unpredictable nature of teaching and learning. What's more, the standardization of processes that inherently rely on customization often lead to less than ideal outcomes.

Lest we mislead you into thinking that we have come up with an absolute solution to such challenging and systemic issues central to both literacy and professional learning, we want to be clear. We are making a case in this book that answers will emerge when we collectively immerse ourselves in questions that cannot be readily answered. Solutions require *time, dialogue*, and *reflection*—factors we are not used to allotting to professional learning—as well as a degree of trust that we aren't used to appropriating. This is not a book of quick fixes because chasing them may well lead to disaster. We argue instead for a reassessment of literacy learning for both teachers and students.

Research, as well as our experience, creates the central message. It *is* possible to reenergize effective teaching in every content area by utilizing literacy skills such as reading, writing, thinking, discussing, inquiring, and evaluating in *discipline-specific* ways. And when teachers work in true professional learning teams where they model the practices they want their students to employ, particularly collaborative inquiry and problem solving, the recursive cycle of change will become powerful and self-sustaining.

Solutions require time, dialogue, and reflection— factors we are not used to allotting to professional learning—as well as a degree of trust that we aren't used to appropriating.

What to Expect From This Book

Disciplinary Literacy in Action follows ReLeah's book on disciplinary literacy (*This Is Disciplinary Literacy: Reading, Writing, Thinking and Doing . . . Content Area by Content Area*, 2016) but differs in significant ways. Here, we first offer a primer on disciplinary literacy and learning, specifically in the first five chapters, while we examine how this shift has moved "across-the-discipline" generic literacy strategies to "within-the-disciplines" learning that utilizes literacy as a tool for content understanding. We ask readers to consider literacy in the 21st century and what it means for students to engage in content learning as experts might. We argue that students must be able to use literacy in flexible ways as they navigate various disciplines and the demands these disciplines make on learners. It is no longer enough for students to memorize material and call it learning or answer questions and call it passing; we call for a shift in how we think about learning overall and learning within the contents in particular.

The research supporting this model as well as the comprehensive "picture" provided in the first half of the book offers a foundation that teachers, coaches, leaders, and administrators might seek to create as they move toward a disciplinary literacy/learning approach, especially as they read the many examples we provide from various content areas.

While not offering as many specific lesson ideas as appeared in *This Is Disciplinary Literacy*, we do provide clear understandings of the skills required for reading, writing, and reasoning (which encompasses speaking and doing) in *all* content areas, devoting one chapter to each of these skills. We know that disciplinary literacy extends to *every* discipline, not just to those classes with the highest number of students enrolled. If we want our students to learn how to move fluidly within and among the disciplines and become self-regulated in knowing how and when to use literacy skills, we must include teachers from courses outside the core math, science, social studies, and English language arts classes. We want this book to be a resource for all content teachers and leaders, including those content areas that sometimes get overlooked. Draper, Broomhead, Jensen, Nokes, and Siebert (2010) remind us that "content instruction cannot be separated from literacy instruction" (p. 33), and if we are

Disciplinary literacy extends to every discipline, not just to those classes with the highest number of students enrolled.

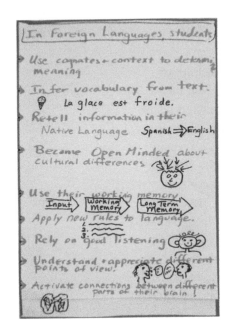

World language teachers brainstorm the literacy skills students need to become successful in their discipline.

seeking systemic, schoolwide change, that means *all* contents. We have, therefore, included examples from art, music, world language, health, and technology throughout the book.

The first two chapters lay the groundwork for subsequent chapters by showing the benefits of a disciplinary literacy approach and how such instruction might look when supported by an authentic professional learning team.

Chapters 3 through 5 focus on the *schoolwide* creation of a disciplinary literacy model as illustrated by the graphic in Figure 0.1.

Chapters 6 through 9 make a transition from informing readers about disciplinary literacy instruction into providing suggestions and logistical underpinnings for how to implement a disciplinary literacy approach not only in individual classrooms but also in entire schools or districts, beginning with the formation of teams, departments, grade levels, or learning communities, as Figure 0.2 illustrates.

Such a shift requires understanding the most effective components of learning communities, such as collaboration, autonomy, supported risk taking, and continuous learning, as well as a consideration of why traditional PLCs have so often failed to meet the goals of professional learning. Specific suggestions and protocols for how to create various disciplinary literacy/learning communities based on your school's unique population are also embedded, as well as ideas for supporting disciplinary literacy leaders, coaches, and administrators.

Finally, in an effort to help teachers expand their literacy offerings, we have included ten appendix items to the companion website, one for each of the major disciplines, as well as one each for health, world language, PE, art, music, and technology as a way to support ongoing dialogue among and within the disciplines. You may download these from http://resources.corwin.com/lent-voigtDLinAction.

Figure 0.1

How to Create a Culture of School-Wide Disciplinary Literacy

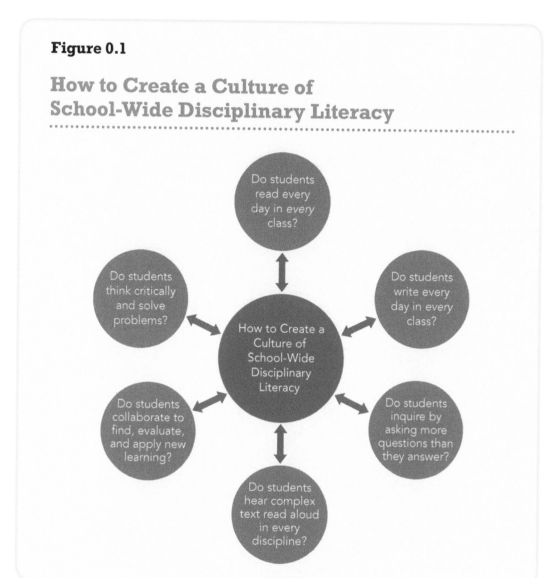

Disciplinary literacy is not just the latest, shiniest thing to hit the educational scene. It is a necessary shift that may well help us synthesize isolated initiatives into a productive whole that can change teachers' lives as well as the lives of their students. A pointed reminder came just the other day when ReLeah was sitting in a café reading through the draft of a chapter of this book when her server, Kaitlyn, asked her what she was doing. ReLeah explained as

Figure 0.2

How to Sustain a Culture of School-Wide Disciplinary Literacy

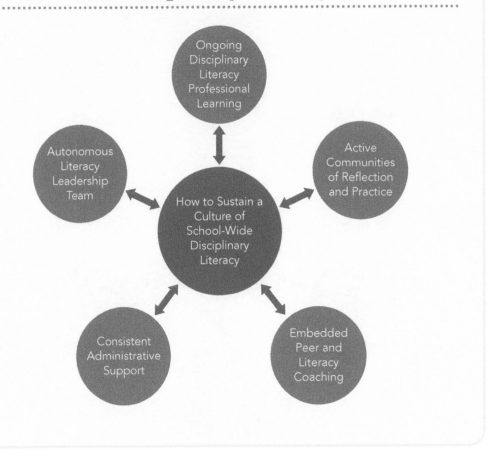

succinctly as possible the concept of disciplinary literacy, trying not to bore the young woman who, she thought, was probably just being polite. Surprisingly, Kaitlyn became extremely interested, saying that she was a junior in college majoring in criminal justice, and she wished she had been taught to read and write in the way that law enforcement officers or legal aids read and wrote. "I did great in English but I wasn't prepared for the technical writing and reading that my instructors expect. We had to do a lot of essays based on literature in high school but not much of the report-type of writing that I have to do now."

ReLeah couldn't help but think of the many ways Kaitlyn might have been better prepared for college and her career if she had been taught to write as experts in various fields write and to actually participate in the literacies of varied subject areas.

It is our hope that this book will enable teachers in every subject area—and leaders in every school—to reimage learning through a disciplinary literacy approach, one that values the knowledge of the teacher as well as the unique literacies that support each content area.

DISCIPLINARY LITERACY AND COLLABORATIVE PROFESSIONAL LEARNING
A PARTNERSHIP THAT WORKS

Professional learning that has shown an impact on student achievement is focused on the content that teachers teach.

Darling-Hammond, Hyler, Gardener, and Espinoza (2017)

The term "disciplinary literacy" may still be unfamiliar to many teachers and administrators. In fact, several educators have told us that when they first heard the words, they thought they had something to do with classroom management—and laughingly said they wished there *were* a literacy for behavioral issues. Others told us that they thought the phrase might be more accurate if "literacy" were replaced with "learning,"

especially in math and science. The 2018 South Carolina Teachers of English Conference theme contained the word "transdisciplinary," and in Alberta, Canada, "interdisciplinary literacy" is an umbrella term for disciplinary literacy because teachers want to emphasize the importance of literacy within disciplines as well as across them. Whatever words we prefer, the time has come to give this approach serious consideration.

The heart of disciplinary literacy is an understanding of the ways in which knowledge is constructed in each content area and how literacy (reading, writing, viewing, reasoning, and communicating) supports that knowledge in discipline-specific ways. An historian, for example, is deeply involved in investigation as he or she seeks to understand events, perspectives, contexts, and language. A scientist, on the other hand, looks at evidence, explanations, hypotheses, new understandings, and data. Mathematicians deal in symbols and abstract ideas, looking for patterns and solutions.

Despite this seemingly forthright explanation, Elizabeth Moje (2008), disciplinary literacy scholar, reminds us that there is no one body of knowledge that can be transferred from teacher to student, the primary mode of instruction in the 20th century: "To learn deeply in a subject area, then, young people need to have access to the ways that conventions of disciplinary knowledge production and communication can be routinely or more explicitly challenged and reshaped" (p. 103). She suggests that we must find "new ways of knowing and practicing" in the content areas, not simply new ways of having students learn "new ideas or bits of information or new texts" (2008, p. 103). We would add that "practicing" in the content areas, what we refer to as *doing*, is virtually impossible when students are sitting silently looking at the backs of one another's heads or copying notes from PowerPoint presentations or lectures.

In short, when content area teachers use literacy as it was intended—as a *discipline-specific* tool to support reading, writing, speaking, and doing—their students become increasingly flexible and independent as they navigate challenging texts and tasks unique to each subject area. Additionally, students learn how to see texts as more than merely conduits for knowledge; texts become windows into how and why knowledge is constructed.

While such a shift does not happen suddenly, especially with an entire faculty, disciplinary literacy instruction offers considerable potential for real change. To realize that change, we must implement this approach differently than we have implemented literacy initiatives in the past, foregoing prepackaged programs, train-the-trainer professional development, or one-size-fits-all approaches. Professional learning about content *and* literacy infused with dialogue, reflection, and collaborative inquiry are the only currencies with which we can purchase the benefits of disciplinary literacy. Going down the same path we have gone in the past with professional development initiatives that aren't embedded or based on continuous learning will cause us to stumble and, inevitably, take us away from our most important destination—increased student learning.

Literacy Initiatives and PLCs: What Went Wrong?

Many teachers, schools, and districts were caught in a movement that was billed as an elixir for comprehension of text: content literacy, a strategy-based approach that emphasized discrete, across-the-board skills such as previewing, activating prior knowledge, annotating, or summarizing, for example. These generic strategies, however, failed to recognize the vast differences among disciplines, their texts, and instructional practices. Worse, they did not emphasize the participation in the disciplines that is necessary for deep content comprehension. (See page 42 in Chapter 2 for an example of how a generic strategy was adapted specifically for math and social studies.)

We now know that despite all the work that went into the reading and content strategies initiative, adolescents' literacy skills did not show significant improvement over a period of years, despite their moderate effect on comprehension (Jacobs, 2008). The National Assessment of Educational Progress (n.d.), for example, reported that in 2015, 12th-grade students had an average score of 287 on the reading scale of 0 to 500. This was not significantly different from the average score in 2013, but it was lower in comparison to the 1992 assessment. The

Learning, for teachers as well as for students, should be joyful, infused with passion and energy.

latest Program for International Student Assessment (PISA) scores also reflect the United States' stagnant performance in reading, ranking behind more than twenty countries, including the top-ranked Singapore, Hong Kong, Canada, and Finland (National Center for Education Statistics, n.d.).

As for professional learning communities (PLCs), vehicles put in place to drive the literacy movement, something was amiss there as well, despite strong evidence of their potential effectiveness (DuFour & Reeves, 2015). The formulaic standardization of PLCs left little room for authentic, recursive professional literacy learning, and often teachers weren't given opportunities to wrestle with and find solutions to the teaching and learning challenges they faced in their own classrooms and schools. As PLCs often devolved into points-based professional development reliant on check-off lists, mandated tasks, and an overriding focus on "interpreting the data," both the enthusiasm for and the effectiveness of PLCs waned. Now, even the mention of PLCs will elicit groans from many of the teachers with whom we work. Learning, for teachers as well as for students, should be joyful, infused with passion and energy, sustained through the "flow" of motivation that results when people are engaged in meaningful, though often challenging work.

Looking at student work samples together is one way math teachers make decisions about the pace of their lessons.

As we mentioned in the introduction, we are not claiming to have found the panacea for literacy learning. What we are arguing, however, is that a reasonable approach to professional learning exists if teachers collaborate within autonomous communities focused on the literacies of their disciplines. To set the stage, consider how you might respond to the questions in Figure 1.1, keeping in mind that simple answers to complex questions often abort deep thinking.

Figure 1.1

Questions That Spur Collaborative Disciplinary Literacy Thinking

- What counts as knowledge in a specific discipline?

- What count as texts in a specific discipline?

- How can we shift our view of literacy teaching and learning so that it is situated as a tool within the disciplines instead of as an add-on to the disciplines?

- To what extent do we trust and value teachers' expertise in their own content? If teacher knowledge is not where it should be, how can we help increase it?

- Are we willing to actively work toward collective efficacy (the collective perception on the part of teachers that they can make an educational difference to their students), the *number one* indicator that affects student learning, according to John Hattie's (2016) research?

- Are we willing and do we have the resources to invest in the time-consuming work of genuine literacy professional learning?

- Do we have the courage to reduce reliance on programs, packaged curricula, and inflexible pacing guides that demand standardization and fidelity instead of differentiation and supported risk taking?

Collaborative Disciplinary Literacy Learning: A Story of Success

We have been extremely fortunate to have been able to grapple with the questions in Figure 1.1 in our work together, specifically in one school district, but also through ReLeah's experiences in schools and districts internationally. When Marsha, a literacy coach in Barrington, Illinois, a suburb outside of Chicago, met with administrators to discuss what they might do to help their population of struggling learners, she argued persuasively for an approach based on collaborative learning, planning, implementation and reflection—a model supported by numerous studies (Darling-Hammond, Wei, Andree, Richardson, & Orphanos, 2009). She believed that when teachers were provided autonomy along with strong disciplinary literacy learning, the result would show positive change in the school culture as well as in student learning. Her insistence on a model that went beyond a menu of literacy strategies, something that had been tried with limited success in the past, along with a belief in the value of teachers' content area expertise, led her to find ReLeah, a consultant and author of several books and articles on literacy and leadership.

The partnership created a literacy initiative that exceeded everyone's expectations. With the full support of school and district administrators, we began with a cohort of twenty high school teachers from various disciplines. The plan was to have four full-day workshops throughout the year with ReLeah bringing new research and practices customized to address teachers' challenges and inquiries, all embedded in a disciplinary literacy approach. Marsha provided individualized coaching and support in between ReLeah's visits. The first full day was a bit rocky, with several teachers openly opposed to "one more thing" and a few resistant to the idea of anything at all having to do with literacy, concerns rather common among secondary educators. They had been *trained* on literacy strategies, they insisted; furthermore, they needed to get back to covering their curriculum.

By the end of that first workshop, we had convinced teachers to try something new, a mantra that drove our work for many years thereafter. Marsha, the consummate note taker, kept a list of any

practices, activities, or suggestions modeled by ReLeah and practiced by teachers as well as any ideas they brought to the table. She created a sort of newsletter (see pages 167–169) that reminded teachers of the new learning that occurred in the workshops and encouraged them to refer back to it when working in their classrooms. All teachers were asked to try at least one "something new" and bring to the next workshop student work samples, observational notes, and any experiences related to a new practice, either negative or positive, that they wanted to share with

Teachers in our first cohort from the world language department share ideas about disciplinary literacy techniques they can adapt in their classes.

the group. After each of ReLeah's workshops, Marsha met with teachers either in small groups or individually, offering support, resources, and suggestions. She shared teachers' comments or struggles with ReLeah so that, together, they could create a workshop that was customized to teachers' needs.

Soon a more organic agenda began to supplement the one we had originally created for the workshops. At the beginning of each session, for example, we allowed plenty of time for cohort members to discuss what they had tried since the last meeting, leaving time for exploring what worked and what didn't, always keeping in the forefront the idea that generic strategies simply weren't enough to support students with the challenging texts and complex tasks they were now expected to tackle. As teachers began to adapt these new suggestions to their own content, they gained confidence in experimenting with and utilizing literacy as tools to reach their students. Their sharing became one of the most valuable parts of the workshop because it tapped into those intangible components that are so often neglected when following a preset model of professional learning: relationship building, collective efficacy, and shared understandings of content literacy. Soon teachers began helping each other find commonalities and differences in their disciplines, a shift that would eventually transfer to classrooms and support students in becoming more flexible learners.

As teachers began to adapt these new suggestions to their own content, they gained confidence in experimenting with and utilizing literacy as a tool to reach their students.

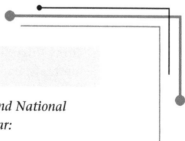

Listening In

Listening in to Katherine Keeler, a veteran social studies (and National Board Certified) teacher, who joined a cohort the second year:

"You would think after 22 years I would feel confident about my practice. It has been said that a great teacher never feels like they've quite gotten it right—the best teachers reflect and adjust and innovate. So maybe I'm in good company. It used to be simple to assign students a chapter reading in their textbook. We no longer use textbooks. Now with the influx of online materials available in many forms (news, blogs, editorials, podcasts, e-books, websites), it is difficult to cull through what is true, necessary, or effective for my students. As an 'old dog' I've done my best to keep up with the tech innovations at my disposal. Technology is a 'foreign language' for many veteran teachers like me. My younger colleagues have grown up learning through technology as part of their 'native tongue.'

"Values and priorities have also changed in the last few decades since I started teaching social studies. The topics we covered 22 years ago and our approaches were very different.

"Students learn differently now. I learned to teach in the 1990s. I can't teach with the same old bag of tricks that I used when teaching their parents' generation. Not only have the methods changed but so has the product. Now, much more is left to a student's interpretation. Students are not given facts to memorize. We ask them to inquire and to reason to find the answer. How can I possibly teach the same old way? Lecture-style teaching has gone the way of chalk and the blackboard. Collaborative grouping and flipped classrooms are more the norm.

"I have always been game for attending workshops and gaining new ideas for my 'toolbox.' At these meetings, I have felt invigorated and inspired working alongside my younger colleagues, but their ready use of blogging, tweeting, posting, and other forms of teaching writing and reading was intimidating and daunting. No veteran teacher wants to feel like she has gone back to her first day of undergrad teacher college. In addition to the number of resources at my fingertips, there were an overwhelming number of strategies, methods, and outlets in which to disburse that information. Where does one begin? And now I was starting to hear about this new framework called disciplinary literacy. Once again I felt like a freshman and my younger colleagues were in the graduate program.

"Nevertheless, I joined a disciplinary literacy cohort in which teachers learned how to use literacy in ways that supported their content. We shared ideas in a collaborative way: A music teacher in the group helped me to rework a lesson on the Civil War. A teaching strategy shared by a world language teacher fit in beautifully with my unit on the Old West. We discussed ideas that incorporated different media types—cartoons, infographics, videos, blogs. I was able to see value and practical uses for a variety of mediums. That successful collaboration between traditional teaching methods and modern innovative techniques requires taking risks, having faith in your peers, and keeping an open mind.

"Slowly and surely they talked me away from the cliff's edge by showing me ways to incorporate these technological innovations. I found myself sharing my tried and true old-school methods and

Katherine Keeler works with one of her students as he looks for articles about the economic forces of American life.

discovered that many of them still have merit. Eventually we morphed the two together into truly effective teaching and learning."

We were also excited to discover that many teachers were leaders in hiding who came out of the shadows when opportunities arose to show others in their departments how their teaching had changed through their participation in the cohort. Within a year, individuals and partners in this group began presenting at conferences, writing journal articles, and creating impressive programs such as schoolwide summer reading initiatives. Traditional, whole-class, lecture-style teaching, so common in high school classrooms, diminished in cohort teachers' classes when their students began to participate in the content as experts in the field might, often through discussions, seminars, and inquiry projects. What's more, discipline-specific reading and writing were increasing in all classes, not only in those of cohort members.

We were also excited to discover that many teachers were leaders in hiding.

The following year, another cohort was added, this time with the inclusion of the library information teachers and technology coaches, all of whom turned out to be invaluable as the groups worked purposefully toward creating a culture of literacy throughout the school. Principal Steve McWilliams's overt support and encouragement lent credibility to the notion that literacy was essential in all subjects, saying that he wanted to "build a sheltered area for literacy and invest in it so it would grow roots." The cohorts did, indeed, become a shelter, not only for literacy growth but also for teachers to engage in collaboration, exploration, reflection, and new learning. For more information on how to form cohorts such as these, see Chapter 6.

Soon a middle school cohort was formed with teachers eager to hone their literacy skills through lessons based on disciplinary literacy practices. One social studies/ELA (English language arts) teacher who joined the middle school cohort, for example, discovered that his colleagues respected his love of reading so much that they began asking him for books their students might like. He is now a favorite presenter at reading conferences, has a serious blog following, and conducts interviews with famous young adult authors. The research on teacher efficacy was exemplified through him and others like him who stepped forward to utilize their talents in a variety of ways.

At the end of four years, we were working with eight cohorts of cross-curricular teachers who made significant changes throughout their schools by sharing and modeling disciplinary literacy practices, especially in having students *do* the work of the discipline rather than merely reading about it.

Eventually, a few teachers from different disciplines began to informally create a literacy leadership team in the high school, something we had advocated from the beginning, but which had not been put in place by the administration. (Read more about how to form a literacy leadership team in Chapter 9, pages 258–259.) You will hear the voices of these teachers throughout this book; they are now an important part of our own learning community, one that enriches our work as well as the work of their colleagues through their insights, classroom experiences, and honest feedback.

Meet Our Disciplinary Literacy Learning Community

Nick Yeager, an English teacher and counselor, was one of the first to "try something new," when he incorporated inquiry and autonomy into his unit on *Romeo and Juliet*, one that he had previously taught in a rather traditional manner. ReLeah asked him to write about this lesson, and it appears in *Common Core CPR: What About Adolescents Who Struggle . . . or Just Don't Care* (Lent & Gilmore, 2013, pp. 156–157). The year following the creation of the first cohort, Nick was approached to create a credit make-up class for students in danger of failing or dropping out, and it ended up being a mecca of reading. Students quickly completed their credits so they could devote themselves to reading the many books that populate Nick's room. His students' successes are truly remarkable and have led to almost all students graduating and some even going on to college.

Nick asks open-ended questions to encourage this student to express his thinking and explore alternative methods. Finding a balance between supportive scaffolding while also encouraging risk taking is something Nick consciously works toward every day.

Kathleen Duffy, a first-year social studies teacher, was also recommended by her principal to join the first cohort. Initially, she appeared reluctant to contribute, but at the end of four years Kathleen was one of its strongest members, advocating for students' active participation in learning and infusing a strong component of project-based learning and critical literacy in all her courses as a way of engaging students in social justice. Her most recent disciplinary endeavor is the creation of a gender studies class where students learn as apprentices in the field, with Kathleen as their coach and mentor.

Janet Anderson, a library information teacher, became an enthusiastic member of each of the high school cohorts, offering suggestions as teachers built multi-modal text sets or asked her for just the right book to engage their most reluctant reader. She began spending more time in classrooms partnering with teachers and became especially valuable in terms of technology as teachers moved from single "textbooks" to a variety of

Kathleen works one-on-one with a student who is researching a topic for a project.

digital resources. Janet created and maintained a Google Community where cohort teachers could share documents and ideas during and in between workshops. Perhaps most important, she helped teachers as well as students find or return to the joy of reading.

Janet offers suggestions to a student who hopes to find that perfect book for his next read.

Caroline Milne, science teacher and ardent supporter of active learning, was fortunate to be a member of a department that valued the *doing* that is a hallmark of disciplinary literacy. She began presenting at science conferences and encouraged others to join her. Quickly recognizing the connection between disciplinary literacy and the Next Generation Science Standards, she was instrumental in melding the two together in practical ways, acting as a peer coach for her colleagues. Her department head supported her endeavors and also provided the autonomy for teachers to engage in risk taking as they incorporated scientific literacy into lessons. Not surprisingly, this department's cohesion led to a type of collaboration that increased collective efficacy and, thus, student learning.

Caroline uses a device that replicates a smoker's lung so a student can experience the breathing challenges felt by individuals with limited lung capacity.

This leadership team has taken on the work of disciplinary literacy within the school, as you will see in later chapters. For now, however, we simply want you to be aware of the members of the team so you will recognize them as they drift in and out of the pages that follow.

Benefits of Collaborative Disciplinary Literacy Professional Learning

A move toward professional learning based on disciplinary literacy offers immediate as well as long-term benefits to students, teachers, and the school overall. Because the approach isn't standardized or prescriptive, teachers are responsible for adapting literacy learning to their content in ways that best serve their teaching goals, curriculum, and students. This authentic accountability engenders efficacy, intrinsic motivation, creativity, and increased content knowledge with a natural emphasis on civic responsibility—all of which ultimately benefits students.

Quoteworthy

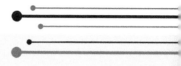

"Several studies, which have been conducted across multiple content areas, have demonstrated that content area literacy instruction can lead to positive outcomes for diverse students on measurements of content knowledge and literacy achievement" (International Literacy Association, 2017).

INCREASED INDIVIDUAL AND COLLECTIVE EFFICACY

Perhaps the most compelling reason to introduce collaborative disciplinary literacy learning is because of its potential to increase collective teacher efficacy, the *number one factor that affects student learning* (Hattie, 2016). We understand collective efficacy well because we have been privy to its power through cohorts of teachers working together to create and sustain disciplinary literacy practices. We refer to this concept throughout the book, so let's make sure we have a working definition: "Collective teacher efficacy refers to the collective perception that teachers in a given school make an educational difference to their students" (Tschannen-Moran & Barr, 2004).

We found Jenni Donohoo's book *Collective Efficacy: How Educators' Beliefs Impact Student Learning* (2017) to be a comprehensive and practical guide for understanding this phenomenon. Donohoo makes clear its importance on the first page of her book when she writes,

> When teachers share that belief [that they can make an educational difference to their students beyond the impact of their homes and communities], it outranks *every other factor* in regard to impacting student achievement including socioeconomic status, prior achievement, home environment, and parental involvement. (p. 1, emphasis in original)

Because disciplinary literacy honors the expertise of teachers and asks for their participation instead of their compliance, it infuses self-efficacy into the mix, frequently "unleashing" the willingness of teachers to try new practices and set higher goals for students, with some making remarkable contributions to the field. We were surprised to find how many teachers

Because disciplinary literacy honors the expertise of teachers and asks for their participation instead of their compliance, it infuses self-efficacy into the mix, frequently "unleashing" the willingness of teachers to try new practices and set higher goals for students.

in our cohorts demonstrated these characteristics soon after joining. Some teachers discovered a new area of expertise in the classroom, and in other cases teachers developed the confidence to act on a leadership skill that had been previously untapped.

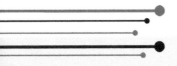

Quoteworthy

"Ashton and Webb (1986) found that when collective efficacy is high, teachers are less critical of students who make mistakes and work longer with students who have difficulty" (Donohoo, 2007, p. 15).

As we noted earlier, many PLCs have not managed to make significant transformations in student learning. There are various reasons for this lack of success, but what we have found is that the efficacy piece is often missing. In fact, PLCs can actually diminish collective efficacy when members of a PLC have little autonomy or teachers perceive that their tasks are a waste of time. Conversely, teams engaged in disciplinary literacy learning tend to gain both individual and collective efficacy, especially when they meet for extended periods of time to reflect on lessons, share ideas, and discuss the challenges and progress they have made with students. Teachers who gain such efficacy are more flexible regarding change and more willing to try new instructional approaches in their classes, a form of encouraged risk taking.

Listening In

Listening in to Scott Sheib, high school health teacher:

"I had been teaching health for seventeen years and felt satisfied that I had developed a curriculum that did a good job of teaching kids the important content of the health curriculum, at least as much as I could accomplish in a one-semester class. There was little time for reading and writing, however, because I felt pressured to cover a great deal of content in a short amount of time. After spending a year with my disciplinary literacy cohort, my entire philosophy changed. I began to incorporate reading and writing activities related to health as a way for students to learn more deeply.

Probably the biggest change was when I brought in young adult novels related to health issues such as *Out of My Mind* [a fictional story of a girl who has cerebral palsy and is unable to speak] by Sharon Draper (2010). I never would have made this shift had it not been for the encouragement from my cohort. I was completely outside my comfort zone, but everyone was experimenting with new approaches or modifying old strategies, and it was contagious. With their support, I had the confidence to try something I had never tried before. It really paid off."

For the Curious

HOW MUCH DOES EFFICACY REALLY MATTER?

Research cited by Donohoo in *Collective Efficacy: How Educators' Beliefs Impact Student Learning* (2017, p. 15) show students of teachers with high efficacy

- enjoy higher achievement,
- are better able to build a strong sense of academic efficacy,
- set more challenging goals, and
- have stronger commitments to accomplish and maintain goals.

A disciplinary literacy method is a natural lightning rod for teachers to coalesce around, one that doesn't set up coerced communities for "professional development" purposes. What's more, once teachers begin collectively solving problems within their discipline, they become enthusiastic about employing these methods because they see increased student engagement. Teams of teachers who have the autonomy to pursue learning relevant to their content have a common purpose and interest,

Photo by Marcia Wingfield.

McNair High School in DeKalb County, Georgia, created a strong literacy learning community with a focus on literacy within the content areas. The team's collective efficacy spilled over onto their students. Here, students demonstrate how their own sense of confidence in literacy has increased due to the creation of a pervasive culture of reading and writing at the school.

which we have found to be a steadfast and enduring foundation for collective efficacy.

INCREASED TEACHER CONTENT KNOWLEDGE

In an article on ways to respond to the disciplinary literacy needs of students, Wilder and Herro (2016) write,

> As coaches and teachers interact around pressing questions of practice, they inevitably construct expertise and uncertainty, collectively problem solve and develop situation identities unique to the collaborative context. In the study, collaboration was viewed as a process of co-constructing knowledge about disciplinary practices related to disciplinary literacy, teaching and students. (p. 541)

Our experience supports the results of this study. Not only did teachers in our cohorts increase their knowledge by digging more deeply into their content as they looked at ways to use literacy, but they also discussed in more depth teaching practices and how they might differentiate content for the varied needs of their students.

The increase in teacher knowledge is especially apparent when teachers work in content-area groups on a specific challenge or area of improvement. ReLeah is currently working with a high school English department as they implement reading and writing workshops. While the teachers are all competent, experienced teachers, she found that their knowledge of reading and writing skills increased dramatically as they began to explore how to facilitate student conferences, provide feedback, create book clubs, utilize engaging practices for mini-lessons, and implement differentiated writing instruction. Their collaborative learning not only led to collective efficacy but also significantly increased their content knowledge.

INCREASED MOTIVATION AND ENGAGEMENT

Draper and Seibert's (2010) explanation of disciplinary literacy taps into the active *doing* that is often characteristic of disciplinary literacy instruction,

Teachers in disciplinary groups read a subject-area article in preparation for engaging in a collaborative activity that they can adapt for classroom use.

the ability to negotiate (e.g., read, view, listen, taste, smell, critique) and create (e.g., write, produce, sing, act, speak) texts in discipline-appropriate ways or in ways that other members of the discipline (e.g., mathematicians, historians, artists) would recognize as "correct" or "viable." (p. 30, as cited in Brozo, Moorman, Meyer, & Stewart, 2013)

Listening In

Listening in on middle school teachers who increased content knowledge while engaging in disciplinary literacy:

- A group of ELA teachers felt strongly about having time for independent reading during the school day. They researched the benefits of free choice reading and best practices for implementation and then created a bulletin with research, activities, and a structure for administrators and teachers. Their plans led to the development of a "Literacy Café" for schoolwide independent reading once a week.

- Content teachers became excited about using picture books to build subject background knowledge and vocabulary. They developed a spreadsheet of picture books complete with lesson ideas, concepts to highlight, and notes from teachers. Others contributed to this resource throughout the year.

- Several math teachers wanted to explore ways of helping students learn from their mistakes. They worked with the technology coach to set up a poster walk. Students prepared a correct and incorrect version of solving a problem with QR codes that students could access for the correct answer.

- Teachers organized professional book study groups to build their content knowledge regarding inquiry projects, digital texts, and blended learning. Mary Stec, technology coach, commented, "Although each of the book studies has been structured a bit differently, overall, all teachers have achieved the goal of reflecting on their practice, gaining additional support for implementation of new strategies from colleagues, and instilling a culture of learning within the content-areas." (See Chapter 9, Figure 9.5 for a sample of a professional Book Study Guide.)

As we visited the classrooms of teachers in our cohorts, we saw lessons where students were motivated to read challenging texts in a seminar, utilize technology to interact with a class in another state, solve "real-world" problems such as how to eliminate the Zika virus, interview a panel of characters (their classmates) from a novel, debate the cultural influences on a piece of blues music, and work in partners to give each other feedback about their written analysis of a football game. Not only was the engagement in these classes palpable, but students were eager to talk about their learning when we asked them.

The physical environment of this world language classroom mirrors students' engagement in the content. After students reviewed definitions of words in their groups, their teacher led them in a vocabulary activity to reinforce the correct pronunciation of targeted words.

The participation in the disciplines, this *doing*, moves teachers from front and center and shines the light on students as they become immersed in the content work. That doesn't always mean that students are up and physically active, of course. They may be deeply involved in figuring out how a mathematical principle can be applied in architecture or how a new finding in science—such as the *Science News* article that shows dogs having more brain neurons than cats—can be tested through behaviors.

Listening In

Listening in on Ginger Montgomery's ecology class as students become fully engaged in scientific learning:

"During the first week of the semester, I gave my students a copy of the Tennessee Ecology Standards and asked them to go online and choose several activities they would like to complete that meet state standards. I also gave them a stack of ideas that I had already pulled, including one about a raptor adoption. They wrote out their activities and topics on paper, and we then placed all the papers on two tables in the room. Students went from idea to idea, voting with a check or a minus to indicate their interest in a topic. Based on their ideas, I developed a semester-long pacing guide that incorporated their topics. It is hard to be unengaged in a class that you help construct.

"They chose to adopt a raptor from the local raptor center in Maryville, Tennessee. I went online and printed off a list of birds that they had available for sponsorship. Each team of three or four students had to research every bird option, if possible pulling up actual footage of the bird. It was amazing what all they were able to find online—not only about the species but also the individual bird. After two days of research, they had to choose a bird to promote.

"Each team made 'vote for' posters listing the qualities of their bird choice and presented to the class why their bird was the best for our class to adopt. It was a close race between a barn owl and a red eastern screech owl. In the end, the red eastern screech owl won. Edie was our bird!

An owl from The Smokey Mountain Raptor Center visits a high school ecology class.

"We sat down with the school calendar and made a list of possible dates for our bird visit. Once the date was set, we began discussing ways to fund our adoption. We opted for a 'Hat Day' to earn our money. A hat day works like this: Students pay two dollars for a sticker that allows them to wear a hat all day inside the school.

"Two days before our owl visit (Monday and Tuesday) we began looking at the food web of an eastern screech owl. Each student created a food web poster that represented what an eastern screech owl would eat in East Tennessee.

"The owl (Edie) that we chose ended up being unable to visit due to medical issues, so two other owls came to our class instead. The Smoky Mountain Raptor Center representative did a great hour-long presentation about raptors, focusing on owls. We also purchased owl pellets for class dissection the next day.

"On the day after the owl visit, I asked the kids to use the dry erase markers to make a list on the table of what they thought the owl pellets we had purchased from the raptor center would have in them, given their understanding of owl food webs. They were allowed to walk outside into the hall to look at the webs they had drawn at the beginning of the week.

"We then watched a sci.spot video clip about what owl pellets are and a YouTube clip of an owl hacking up a pellet (kids love that). We dissected the pellets and then checked off or circled the organisms we had on our tabletop list. Students were excited to see that they had chosen organisms that showed up in their pellets.

"Our Hat Day was a success! We raised enough money to cover Edie's adoption, pay for our pellets, and send a little extra just because! If I had time I would have asked the students to each write down something from the presentation that they were interested in, such as why red screech owls and grey screech owls seem to live in certain areas, or ways to prevent owl poisoning due to mouse poison. We would have then taken a few days to dive deeper into the topics they had chosen. I could have extended this activity into several different avenues, but my time was up. We had to move on to Triops and Dam Construction.

"This is an important point: This year we had NO budget for the science department. This activity was completed with basic classroom supplies and a small school fundraiser. We used old calendar backs for our posters and many of our markers and crayons are donated from my mom's first-grade classroom leftovers. We do have a set of second generation iPads, but they have not been updated in over 200 weeks, and we have to share them with other classrooms. It is not about funding; it is about using what you have, where you are, and most of all, engaging the students in real scientific learning."

INCREASED CIVIC UNDERSTANDING AND ACTION

One important aspect of disciplinary literacy is its tendency to motivate students toward becoming active participants as members of a democratic society because it encourages students to challenge and question texts, norms, and traditional understandings, just as experts do when engaged in their work. Jacobs (2008, citing Freire, 1998) writes about how, by capitalizing on literacy skills and processes, teachers are helping their students "become independent learners who are able to comprehend the 'world' as well as the 'word' of their disciplines."

Kathleen, our social studies team member, put into practice this aspect of disciplinary literacy *doing* by helping her students become agents of change through projects that involve civic engagement. She describes how initial learning in social studies supported their "construction" of new knowledge that then led to action that made a real difference in their school and community:

> I designed and taught a new class called gender studies. In my disciplinary literacy professional learning community we had

One important aspect of disciplinary literacy is its tendency to motivate students toward becoming active participants as members of a democratic society because it encourages students to challenge and question texts, norms, and traditional understandings.

Initiatives that utilize the expertise of content teachers within learning communities where they are afforded autonomy and time to collaborate have the best chance of gaining the benefits intrinsic in disciplinary literacy instruction.

been experimenting with project and problem-based learning and I knew, with this approach, my students' learning would increase dramatically, going far beyond memorization for a test. At the beginning of each unit, I built students' background knowledge through lectures, readings of primary and secondary sources, guest speakers, excerpts from historical fiction and nonfiction, videos, and documentaries. This work is essential in laying the groundwork of content knowledge so students' curiosity and creativity can be ignited. Once they were exposed to the basics, students continued to learn in a hands-on manner through a variety of mediums of their own choosing. I am always amazed with the projects they pursue and how their understanding of the curriculum guides their actions.

Some of the projects Kathleen's students chose included

- Advocating for equality in girls' lacrosse by amending rules and altering the sexist uniform. The students petitioned online, in a lacrosse circle, and in phone meetings with state representatives of the athletics association. Due to this project, the high school girls' lacrosse team will be wearing shorts, not skirts, next season.

- Promoting safety and consent in teenage behavior by pushing the administration to install a camera in a known blind spot in the school. One student, who had witnessed an incident of sexual harassment at this spot spoke to the staff about the issue. Another engaged the student National Organization of Women Club to spread awareness and raise funds to buy a camera. Still another student involved the school board, which led to the school's purchase and installation of the security camera.

- Conducting a cross-generation interview and script with a mother and grandmother about being a girl and woman in various time periods.

- Organizing a 5K fun run/walk to raise money for WINGS, an organization that helps women and children who have been assaulted. This was not even done for credit, but was completed during the summer before this student left for college.

One might think this advantage would more readily be seen in social studies than in other subjects, but every subject has the potential of propelling a student's ability to be prepared to lead a successful life in an innovative and changing world. We found students engaged in such critical thinking in science regarding new policies on climate change or protection of endangered species, in English as students evaluated opinion pieces and then wrote their own, and in subject areas such as health when considering governmental oversight of sugar in children's cereal, for example. In Chapter 8, we describe a project that resulted from English teachers' work with disciplinary literacy where students raised money to send to countries struggling with water issues after critically reading *A Long Walk to Water* (Park, 2011).

Photo by Kathleen Duffy

Students from Kathleen's Gender Studies class, motivated by class readings and discussions, organize a 5K walk to raise money for women and children who have been victims of assault.

Perhaps these advantages point to why there is a call for literacy experts to assist content teachers in building disciplinary literacy programs rather than focusing professional learning on generic literacy practices and strategies (Moje, 2008). As we explore in later chapters, initiatives that utilize the expertise of content teachers within learning communities where they are afforded autonomy and time to collaborate have the best chance of gaining the benefits intrinsic in disciplinary literacy instruction.

Fostering Disciplinary Literacy Dialogue

1. To what extent do the teachers in your team or school have difficulty moving from a model that transfers knowledge to a new paradigm that emphasizes students participating in the work of the discipline? How can you facilitate this move?

2. On pages 15–17, Katherine Keeler talks about feeling left behind because of the way technology is used by those considered "natives" to digital ways, yet she discovered that she has much to contribute. How can disciplinary literacy instruction unite technology "natives" and "immigrants" in ways that will benefit students?

3. Consider what a disciplinary literacy leadership team in your school might look like.

   - What role would it play?
   - Who might be on this team?
   - What challenges do you see in the implementation of such a team?
   - How might you address those challenges?

   See pages 258–259 for information on how to create a disciplinary literacy leadership team.

4. In looking over the advantages of a disciplinary literacy approach, which do you consider most pressing in your school? Why?

   - increased individual and teacher collective efficacy
   - increased teacher content knowledge
   - increased motivation and engagement
   - increased civic action and understanding

Notes:

Resources for Continued Learning

ASCD. (2017, February). Educational leadership: Literacy in every classroom. *ASCD, 74*(5).

Donohoo, J. (2017). *Collective efficacy: How educators' beliefs impact student learning.* Thousand Oaks, CA: Corwin.

National Council of Teachers of English. (2007). "Adolescent literacy: A policy research brief." Washington, DC: Author. Retrieved from http://www.ncte.org/library/NCTEFiles/Resources/Positions/Chron0907ResearchBrief.pdf?_ga=2.84598617.1335543564.1525721188-1198754886.1525721188

Shanahan. T., & Shanahan, C. (2015). Disciplinary comes to middle school. *Voices From the Middle, 22*(3), 10–13.

2

UNLOCKING DISCIPLINARY LITERACY

Disciplinary literacy instruction does not seek to make experts of teenage students. Rather, disciplinary literacy instruction begins to help students to read, write, and think in ways that are aligned with experts in the field.

Rainey and Moje (2012)

In little over twenty years the meaning of the word "literacy" has changed so much that it may be unrecognizable even to those who were once immersed in its study. Not so long ago, literacy was simply the antidote to "illiteracy", often with the words "adult" or "family" preceding it to denote tutoring or second language reading programs. Today, the multi-literacies that are a part of our everyday lives (digital literacy, financial literacy, collaborative literacy, media literacy, and mathematical literacy, for example) make simple reading and writing seem like stone-age skills. Many teachers are still scrambling to keep up with students whose out-of-school literacies and technological prowess seem more inborn than learned. They face a challenging task: How to keep literacy relevant and engaging day after day. This task is much less daunting, however, when literacy is used as a tool for active content-area learning.

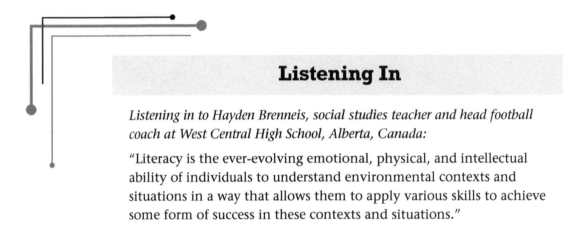

Listening In

Listening in to Hayden Brenneis, social studies teacher and head football coach at West Central High School, Alberta, Canada:

"Literacy is the ever-evolving emotional, physical, and intellectual ability of individuals to understand environmental contexts and situations in a way that allows them to apply various skills to achieve some form of success in these contexts and situations."

What Is Literacy in the 21st Century?

Let's take a look at some of the more common 21st-century literacies and how they seamlessly interconnect with disciplinary literacy:

- **Media literacy** may be the hottest literacy on the classroom burner today thanks to the profusion of "fake news." The National Council of Social Studies (2016) released a position statement on media literacy, in part because of the "deluge of unfiltered information that streams through the Internet," social media, and other sources. The council asks teachers to help students analyze and evaluate information while calling for a renewed focus on critical thinking skills that include asking questions, comparing competing claims, assessing credibility, and reflecting on one's own process of reasoning (p. 183). A disciplinary literacy approach encourages teachers to incorporate such skills in content-specific ways.

- **Critical literacy**, similar in ways to media literacy, requires that students recognize literacy as a tool for social action "understanding the ways in which language and literacy are used to accomplish social ends" (Dozier, Johnston, & Rogers, 2006). Students who have developed critical literacy skills are able to interpret embedded messages in all sorts of texts (i.e., print, television, songs, novels, movies), especially those of social or political relevance, as well as texts with undertones of discrimination, sexism, or racism. They also are able to reflect on and discuss what those messages send about power, inequality, and injustice, for example. This approach asks readers, viewers, and listeners to assume a critical or questioning stance, always on the lookout for underlying attitudes or inequalities. This literacy has less to do with traditional reading skills than with a reader's ability to infer the author or creator's intentional or unintentional bias. One of the tenets of disciplinary literacy is that it encourages questioning, challenging, and understanding in ways that go beyond superficial content knowledge.

One of the tenets of disciplinary literacy is that it encourages questioning, challenging, and understanding in ways that go beyond superficial content knowledge.

- **Visual literacy** targets the ability to "read" visual images—that is, to interpret, evaluate, and understand the creator's subtle, symbolic, or obvious meaning. Just as with media literacy, students who are proficient in visual literacy understand more than what is immediately apparent. Such skills may include analyzing conventions (such as flashback or time lapse) used in movies; color, line, or shapes in art; choice of images in magazine covers or print media; or simply understanding the message in an infographic. Because visuals are discipline specific, students must learn how content-area tools (such as figurative language in ELA, symbols in math, context in history, or objectivity in science) can influence meaning in a visual text.

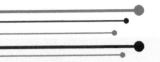

Brain Connection

WHAT IS THE CONNECTION BETWEEN VISUAL LITERACY AND COMPREHENSION?

"The ability to transform thoughts into images is often viewed as a test of true understanding. But some people seem to process information the other way around, literally seeming to comprehend information by visualizing it" (Wolf, 2001, p. 153). Albert Einstein was one of those people. He wrote that his ideas came to him in images, and he had difficulty putting his ideas into words (Shaw, 2000).

- *"Multi-literacies"* is a term that ties many literacies together and expects students to go beyond print to enhance conceptual understanding. Such literacies may include video games, hypertext, film, images, and Internet. Today's literate students will analyze conceptually and bring meaning to all sorts of content that might otherwise be vague or abstract, understanding various modes of representation such as visual, auditory, and kinesthetic expression. Teachers may expand students' use of multi-literacies by creating multi-modal text sets that include a main text along with supplemental books, documentaries, photographs, videos, song lyrics, or drama. Critical literacy plays a role in multi-literacies because it asks students to look behind texts to find underlying meanings, whereas disciplinary literacy informs the function of the texts and shows how they can take on different meanings in various subject areas.

One of the reasons we advocate for a disciplinary literacy model is because it incorporates multiple literacies and utilizes them in pursuit of its goal—supporting students as they become immersed in learning in ways that experts recognize and value. In place of learning

In place of learning about the content, students actually use subject-based literacies to participate in that content.

Students in Tina Reckamp's class use math literacy to explain the steps they used for solving problems.

For the Curious

about the content, students actually use subject-based literacies to *participate* in that content.

Content Area Literacy Versus Disciplinary Literacy

Why and how did disciplinary literacy become so important? Let's back up a bit and consider what happened to propel it to the forefront.

While our digital literacies increased exponentially, the basic skills of reading and writing remained problematic, especially in the content areas where increasingly challenging texts were proving more and more

difficult for students to access. As we mentioned in Chapter 1, the answer to this "literacy" problem came in the form of generic strategies, a sort of magic potion that involved an across-the-disciplines approach intended to increase the reading scores of students in all subjects. Unfortunately, the vast differences among disciplines, their texts, and disciplinary instructional practices rejected the one-size-fits-all model of literacy that tried to uniformly thread together the content areas.

The clog in the wheel became apparent pretty quickly: unless students recognized how and when to use strategies in specific disciplines, the strategies became more like isolated exercises than embedded content tools. And disciplinary teachers continued to feel they were being asked to subjugate content area learning to the greater good of enhanced literacy skills. Figure 2.1 shows a quick comparison of content area literacy and disciplinary literacy.

Figure 2.1

Content Area Literacy Versus Disciplinary Literacy

Content Area Literacy	Disciplinary Literacy
Focuses on the "what"	Focuses on the "how"
Utilizes generic reading and writing strategies as study skills	Utilizes teachers' expertise in locating literacy practices appropriate to text and learning goals
Shows students strategies for reading and writing across the content areas	Shows students how to use reading and writing as tools to engage in the specific work of the discipline
Uses strategies to improve test scores	Uses literacy to build deep, conceptual understandings
Relies on teachers to make decisions about which strategies to teach when	Relies on students to become independent in using strategies as needed
Scaffolds content-area reading and writing	Scaffolds content-area participation through reading, writing, viewing, and speaking
Conceptualizes literacy "across" disciplines, often with little differentiation	Conceptualizes literacy as highly discipline-specific and seeks to capitalize on those differences and commonalities

Content Area Literacy	Disciplinary Literacy
Relies on teacher understanding of universal reading and writing skills along with associated strategies	Relies on teacher content expertise and understanding of how specialists in field read, write, think, reason, and do
Builds reliance on strategies and techniques for studying texts	Builds flexibility in learning which strategies to use when
Incorporates general collaboration activities	Incorporates inquiry and collaboration in discipline-specific ways
Addresses, for the most part, reading and writing	Addresses a wide variety of literacy skills, including communicating and reasoning

Quoteworthy

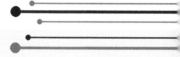

"If content area literacy focuses on study skills and learning from subject-matter-specific texts, then disciplinary literacy, by contrast, is an emphasis on the knowledge and abilities possessed by those who create, communicate, and use knowledge within the disciplines. The difference is that content literacy emphasizes techniques that a novice might use to make sense of a disciplinary text (like how to study a history book for an exam), while disciplinary literacy emphasizes the unique tools that the experts in a discipline use to participate in the work of that discipline" (Shanahan & Shanahan, 2012).

Even as we have attempted to show the difference between disciplinary literacy and general literacy strategies, it is not as cut and dried as we might have implied. Strategies used in content-specific ways actually support a disciplinary literacy approach, but it is the teacher, as the subject expert, who customizes (or adapts) appropriate strategies and practices to fit the discipline with the ultimate goal of students independently using a strategy to help them access content. And when collaborative inquiry dovetails with disciplinary literacy, the result can significantly increase student learning, as you will see in Figures 2.3 and 2.4 where teachers in math and social studies transformed a general

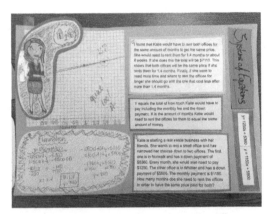

Griselda Manzur's student, Ilena Carrillo, shows how she makes sense of a disciplinary text, in this case a math problem.

strategy into a tool to help students engage more deeply and meaningfully with their content.

DISCIPLINE-SPECIFIC "STRATEGIES" FOR MATH AND SOCIAL STUDIES

As an example of the difference between content area and disciplinary literacy, let's look at a well-intentioned initiative in a school where standardized test results and teacher observation indicate that many students in the school are having difficulty summarizing and finding the main idea in informational texts, an important skill in reading. The literacy team decides that students should practice this skill through a cleverly titled "Finding the GEM" (*G*eneral concept + *E*ssential words = *M*ain idea) that all teachers will use in all classes. They create a graphic organizer that supports students' learning of this strategy with one circle asking for the "general idea" of the article after a quick skim, the second circle asking for "essential words" students identify after another closer reading with highlighters for annotating, and a third circle for writing the "main idea" of the article.

While the activity is certainly not harmful—and math teachers appreciated the equal symbol in the title—this type of strategy doesn't address the variables in different content areas or help students understand how the main idea in a primary document or a short story differs in important ways.

While using the same data that led to a whole-school GEM strategy, suppose we were to ask math teachers how they might help students find what we are calling the "main idea" of a word problem by utilizing literacy skills (reading, writing, speaking, reasoning, and doing). Because math teachers are so good at . . . well, numbers . . . they might at first have difficulty pinpointing how literacy plays an essential role in solving mathematical problems. A disciplinary literacy approach would have teachers think about and discuss together how a mathematician might approach a complex problem. What skills would she need? What mathematical reasoning would she use? How would she speak or write about the problem?

We actually did ask several math teachers to incorporate a disciplinary literacy approach in their lessons and explain how that might help students solve a challenging word problem. Figure 2.2 shows their thinking.

Figure 2.2

How Math Teachers Use Literacy With Word Problems

Have students

1. Read the word problem silently and jot in their notebooks what the problem is asking.

2. Talk about the problem with a partner and compare their notebook quick-writes. If the responses are different, have them read the problem again or ask for clarification from their teacher.

3. Determine, together, what steps are needed to solve the problem.

   • Jot down the information that has been provided and decide what information is needed to solve the problem.

   • Identify *how* the problem can be solved.

4. Attempt to solve the problem individually.

5. Compare solutions. Ask: Does each make sense? Can the results be checked?

The teacher then leads a whole-class discussion where students offer mathematical reasoning related to their solutions with the teacher expanding understanding.

Math students compare solutions and explain reasoning behind their methods.

Math-Specific GEM (General Concept + Essential Words = Main Idea) Strategy

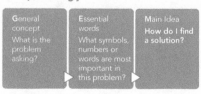

General concept	Essential words	Main Idea
What is the problem asking?	What symbols, numbers or words are most important in this problem?	How do I find a solution?

Quoteworthy

"Mathematics texts contain more concepts per sentence and paragraph than any other type of text. They are written in a very compact style; each sentence contains a lot of information, with little redundancy. The text can contain words as well as numeric and non-numeric symbols to decode. In addition, a page may be laid out in such a way that the eye must travel in a different pattern than the traditional left-to-right one of most reading" (Metsisto, 2005, p. 11).

Now let's compare the math teachers' response to the thinking of social studies teachers when we asked them how they would use literacy as a tool to help students read a primary document about the genocide of Native Americans. Figure 2.3 shows their plan.

Math teachers brainstorm how students read in math.

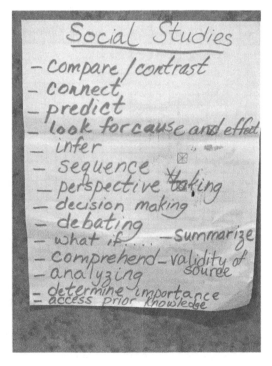

Social studies teachers brainstorm how students read in social studies.

Figure 2.3

How Social Studies Teachers Use Disciplinary Literacy With Primary Documents

1. Provide groups of students with different guiding questions based on their previous learning about the topic and ask them to engage in a discussion related to the question.

2. Have students read the document with a partner to ensure they understand the basics: Who? What? When? Where? Why? They may choose to read silently or take turns reading aloud. Ask them to circle any words with which they are not familiar.

3. Bring students into a whole-class discussion to assess students' comprehension of the document and understanding of essential words. Provide definitions if necessary.

4. Have students read the document again and write questions they would like to ask the author. Before they begin, model how to construct good questions with the entire group.

5. Place students in small groups to share their questions and come up with one or two that they would like to share with the rest of the class.

6. Create a fishbowl or seminar with the students' questions as discussion starters, leading students into thinking like a historian as they analyze and respond to the document.

Social Studies–Specific GEM (General Concept + Essential Words = Main Idea) Strategy

General concept	Essential words	Main idea
Have students	1. Students identify unfamiliar words.	Students gain deep understanding through seminar based on their own questions.
1. Review prior learning on topic.	2. Teacher provides meanings of words within context.	
2. Read for basic information.		
3. Question the author.		
4. Engage in discussion.		

Quoteworthy

"Historians have long defined history as investigation, casting themselves in the role of detectives seeking plausible explanations for historical events, trends, and controversies" (Bain, 2006, p. 2080).

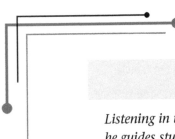

Listening In

Listening in to Clay Francis, high school social studies teacher, discuss how he guides students to read, write, and think like historians:

"Encouraging students to think like social scientists or historians may seem like a difficult task since our discipline cobbles together a diverse set of research methods and modes of inquiry. Investigating population growth in a geography course requires different skills than explaining the causes that led to the War of 1812. Yet both tasks require that students engage deeply with a text like a map or a primary source document, make inferences about that text, and then synthesize or develop some conclusions using information they have learned in class.

"To help students go through these steps, I have incorporated into my classes a three-step writing and discussion process that is highly adaptable to different content areas. I first provide an article from the *New York Times*, a map, a short video, or section from a podcast that is relevant to the unit. For example, in an introductory unit in my world religion class, I use the *Times'* topics aggregator to choose current events related to the religions of the world. Students had the opportunity to read one of the following: "The Jerusalem Issue, Explained," "Across Myanmar, Denial of Ethnic Cleansing and Loathing of Rohingya," or "Dalai Lama: Behind Our Anxiety, the Fear of Being Unneeded." These texts show students that the topics we discuss are living and changing, and this first step is critical to help students build their knowledge base and move beyond their opinions on a given topic. Then I ask students to reflect on the text—was it new information? Does it contradict something they have learned previously? What other thoughts or questions do they have after reading? They write for five to ten minutes, and in this process, they also evaluate whether the source for this information is credible.

"Next, we engage in a group discussion activity to help students flesh out their ideas, evaluate others' comments and opinions, and begin to synthesize different strands of information. In one activity, students line up on a spectrum based on whether they agree with the text or a statement related to the text. I ask probing questions along the way and help guide students to ask deeper questions of their peers. If the topic does not lend itself to a simple agree or disagree statement, then I arrange the students in two groups for a Fishbowl activity. Students inside the fishbowl ask questions and share opinions—those standing outside listen carefully to the ideas presented (and take notes) but do not speak in the conversation.

"After the discussion activity, students expand on their original writing. They may use comments from discussion, provided they cite their sources, and I ask that they also include the original article or video as a source. Typically, I provide an essay prompt that builds from previous course material, but this more formal assessment need not be a written response. Instead, try creating an infographic, filming a PSA, or recording a podcast."

——●

While the generic GEM strategy may be entirely appropriate in a reading class for students who have problems with comprehension and summarizing, its undifferentiated use in a math or social studies class may detract students from the way experts in those fields read, analyze, and reason through text. Given the GEM structure, math teachers made it fit their discipline by asking students to monitor their comprehension, engage in discussion, and work collaboratively in a way that supported students' understanding and solving of a problem.

This photo from Mercedes Beltran's Spanish class shows the inner "fishbowl" circle and the outer circle of students listening and preparing to participate.

The social studies teachers contextualized the document through prior learning and asked students to read and discuss the document as questioners, a major skill utilized by historians. They provided definitions for unfamiliar vocabulary since students only needed to know words as they applied to the document, and then they asked students to use their own questions as the basis for a seminar. Because each group of content teachers had a good understanding of literacy *and* their content, they were able to effectively create a lesson that precisely targeted their learning goals in place of plugging in a general literacy strategy.

A LITERACY PROGRESSION

Because each group of content teachers had a good understanding of literacy and their content, they were able to effectively create a lesson that precisely targeted their learning goals in place of plugging in a general literacy strategy.

It might be helpful to think of literacy in terms of a sort of progression: beginning literacy (where students learn how to read), content area literacy (where students utilize tools to help them with content area texts), and disciplinary literacy (where students take on the mantle of the disciplines, often by using content area literacy in discipline-specific ways). Figure 2.4 shows a graphic of this progression. Note that depending on a text's complexity or a reader's unfamiliarity with the text, we all may find ourselves at the "beginning literacy" stage of reading. Similarly, those who read as disciplinary experts may utilize content literacy skills to help them comprehend especially challenging text. The arrows show how stages of reading can be recursive rather than linear.

We look at disciplinary reading in more depth in Chapter 3 and how it can be implemented in content area classes as well as including a section on the best strategies to adapt for discipline-specific use, on pages 76–80. Generally, activities that require students to engage in metacognitive

High school social studies students discuss questions they have written about a primary document.

Quoteworthy

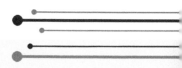

"[A]n exclusive focus on common literacy strategies, without a concurrent emphasis on discipline-specific content and practices, does not produce optimal results in students' learning" (International Literacy Association, 2017).

thinking about their learning instead of plugging in a strategy assigned by the teacher are most effective. Perhaps instead of worrying about the semantics of content literacy versus disciplinary literacy, we can all agree that literacy and content are not separate components of a lesson or unit but are inherently infused—and active participation in the discipline-specific literacy practices and strategies will enhance that partnership.

Figure 2.4

Progression of Literacy Development

Beginning Literacy	Content Literacy	Disciplinary Literacy
• Unlocking Literacy Code • Students learn "how" to read Letter Sound Relationships Encoding (spelling) Decoding (learning to attack new words) Sight Words Fluency These skills lead to the development of *automaticity*, freeing the learner to focus on meaning.	• Literacy Across Subjects • Students learn "generic" skills to read, write, speak, and think Making Connections Predicting Asking Questions Determining Importance Summarizing Visualizing Text Structure Monitoring Comprehension These skills propel a learner to *proficiency* and are essential skills for all subject areas. The skills are developed from the "outsider" view of the discipline.	• Literacy Within Subjects • Students learn to read, write, speak, and think as a specialist or "insider" of the discipline, often while utilizing content area literacy skills Scientist Artist Mathematician Literary Specialist Historian Economist Musician These skills are determined by the text and practices of the discipline. Learners continue to develop these skills throughout middle school, high school, advanced education, and into vocational programs and careers as they become members of a disciplinary culture.

Source: Adapted from Shanahan, T., & Shanahan, C. (2008). Teaching disciplinary literacy to adolescents: Rethinking content area literacy. *Harvard Educational Review: Adolescent Literacy, 78*(1), 40–59.

Disciplinary Literacy Instruction in Action

Through disciplinary literacy instruction, we may be closer to reaching our literacy goals than ever before. The evolution from "reading" to the colorful spectrum of literacy, which includes reading, writing, speaking, reasoning, and thinking, with all the digital tools available to us has empowered both teachers and students to incorporate multiple literacies into content area learning. Disciplinary literacy instruction asks teachers what they can do to help their students learn in the unique ways that experts in their fields learn. Some experts use the phrase "inducting students into the disciplines" to describe what happens when teachers welcome students as insiders rather than outsiders to their content (Shanahan & Shanahan, 2015, p. 12). Others warn that comprehension barriers may arise if students are not invited to experience "insider knowledge" or the discourses of a certain discipline (Greenleaf, Cribb, Howlett, & Moore, 2010–2011, p. 291). This approach is in stark contrast to students "dropping in" for course credit. Let's look at a few examples of how teachers have invited their students to act as experts in the field.

Literacy and content are not separate components of a lesson or unit but are inherently infused—and active participation in the discipline-specific literacy practices and strategies will enhance that partnership.

INVITING BIOLOGY STUDENTS IN

Dr. Lynn Moore, science teacher at Rocky View School Division in Alberta, Canada, with the help of her student intern Lucy Engelman, asked their science and biology students to begin the year by participating in an activity that immersed them in the work of scientists. She created four centers or stations that focused on skills that all scientists must develop.

1. How to interpret experimental data

2. How to use a flow chart

3. How to understand a scientific figure

4. How to understand a biochemical cycle

Each center had a large chart, figure, or diagram with associated questions to help students interact with the graphic. Students were placed in groups and asked to rotate through the centers as they worked together to address the questions. By participating in each center, students jumped into the authentic work of science as insiders. Lynn explains that having students wrestle with these skills in active, collaborative ways before they begin learning about, for example, cellular respiration, will help them have an easier time with scientific concepts. Figure 2.5 shows one of the center tasks for students.

Figure 2.5

Students Collaborate to Understand a Scientific Figure

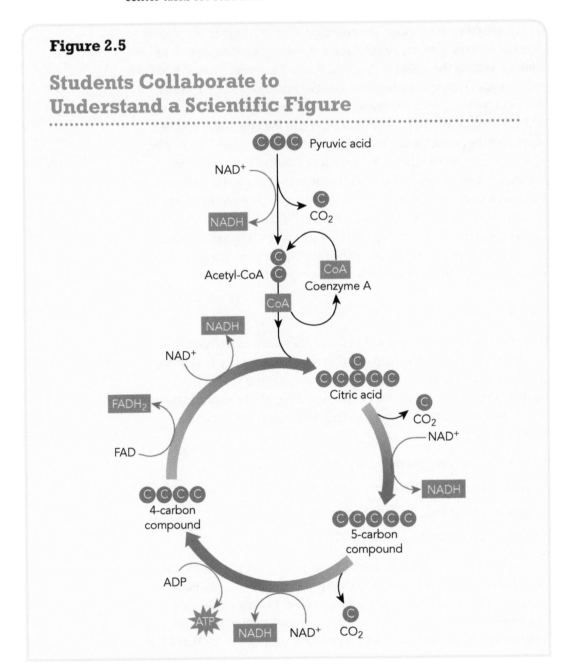

Answer the following questions with your group, using the graphic as a reference.

1. Why do you think there are different colors and thicknesses of arrows?

2. Using the symbol surrounding the ATP, what conclusion could you draw about that molecule?

3. Following the route from citric acid to the 5-carbon compound in the top right of the diagram, where did the carbon go? (There were 6 in citric acid, and now there are 5.)

4. Starting with acetyl-CoA (2 carbons) at the top of the diagram and following the route to citric acid (6 carbons), where did the other 4 carbons come from?

5. Write a figure caption for this diagram.

Lynn's activity situates students as apprentices (rather than as visitors) who engage in "on-the-job training," or as Monte-Sano & Miles (2014) coined it, a "cognitive apprenticeship approach." We like the word "apprentice" because it implies a dynamic rather than a static type of education that positions learners as members of a disciplinary community who are expected to use the tools of the trade. This student-driven approach also offers significant advantages over a teacher-driven lecture or PowerPoint format prevalent in many secondary classrooms.

We like the word "apprentice" because it implies a dynamic rather than a static type of education that positions learners as members of a disciplinary community who are expected to use the tools of the trade.

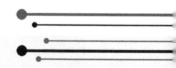

For the Curious

WHAT IS THE DIFFERENCE BETWEEN TRADITIONAL APPRENTICESHIP AND COGNITIVE APPRENTICESHIP?

In traditional apprenticeship, the apprentice observes as an expert performs portions of the task and then takes on more and more responsibility until he or she can accomplish the task independently.

In cognitive apprenticeship, both the teacher's and students' thinking must be made visible, actually brought to the surface.

Classroom practices such as reading, writing, or problem solving may be less observable than traditional apprenticeship tasks so teachers must deliberately and explicitly engage the student in cognitive processes that support the learning—that is, making the thinking visible. Teachers can do two additional things to help students with this apprenticeship process: place abstract tasks in authentic contexts so students see the relevance of the work, and vary tasks while finding commonalities so students can transfer what they learn (Collins, Holum, & Brown, 1991).

STUDENT APPRENTICES IN SPANISH CLASS

We observed another example of apprentice-style teaching in Marta Constenla's Spanish class. As a member of one of our cohorts, Marta had shifted from a more traditional way of teaching Spanish toward a disciplinary literacy approach. Students were using their new learning to engage in the work of the discipline: reading, making notes, and formulating arguments in Spanish.

When we entered her class, we actually *felt* energized and motivated to learn more about the language and people who spoke Spanish. Marta had student work posted on the walls, a Spanish word wall, photographs of students from field trips, and interesting articles, all in Spanish, of course.

On this particular day, students were involved in a debate as part of a unit titled "Beauty and Aesthetics," one of the six AP themes in all world language classes. Students were to debate the question: *Is it essential to wear brand-name clothes not only for the quality but also as a sign of social status and prestige?*

Marta's class after the debate with the judges in full dress front and center.

Marta was a whirlwind of activity herself, not wasting a moment of learning time. "You have five minutes to research information related to the question," she told her students, who enthusiastically retrieved their devices.

Since they had already discussed the question in class, she considered the limited time a sufficient review.

She then randomly assigned each student to one of three groups: Group in Favor (*grupo a favor*) of wearing name-brand clothes, Group Opposed (*grupo en contra*), and three judges (*tres jueces*) with their official robes. Students moved quickly to their assigned side of the room.

Marta set the expectations for students—they were to speak at least twice and use vocabulary or information from the unit when making their argument—and then she gave each group a few minutes to plan their specific arguments.

The contest began in earnest. Students spoke one at a time, but they often paused or hesitated to find just the right word in Spanish. A comment from one side prompted an opposing opinion from the other side and on it went. Judges intervened when necessary for clarification.

Two components of this targeted disciplinary literacy activity quickly emerged. First, there was laughter and a respectful comradery among the students. Second, the teacher did not need to direct the activity; students knew what they were expected to do and had been granted the independence to do what was expected. It was clear that they were accustomed to *doing* instead of just watching Marta do.

During the debate Marta took notes on the board as students spoke, writing phrases and words. After the lesson, she came back to her notes, using them to expand or reinforce students' Spanish learning and pointing out positive examples of students who took risks.

At first glance, disciplinary literacy may appear simplistic, teaching from a content-specific point of view with a dash of literacy to spice things up. But Marta's lesson reminds us that disciplinary learning is much more than merely increasing knowledge as it actually produces or constructs knowledge (Moje, 2008). Such a construct allows students to be "in on" the ground floor of knowledge acquisition and, as a result, allows them to better critique information, such as political claims or news they read on Facebook, examples of the media literacy we discussed earlier. Moje also points out that knowledge production is the result of human interaction, an approach that is very different from employing general strategies for the purpose of text comprehension or what is often called the "pedagogy of telling" (Sizer, 1984).

For readers who want a more comprehensive explanation of disciplinary literacy, specific practices that support it, and examples of a school that is utilizing it, take a look at ReLeah's book titled *This Is Disciplinary Literacy: Reading, Writing, Thinking and Doing . . . Content Area by Content Area* (2016). For our purposes in this book, however, we move on to examine what it means to read, write, and reason in various disciplines and how teams, departments, grade levels, schools, and entire districts can utilize disciplinary literacy to transform learning for both students and teachers.

Fostering Disciplinary Literacy Dialogue

1. What experiences with literacy, both negative and positive, have you had either as a student or as an educator?

2. If you could identify one issue regarding literacy (defined broadly as reading, writing, speaking, reasoning, and doing) that continues to be problematic in your department, school, or district, what specifically would that be?

3. Some literacy scholars suggest that content literacy (which relies on study skills and reading strategies) could be balanced with disciplinary literacy (which focuses on how experts in the field approach and participate in the work of the discipline). What approach—or combination of approaches—do you see as most valuable in your discipline?

4. Many states in the United States and provinces in Canada have created their own definitions of disciplinary literacy. Wisconsin defines disciplinary literacy as "the confluence of content knowledge, experiences, and skills merged with the ability to read, write, listen, speak, think critically, and perform in a way that is meaningful within the context of a given field" ("Literacy in All Subjects," Wisconsin Department of Public Instruction, n.d.).

   Alberta, Canada, looks at numeracy as a separate component of literacy and defines it as "the ability, confidence and willingness to engage with quantitative and spatial information to make informed decisions in all aspects of daily living" ("What Is Literacy?," Alberta Education).

   Together, create a teacher-friendly definition of disciplinary literacy or content-specific literacy (i.e., scientific literacy, historical literacy, mathematical literacy) that could be shared with others in the building or district.

Resources for Continued Learning

Dobbs, C., Ippolito, J., Charner-Laird, M. (2016, September/October). Layering intermediate and disciplinary work: Lessons learned from a secondary social studies teacher team. *Journal of Adolescent & Adult Literacy, 60*(2), 131–139.

Draper, R. J. (Ed.), Broomhead, P., Jensen, A. P., Nokes, J. D., & Siebert, D. (Co-Eds.). (2010). *(Re)imagining content-area literacy instruction.* New York, NY: Teachers College Press.

Fisher, D., & Frey, N. (2017). Show & tell: A video column/modeling disciplinary thinking. *Educational Leadership: Literacy in Every Classroom, 74*(5), 82–83.

Goble, P., & Goble, R. R. (2015). *Making curriculum pop: Developing literacies in all content areas.* Golden Valley, MN: Free Spirit.

Lent, R. C. (2016). *This is disciplinary literacy: Reading, writing, thinking, and doing . . . content area by content area.* Thousand Oaks, CA: Corwin.

Moje, E. (2008). Foregrounding the disciplines in secondary literacy teaching and learning: A call for change. *Journal of Adolescent & Adult Literacy, 52*(2), 96–107.

Shanahan, T., & Shanahan, C. (2017). Disciplinary literacy: Just the FAQs. *Educational Leadership, 74*(5), 18–22.

Notes

Creating a schoolwide culture of disciplinary literacy is the first step in the systemic transformation of student learning. In every class, every day, students should be immersed in literacy skills specific to each discipline—which means having students read, write, think, collaborate, and participate in content learning similar to the ways experts in the disciplines might engage in their practice. When schools are successful in this endeavor, they will prepare students well for the challenges of career, college, and life. Chapters 3, 4, and 5 address this challenge.

CHAPTER

3

CREATING A SCHOOL-WIDE CULTURE OF DISCIPLINARY READING

Adolescents entering the adult world in the 21st century will read and write more than at any other time in human history. They will need advanced levels of literacy to perform their jobs, run their households, act as citizens, and conduct their personal lives.

Richard Vacca (Moore, Bean,
Birdyshaw, & Rycik, 1999, p. 3)

Janelle, a middle school social studies teacher who is also certified in English language arts (ELA), could be considered a bibliophile. She knows the latest bestsellers, has a comprehensive classroom library, and spends much of her free time engaged in—you guessed it—reading. Her enthusiasm for literacy often transfers to her students, even those who might be considered struggling or reluctant learners. What's more, she supplements her curriculum with impressive multi-modal text sets related to her unit of study: historical novels, nonfiction, infographics, videos, blogs, and websites. She incorporates writing into her lessons, and each student must complete a history fair project even if they choose not to participate in the event. Her students respond well to this method of instruction and consistently score higher on standardized tests than most other students in their grade level. Janelle's principal told us that he would like to clone her.

In a classroom off of an adjoining hall, Mia teaches science. She majored in biology and, during a stint as a substitute teacher, found that she enjoyed the middle school classroom so much that she took the necessary coursework to become certified to teach. Mia likes the lecture format and sticks pretty closely to the table of contents in the science textbook. She creates labs to enhance lessons but utilizes the textbook as the major source of information for her students, even while acknowledging that many of them won't read outside of class. That understanding reinforces her belief that she must cover the material thoroughly in class, often through videos and PowerPoint. Her students also don't write very much other than taking notes or answering questions on an exam. Mia is a knowledgeable teacher, and students generally enjoy her class, saying that they know what is expected of them and that the class isn't boring. Her principal has no complaint with Mia's performance as a teacher and is pleased to have someone with such a strong science background on the faculty. He doesn't, however, say that he would be interested in cloning her.

What is the point of this comparison? One teacher has certain strengths and another has different strengths; one engages students in reading; another is better at technology and conducting labs. This is all pretty typical for most faculties. But for teachers and administrators who want more than "typical," we propose shifting toward a synergistic approach that ensures not only the benefits of collective efficacy (see Chapter 1, pages 21–24), but also the advantages that come when a strong schoolwide culture of disciplinary literacy is in place. What this means is that every single teacher is aware of how experts in his or her field read, write, speak, think, and do—*and* that every teacher has both the content knowledge and the teaching expertise to help students with these skills.

A shift to disciplinary literacy means reimagining literacy in light of *discipline-specific* literacy tools. If each teacher in each class shows students how to use literacy as a way of participating in the subject—not just learning *about* the subject—students will become flexible and independent users of literacy in a wide variety of fields. In this chapter we focus primarily on reading in every discipline.

Why Read in Every Discipline?

The research is clear. Academic performance is closely related to reading ability, according to a review of research about reading from the U.S. Department of Education. "The premise that literacy is associated with school achievement, participation in a democracy, and self-fulfillment is widely held," says the document's author (Cullinan, 2000). In fact, the benefits of wide and frequent reading are nothing short of amazing. They include

- Increased vocabulary (Nagy, Anderson, & Herman, 1987; Nagy, Herman, & Anderson, 1985)

- Increased fluency, knowledge of text structures, and ability to construct meaning from challenging text (Ivey & Fisher, 2006)

- Higher standardized test scores (Anderson, Wilson, & Fielding, 1988)

- Broader academic background knowledge (Marzano, 2004)

- Increased writing, spelling, and grammar skills (Krashen, 2004)

- Increased comprehension in content area subjects (Allington & Johnson, 2002)

- Increased self-confidence as readers and motivation to read throughout life (Allington & McGill-Franzen, 2003; Eurydice Network, 2011)

For the Curious

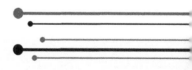

HOW IMPORTANT IS READING STAMINA?

Hiebert (2014) noted that the problem facing many students is not that they cannot read, but rather that they cannot focus on a reading task over time. This is particularly important for college reading preparation. Without the stamina, it is difficult for students to keep up with the increase in a college reading load.

If each teacher in each class shows students how to use literacy as a way of participating in the subject—not just learning about the subject—students will become flexible and independent users of literacy in a wide variety of fields.

The first step in creating a schoolwide culture of literacy is to ensure that students are reading some sort of text in every single class.

Everyone knows there is no downside to reading, yet we have seen students go through an entire school day without reading a word, thanks to PowerPoint, lecture, and other activities that promote nonreading content acquisition. The first step in creating a schoolwide culture of literacy is to ensure that students are reading some sort of text in every single class. That means music students are reading musical notes, lyrics, or reviews of new songs, albums, or musical performances. In art, students are reading visually and understanding symbolism as they make meaning from images and other forms of artistic expression. And on it goes for every course in the school.

It is not up to our reading coaches or commercial programs to determine these varied ways of reading; it is, instead, the responsibility of each teacher to work with others in his or her field to determine how to best help students read in that specific discipline. Let's take a look at some of the most effective practices that can be adapted to each content area as teachers transition to disciplinary literacy instruction.

In the culinary arts program at McNair High School, DeKalb County, Georgia, students read about regional cuisine before they cook.

Photo by Marcia Wingfield.

Wide Reading in All Disciplines: There's No Downside

Drop everything and read? Not quite. Independent reading in all content areas? Absolutely. Independent reading is the reading that students do on their own; in the classroom that means teachers allow students to read for a certain length of time several times a week (or each day if possible) but teacher support is critical. That's the difference between the old "Drop Everything and Read" where every staff member enjoyed a reading siesta and research-based independent reading where the teacher interacts with students while they are reading. It isn't necessary to do anything more than provide reading time, a classroom library if possible, and one-on-one dialogue with students about what they are reading, all while encouraging them to branch out or choose more complex text. No assignment is necessary, though a reading log (see the following photo for an example) is a good way for students to keep track of their reading, both in and out of school. Thankfully, completion grades are the preferred assessment. In fact, such a log doesn't need to be an additional form or assignment for teachers to keep up with; it can be easily assimilated into existing classroom structures, such as in notebooks or along with other digital record-keeping forms. In ELA classes, students can choose from any genre or subject, but some content area teachers like to have students read books, articles, or websites closely related to their content. An added benefit to content area independent reading is that students' background knowledge soars, creating a sort of Velcro-like attachment for new learning.

Teachers often say they don't have the extra time to devote to independent reading or that they won't be able to cover their curriculum if they take even a small chunk of time for such an instruction-less activity, but that thinking does not support the growth of independence or the old axiom that when you give someone a fish they eat for a day, but when you teach them to fish they eat forever—and this holds true for all disciplines. If you doubt the value of this practice, consider Wilhelm and Smith's (2016) finding that leisure reading is even correlated with increased math performance. Other studies show that achievement gains are associated with reading overall and more strongly associated in classrooms when teacher support is present (Topping & Samuels, 2007). And think about this: Pleasure reading is three times more significant in contributing to a child's cognitive progress than the parents' educational attainment (Sullivan & Brown, 2013), making this study, according to Wilhelm and Smith (2014), an absolutely compelling argument for teachers to make pleasure reading more central to their practice.

Title of book, article, or website	Date	Pages read	Brief Response I agree or disagree with. . . I thought. . . I would like to ask the author. . . I wonder. . . I want to copy this passage to refer to later. . .
Hitler Youth	Feb. 20	93-98	I know someone who is handicapped. What if she had lived in this time? Euthanasia = word to know
Hitler Youth	Feb. 20	99-102	This is the sadest thing I have ever read. How could this happen? I would have fought back.
Article - The Youngest Schindlers List survivor is still Telling Her story	Feb 21	2 pages	I saw the movie Schindlers List & I wanted to know more. This lady saw terrible things.
Hitler Youth	Feb 22	103-107 end of chapter	When I finish this book I want to read Boy In a Wooden Box about a Kid Schindler saved.
Hitler Youth	Feb. 25	129-131	Kids 16 + 17 went into battle. "Hitler was impressed with them." He didn't fight though. P. 130

A page from an eighth-grade student's daily reading log in a social studies/ELA team-taught class.

High school science teachers pull books from the school library related to their content as a way of encouraging students to read outside of class.

Listening In

Listening in to Kelsey Sullivan, student of our team's social studies teacher, Kathleen Duffy:

"I was not much of a reader as a kid, as I tended to wait and find the perfect book instead of actually reading one to judge it for myself. In fact, I would rarely read anything beyond assigned books until high school. In Ms. Duffy's global studies class, we explored reading through nonfiction text, activities, and news articles relating to the topics we studied. Having multiple sources was one of the things Ms. Duffy emphasized as being important because it opened more doors on the opinions we had. I learned that the more you read the more you can voice your opinion because of the vast knowledge you have to back it up. In her class, we did one book report where she gave us a time period and we got to choose whatever book we wanted. I absolutely loved mine, *Code Name Verity* by Elizabeth Wein (2012), and ever since then I have had a greater thirst for knowledge and reading. I am a very busy person between dance and school, but I always use my breaks to read a good book!"

Not surprising, young people who view reading as enjoyable and read outside of class on a daily basis are much more likely to experience success as readers overall, according to a report from the International Reading Association (2014). Another study found that high school students who regularly engage in leisure reading scored significantly higher in reading than did peers who did not regularly read for pleasure (National Center for Education Statistics, n.d.). Research results also suggest, however, that reading enjoyment declines as students

Photo by Janet Anderson.

This unstaged photograph shows every student in this high school ELA class fully engaged in independent reading.

advance through school, a finding to which most teachers and parents can attest. One teacher recently told us a familiar story: Her 14-year-old son used to love to read and now will barely touch a book unless forced to do so. He's not alone. Over one third of students reported that they did not read for enjoyment, 41 percent indicated that they read only when they had to, and 24 percent considered reading to be a waste of time (OECD, 2010). This trend was repeated in a study of middle-grade students in which attitudes toward recreational reading tended to decline as students progressed through the grades in school (McKenna, Conradi, Lawrence, Jang, & Meyer, 2012). Our experience shows us that schools intentionally working to create a culture of reading throughout the disciplines are revising these statistics in positive ways.

HOW TO ENGAGE STUDENTS IN DISCIPLINARY INDEPENDENT READING

It's easy to begin an independent reading program—so easy, in fact, that teachers often report that they feel like they are "slacking" due to the little effort it takes. (See tips for creating an independent reading program on pages 69–72.) Those who have invested in a sustainable reading initiative wouldn't trade it for any amount of extra instruction, and their students' increased achievement backs up that commitment. "My students have learned so much about history just by giving them time to read. The most surprising thing is that they often develop what I think will become life-long interests by following up with something interesting that they have chosen to read. One of my kids practically became an expert on the Civil War when I suggested he read *Gods and Generals*, a book I loved in college," a history teacher told us. As standards demand that students read increasingly complex text, comprehend academic language, and engage in critical thinking, there is no better way to scaffold those skills than through wide reading.

Listening In

Listening in to Nick Yeager, our team's English teacher, as he discusses how independent reading changed the lives of students in his credit-makeup course. Many would not graduate without this course, but they gain much more than simply a credit when they walk through the door of his classroom.

"We have all heard it before (probably from a parent), 'Freedom is not a right. It is a responsibility. It is a privilege.' I subscribe to this notion. In fact, it is the very essence of how I use independent reading to empower my students. Ten minutes of independent reading at the start of every period is the standard in all of my classes. Wednesdays are typically 100 percent dedicated to what I call *book love*. (Thank you, Penny Kittle!) Time for Independent Reading includes conferencing, journaling, book talking, and/or some combination. Once I made independent reading a part of our routine, my students were suddenly more engaged, they were more willing to take academic risks, and their progress accelerated. The way I see it, it is not so much that I am giving my students permission to choose their own books; rather, I am trusting them with this vitally important task.

"In *Readicide*, Kelly Gallagher quotes Kenneth Burke (2009) who once said, 'When children read books, they are not just reading stories. They are being given an opportunity to understand the complex world they live in' (p. 66). Independent reading provides my students with just that opportunity. Their reading informs them that they are not alone in the world—that they are 'not the only one.' Granting them 'permission' to understand that about themselves is a risk that I am willing to take every single day. For my students, and all adolescents, the end is self-discovery; therefore, the question that I constantly ask myself is, 'How can I help my students use the content of my class to get just a little closer to understanding something about themselves and their world?'"

What about reading in classes other than English? How are we to help content area teachers incorporate reading as an integral part of their curriculum? In our work with our cohorts, we found that the inclusion of wide and varied reading did not constitute a huge shift, especially in middle school. Many high school teachers also discovered ways to incorporate reading and found that it supported their curriculum more than they expected by expanding content knowledge, supporting learning about difficult topics, creating avenues for differentiated instruction, and increasing motivation for content learning overall.

Nick works with an ELL student who has discovered the joy of independent reading in his native language. Here he has just finished reading *Las alas de Leonardo* by Fernardo Morillo and shares how he identifies with Leonardo's efforts to overcome adversity.

TIPS FOR IMPLEMENTING INDEPENDENT READING IN THE DISCIPLINES

- Develop a classroom library of books, articles, websites, and resources related to your content and provide time at least once a week (or more if possible) for students to read. Try to have a range of texts that reflect various reading abilities. If you don't have a classroom library, ask your library information teacher to create a cart of books or magazines related to your current topic or find out what digital reading resources are available schoolwide for students. It generally works better to have texts in the classroom rather than taking the entire class to the library.

- Walk around the room as students read, and take advantage of this time to engage in formative assessment and individualized instruction. Teachers find that listening to students' conversations or reading their learning-log reflections provides valuable anecdotal information about student learning.

- Encourage students to keep track of and then follow up on questions they have from their reading through independent research (or class research projects). Read their questions periodically and suggest other texts related to their interests.

- Allow students to share interesting (or confusing) passages or facts from their reading in small groups or with the entire class.

- Provide opportunities for students to blog, tweet, or write reflections in other digital ways about their reading. Encourage students to respond to each other's comments. See pages 113–114 for an example of a Twitter project in history.

- Post links (or have students post links) to articles related to your subject from the *New York Times* Learning Network, Smithsonian, U.S. Library of Congress, or Mathalicious to encourage students to read related informational text. See Appendices A–I for additional content-specific websites.

- Don't worry about reading levels, lexiles, or fluency. Students will gravitate to what they can read, and you can move them toward more complex reading as they broaden their interests, knowledge, and reading practice.

- Read text (especially engaging, complex text) aloud from your discipline to increase students' comprehension, vocabulary, and motivation to learn more about content area topics.

Figure 3.1

Try This: Independent Disciplinary Reading

Instead of . . .	Try . . .
Grading independent reading	Checking in with students as they are reading or read over the comments they have written in their reading logs as you walk around the room
Giving worksheets or pop quizzes related to independent reading	Allowing students to share what they are reading with their learning partner or in small groups
Using lexiles to rate books or guide students' reading	Providing a wide range of texts from various genres and helping students learn how to choose texts based on interest and ability
Mandating whole-class texts without consideration of individual abilities	Utilizing different texts for individual or small group reading as well as in book clubs or inquiry circles
Assigning questions or study guides that encourage superficial or fake reading	Providing opportunities for relevant discussions or written responses with authentic audiences.

CREATING A SCHOOL-WIDE CULTURE OF INDEPENDENT READING

While independent reading within classrooms has its place, many schools also create schoolwide reading initiatives that encourage students to increase their volume and range of content area reading. Following are some initiatives that we have seen successfully implemented in schools, elementary through high:

- Departments or grade levels are asked once a month to provide a digital or print-based text for all students (and often parents) to read and discuss.

- Schools sponsor a "One Community, One Read" book choice from various content areas to encourage community participation and expand disciplinary learning.

- Student book club members do book-talks on texts from different disciplines or create blogs highlighting various texts. In Franklin County High School, students in the book club are making posters of books from the Georgia Peach Teen Books to display around the school. The student body will vote on their favorite book at the end of the year.

- Students are required to create a Goodreads.com account and post to it on regular intervals.

- Teachers in various disciplines lead the school's student book club one period a month to encourage reading of content texts (see a description of such a club on page 230).

- Library information teachers create author or "expert" events through Skype or in person.

- Teachers or leadership teams write grants to stock classroom libraries.

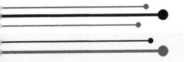

For the Curious

WHAT IS THE MIGHTY SMACKDOWN?

During one of our workshops when ReLeah was carrying on about books, Brad Smilanich, assistant principal at Bellerose Composite High School, told us about an amazing blog that features a tournament-style reading competition. We were intrigued, to say the least, and went to the website right away. What we discovered was one of the liveliest blogs about books for students that we had seen in a long time. The founder, English teacher Dia Macbeth, created a way to "read a few books, learn about many titles and have fun doing it." In her introduction she explains that the tournament-style reading of the Mighty Smackdown means that in the first round each participant reads two books, discusses both in a blog post, and then selects one book that will move on to the next round. Teachers are asked to commit to one round but most, if not all, continue on. What happens then? "We will read to the end when we will have only one book left standing!" You simply must take a look at this: http://mightysmackdown.blogspot.ca/.

The following "Listening In" pieces from teachers show two different ways of creating schoolwide cultures of reading. In the first example, an ELA teacher from a mid-sized middle school talks about how teachers worked together to create a discipline-specific culture of reading that supported content learning. You'll see that such an approach blurred the lines of discrete classes, helping students understand different purposes and genres within and across disciplines.

Then the "Listening In" piece on page 75 describes how a library information teacher in a very large high school wanted to increase reading not only with all students but also with as many staff members as she could hook. Her approach was ambitious and required the support of administration and a team of teachers committed to this goal. She was convinced that wide and frequent reading overall would "trickle down" into the content areas, increasing student learning as well as content knowledge. As you will see, her instincts were correct.

Listening In

Listening in to Tracy Kalas, ELA teacher, as she discusses how her school incorporates wide reading every day in every subject:

"We know Lexile scores, Map scores, PARCC scores. We have access to ECRISS and incredibly detailed numbers that give us information about our students and may inform our teaching. But none of these data are helpful in getting to know the reader inside every student. In every class, every day, we now better understand our students as readers and learners.

"For instance, math teachers in our school realize the importance of solid reading skills. They provide examples of math in texts and challenge students to do the same as they introduce or read aloud math-based novels such as *Flatland*, by Edwin Abbott (2017) or *Math Curse* by Jon Scieszka and Lane Smith (1995). They also read nonfiction that shows how math is used in the real world and engage kids in activities such as creating an ongoing list of all jobs that require math skills. They challenge kids to write and share in math as well: narratives, explanations, or reflection pieces. Teachers also ask kids to research a mathematician and present their findings, pretending to be the mathematician. Such discussions do not take the place of learning math but simply make it more meaningful.

"In science, reading is promoted seamlessly without deviating from the curriculum. Our students bring in unit-related articles and share those with each other. Teachers read aloud short excerpts from articles and give students access to the entire article for them to finish. They then begin the next class by asking for feedback on the article, and everyone is expected to participate in some way.

"As an English teacher, I also promote science reading, often through my 'Literacy Lunch' program. Students read a story or article, answer a question or create one, come in for lunch (and snacks), participate in discussion, and view a video related to the topic. I use the science curriculum for the topics of the reading. They often bring the literacy lunch discussion back to science and suggest future topics. In addition, our science teachers read science-related texts or science fiction novels to the class throughout the year as bell ringers. Students are invited to read as well, and they often suggest novels related to science.

Middle school science students take time for independent reading related to space exploration.

"Literacy is one of the most important aspects of every subject. Teachers generally agree with this goal but they sometimes say they find it hard to fit reading in. Reading should not be fit in. Reading should be a fit for every class, every day. Reading in all subjects exposes our students to a variety of genres so they become balanced readers. Our teachers have amazing ideas about using literacy in their class; sharing those great ideas is key to building stronger content learning through reading."

Listening In

Listening in to Janet Anderson, the library information teacher on our team, as she discusses a way that she and her colleagues built a schoolwide culture of disciplinary reading:

"Creating a culture of literacy begins with a lot of small steps. In our case, we started with advertising and promoting the Illinois High School Lincoln Award list of books (https://www.aisled.org/). By coordinating with our technology department, we were able to put the cover of every book on this list on every computer throughout the building. Students began coming to the library asking for 'that book on the computer. . . .' We put posters of book covers depicting new books, trending books, or just fun books in bathrooms. Yes, bathrooms—one of the few places in the school that students aren't glued to their phones.

"We also invited content teachers who like to read and discuss books to join a summer online reading community. Teachers committed to reading twelve of the twenty-two books (of various genres) from the Illinois award list over the summer. As they read, they would discuss the books, complain about them, shed tears over them and, most important, share how they planned to use these books the following year with students.

"What an amazing effect this initiative had on literacy and reading in our school! Teachers from all disciplines not only discussed the books with students but also with each other in hallways or the faculty cafeteria. They were so enthusiastic that they motivated teachers who weren't even in the online community to read some of the books. And our circulation rates increased substantially, especially for the targeted books.

"We purchased extra copies of the books for our library. We contacted area book stores and public libraries to make them aware that they may experience an increase in demand for these books. We also purchased them in audio format and preloaded Kindles for checkout. One year we had over 80 teachers taking the online reading course. What happens when 80 teachers get excited about reading? Transformation.

"Teachers who loved to read fell a little more in love with reading. Teachers who confessed that they honestly didn't remember when they had last read a book became readers again. One teacher said that books allowed her to see things she didn't know she needed to see and, as a result, changed not only the way she viewed her students but also the way she taught them."

Reading Strategies: When and How

As we pointed out in Chapter 1, most reading strategies used en masse simply have not served us well if our goal is to help students learn to read more complex disciplinary text. While national reading scores in lower grades have risen since 1992, this early success has not led to later growth in literacy. In fact, early learning gains largely disappear by the time students reach eighth grade. And research shows that it takes more than strong early reading skills to help students deal with the challenging demands of disciplinary reading (Perle, Grigg, & Donahue, 2005), which is why disciplinary literacy instruction is essential for helping students become successful in advanced grades.

Strategies may be a piece of the puzzle—but only if they are used as discipline-specific tools that encourage metacognition.

How are we to move students toward these extremely sophisticated levels of literacy? Strategies may be a piece of the puzzle—but only if they are used as *discipline-specific* tools that encourage metacognition, which includes not only thinking about one's thinking but monitoring thinking as well and then changing learning behaviors and strategies based on that monitoring. Furthermore, metacognitive practices actually help students solve problems and transfer or adapt their learning to new contexts and tasks (Cambridge International Education Teaching and Learning Team (n.d.). It's best, then, to find strategies that encourage critical thinking and problem solving—and make sure that students know how and when to use them instead of simply knowing *about* the strategies or employing them at a teacher's direction.

Figure 3.2 lists examples of metacognitive reading strategies that are effective in most content areas *if* students understand how the strategy helps them with their goal of comprehending the text.

Figure 3.2

Metacognitive Reading Strategies for Disciplinary Texts

Before Reading

- Help students build or activate background knowledge and make connections between what they already know and new topics of study.
- Activate students' curiosity by previewing text and offering relevant graphs, illustrations, charts, or other texts.
- Have students set goals for reading and learning.
- Have students think about and discuss the author or creator's purpose.
- Show students how to address unfamiliar vocabulary.

Before-reading activities may include small-group discussions, student-teacher conferences, written reflections, or completion of anticipation guides, T-charts, question cards, or learning logs.

During Reading

- Students should monitor comprehension through reflections or questions in a learning log.
- Ask:
  - "What is the author saying?"
  - "What does the author mean?"
  - "What is confusing?"
  - "What makes sense?"
  - "What underlying or hidden messages are contained in the text?"
  - "What is missing from the text?"
  - "What do I think is coming next and why?"
  - "Do I need to know this word? If so, how do I find its meaning?"

During-reading activities may include having students reflect on the text in writing, organize thinking in a graphic form, engage in debates or fishbowl-type discussions, or partner read/think/share.

(Continued)

(Continued)

After Reading

- Solidify students' thinking by having them
    - o Reflect on new learning through discussion or in writing
    - o Clarify confusion
    - o Connect or apply new learning to other problems, situations
    - o Draw conclusions from reading
    - o Classify information
    - o Reorganize ideas
    - o Evaluate and/or analyze information
    - o Teach others
    - o Do something with what they have learned

After-reading activities may include seminars, inquiry projects, collaborative adaptation of new learning to a different situation or text, performances, writing, blogging, or engaging in online discussions with students from another class or geographic area.

Brain Connection

HOW DO ADOLESCENTS THINK?

The Swiss genetic epistemologist Jean Piaget was among the first scientists to understand that adolescence heralds a totally new kind of thinking that is qualitatively different from childhood cognition. This stage, called *formal operational thinking*, brings the "capacity to think abstractly for the first time, to create hypotheses like a scientist, to be able to manipulate abstract symbols (as in $x = 2y$), and most important, to think about thinking itself" (Armstrong, 2016, p. 108). In the past, secondary school teachers viewed their mission as providing content—facts, concepts, and skills. What we now know about the adolescent brain and its relationship to metacognition suggests that we should place as much (or more) emphasis on helping students hone the crucial skills of metacognition (Armstrong, 2016).

One specific activity that engages students in metacognitive thinking is called *reciprocal teaching* (Palincsar & Brown, 1984). Students work in small groups to deconstruct challenging text in any discipline by talking about the text with each other. For an example of an adaptation of this activity for use with nonfiction, see Figure 3.3. While this is a highly effective practice for student achievement according to John Hattie (2017), we might want to consider why this strategy has such an impressive effect size (0.74) and if it would be equally effective in all disciplines.

Figure 3.3

Reciprocal Teaching, Adapted for Nonfiction

Reciprocal Teaching (Palincsar & Brown, 1984) is a way of having students engage actively with a text by using the following skills:

- summarizing
- questioning
- clarifying
- predicting

Students can also practice other skills appropriate to your discipline or topic, such as

- evaluating
- analyzing
- solving
- fact finding
- making connections

Instructions:

1. Place students in groups of four.

2. Provide a challenging article or piece of informational text broken into manageable chunks.

3. Ask students to read the first section of the article and annotate as they read. Show them how experts in your discipline annotate text such as by

   - Circling confusing parts
   - Writing in the margin, especially questions related to the text
   - Noting unfamiliar words, symbols, or concepts

(Continued)

(Continued)

4. Assign or allow students to choose a facilitator who will keep the process moving. Then assign or allow students to choose a role from the list below. It's often helpful to have notecards containing descriptions of the roles to provide to students. Give students a few minutes to read the text and think about the tasks associated with their roles. They will then speak one at a time in the following order.

➢ **The Summarizer** will highlight the key ideas up to this point in the reading (or the important numbers, quantities, etc.)

➢ **The Questioner** will pose questions related to

- puzzling or unreasonable information,
- possible connections to other information, and
- uncertainty or confusion about quotes or "facts."

➢ **The Clarifier** will attempt to address some of the questioner's queries. The point is not to "correctly" answer questions but to consider the questions, think critically about them, and offer plausible and thoughtful responses, often by asking others in the group for their input.

➢ **The Predictor** will "predict" what the next section of the article (or problem) might contain. Where is the writer headed and why?

5. *The roles in the group then switch one person to the right, and the next selection is read.* Students repeat the process using their new roles. This continues until the entire selection is read.

6. If possible, students should do something with what they've read. Different articles may be provided to different groups, for example, and after reading they might write a blog, a PSA, a tweet, or engage in a debate or seminar. They might also delve deeper into the topic, researching unanswered questions.

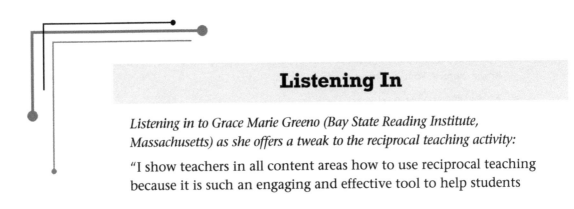

Listening In

Listening in to Grace Marie Greeno (Bay State Reading Institute, Massachusetts) as she offers a tweak to the reciprocal teaching activity:

"I show teachers in all content areas how to use reciprocal teaching because it is such an engaging and effective tool to help students access disciplinary texts. Eventually, we want students to become proficient with all the 'roles' (as good readers do), so after a bit of practice, each student must do all the tasks (as opposed to one at a time): predict, clarify, question, and summarize. They then engage in a discussion about how their responses were similar or different and which response appeared to be the strongest."

It is apparent that reciprocal teaching has much to do with students making meaning through a common understanding of what the text says, thinking about the text in ways that encourage questioning and critical thinking, solving problems related to the text, and then thinking beyond the text as students predict what the author might say next—all through disciplinary collaboration and dialogue. The ultimate goal is *not* to have students learn how to perform their roles expertly or come up with a finished product that can be graded with a rubric but, instead, to "empower students to take ownership of their learning in a systematic and purposeful process" based on metacognitive thinking (McAllum, 2014). Reciprocal teaching provides a scaffold for such thinking, but it is important that the teacher guide students in reading through a content lens. What questions would a scientist ask, for example, or what might an historian predict would come next in a document?

High school science students assume the roles of scientists to facilitate their discussion after reading a short article.

TIPS FOR SPARKING DEEPER LEARNING THROUGH DISCIPLINARY READING

- Ask students to read a section of a text and turn to their learning partner to ask a question, make a comment, or engage in some type of metacognitive thinking or questioning. Model metacognitive thinking so students understand the term.

- Provide many opportunities for partner-to-partner, small-group, and whole-class discussions before, during, and after reading.

- Have students approach text for the purpose of solving a problem or utilizing information rather than merely answering questions.

- Make available to students various types of concept maps during or after reading. Allow them to choose or, even better, create one appropriate to the text. Try concept mapping at Educational Technology and Mobile Learning, a good website that allows students to create mind maps using Google Draw.

- Show students through reading aloud how proficient readers in the field comprehend text. Simply read aloud and stop to explain your thinking as you read. If you read complex text, this practice also exposes students to challenging concepts, academic vocabulary, and disciplinary thinking. See pages 39–42 in *This Is Disciplinary Literacy* (Lent, 2016) for more information about this practice.

- Make the text relevant to students' lives even if it means going off topic.

- Allow opportunities for students to partner read text any way they choose.

- Stop often during videos, demonstrations, or PowerPoints to allow for student interaction.

- Encourage students to ask more questions than they answer while reading.

- Help students devise their own methods of annotation specific to your discipline.

- Provide different texts related to the same topic for small groups and have them share what they have learned with the entire class.

For the Curious

HOW EFFECTIVE IS CONCEPT MAPPING IN HELPING STUDENTS LEARN CONTENT?

Concept mapping is very effective, according to John Hattie's research, ranked 27 out of 150 (ES = .60), when it is used to support cognitive work. Students benefit from seeing their thinking develop on paper or screen, but it's important to remember that it is the transformation, not replication, that is key in its power (Fisher, Frey, & Hattie, 2016).

Vocabulary: The Key to *All* Content Reading

What is reading without an understanding of the words that form the text? Many students can decode quite well, and some can even read aloud like a Shakespearean actor, but ask them a question about what they've read and they look at you with a blank stare. Besides engaging students in the active, discipline-specific reading practices we discussed earlier, vocabulary study that involves showing students how and when to find the meanings of key words can help immensely in comprehension. In fact, vocabulary is among the greatest predictors of reading comprehension—especially in content classes (Simmons & Kameenui, 1998). There is even evidence that vocabulary size in kindergarten is an effective predictor of academic achievement in later years (Scarborough, 2001). Furthermore, we know that students who are exposed to more words per day experience higher levels of achievement (Anderson et al., 1988), which, by the way, also supports the practice of independent reading.

An insufficient amount of explanation and too many bold words per textbook section can cause "vocabulary overload," often shutting down students before they have a chance to internalize or expand a word's meaning.

The trouble may be that many content area teachers have been teaching vocabulary the same way for many years, often the way they were taught: provide a list of words to students, have them look up the word in a glossary or dictionary, and then write their definition. Textbooks often aren't much help either, even in vocabulary-dense content areas where words are in bold within the text. An insufficient amount of explanation and too many bold words per textbook section can cause "vocabulary overload," often shutting down students before they have a chance to internalize or expand a word's meaning. Similarly, vocabulary exercises such as matching words to meanings, fill-in-the-blank vocabulary exercises, or memorization of lists of words are generally not effective if

Tina Reckamp, middle school math teacher, asks students to make an educated guess about the meaning of new terms on Post-it notes. Later in the unit, they revisit their definitions and revise their thinking based on a deeper understanding. Learning, she reminds them, is a work in progress.

our goal is a conceptual understanding of a word's meaning for deep content understanding (Kame'enui & Baumann, 2012).

When students learn specialized vocabulary, their content knowledge solidifies. It is not surprising, then, that a lot of attention has been paid to vocabulary study, leading to many excellent books and articles based on solid research that offer suggestions and practices to teachers of all disciplines. If teachers work together to find and adapt vocabulary instruction ideas, they can create a top-notch plan for vocabulary instruction that works best in their unique content areas. In a science class, for example, students might learn about the prefix *endo–* when studying vocabulary words such as *endobiotic and endocrine*; in an art class they may work in groups to discuss similarities and differences between the techniques used in printmaking platforms such as *linoleum, etching, dry point,* and *photogravure*; and in a history class they might create images to help them associate the meanings of *democracy, autocracy,* and *dictatorship*. As students practice how to access vocabulary in each discipline, they will develop an expansive repertoire of effective strategies for learning—and retaining—academic vocabulary.

Caroline Milne, the science teacher on our team, finds that it is essential for students to deeply comprehend vocabulary related to specific topics in her discipline if they are to understand the scientific processes and principles related to the content.

For a unit on the alimentary canal, Caroline wanted to make sure that her students were very familiar with vocabulary associated with the processes involved in digestion beyond memorizing terms for a test. She had discovered in previous years that the classic gastrointestinal tract diagram in the textbook left her students feeling that the alimentary canal was totally unrelated to their own bodies. This year, after having been immersed in the study of disciplinary literacy, she was determined to do things differently. She first promised her students that they would put to good use their knowledge about the structure and function of the digestive system, but they had to learn the basics first.

Her plan was to involve each student in active learning by having them use their knowledge to try and solve a problem involving a gastrointestinal issue, one that all students had experienced. Her scenario began as follows:

If teachers work together to find and adapt vocabulary instruction ideas, they can create a top-notch plan for vocabulary instruction that works best in their unique content areas.

Harrison's grandmother made a classic goulash for dinner. He sprinkled some cheddar cheese on the goulash and then ate the entire thing! A few hours later, Harrison suddenly experienced sharp pains in his abdominal region. What could be causing this distress in his body?

Caroline asked students to use the anatomy and physiology dictionaries they had created in their learning logs so they would have common language to diagnose the problems. Their first task was to fill out the Goulash Component Chart she had created (see Figure 3.4), including all the components from the column headers.

Figure 3.4

Example of a Problem-Solving Chart in Science

Goulash component	Digested in the (identify all organs)	Enzyme secreted (name/organ) ex: Salivary amylase/ mouth	Organ(s) absorbed in	Macromolecule
Beef				
Tomato sauce/Diced tomatoes				
Elbow macaroni				
Cheddar cheese				

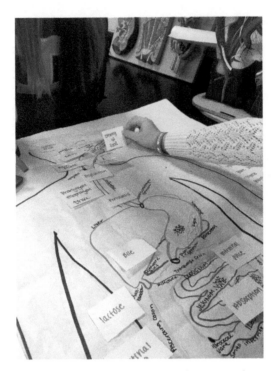

In groups of three, students then drew and described on chart paper the physiological changes that take place en route using proper anatomy and physiology terms.

Next, students were asked to hypothesize the reason for Harrison's distress. In small groups, they entered into lively discussions about the problem and tried to persuade others that their hypothesis was correct. Caroline said that she was amazed at the frequent and appropriate use of science vocabulary that students used in their discussions.

Working in small groups, students used vocabulary terms related to the alimentary canal to label their drawings.

To round out their learning, she employed technology in a new way. "Since students had to identify the macromolecules in the goulash on their chart (as well as how and where the body digests and absorbs them), I assigned each student one macromolecule and had them use the app Chatterpix to give the molecule a voice.

They had to record the 'voice' of the macromolecule as it explained how one component in the goulash was digested by a selected organ on their drawing." While the students might have appeared to an observer as if they were playing with their phones during science class, Caroline said nothing could be further from reality. "A lot of research, application, communication, and organization was needed to accomplish all the requirements. Best of all, students were really engaged in the learning."

Quoteworthy

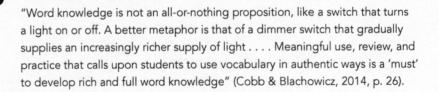

"Word knowledge is not an all-or-nothing proposition, like a switch that turns a light on or off. A better metaphor is that of a dimmer switch that gradually supplies an increasingly richer supply of light . . . . Meaningful use, review, and practice that calls upon students to use vocabulary in authentic ways is a 'must' to develop rich and full word knowledge" (Cobb & Blachowicz, 2014, p. 26).

TIPS FOR CREATING DISCIPLINE-SPECIFIC VOCABULARY INSTRUCTION

Michael Graves (2006, 2009) offers a four-part vocabulary plan that focuses on deep learning of vocabulary. We have added bulleted suggestions under each of his components to emphasize content-specific vocabulary study.

1. Provide rich and varied language experiences [related to disciplinary topics]

   - Increase students' reading. It is the "single most powerful thing teachers can do to increase [students'] vocabularies" (Graves, 2006, p. 5). In content areas, that means increasing the variety and quantity of discipline-specific reading.

   - Engage students "frequently in authentic discussions—give-and-take conversations in which they have the opportunity to thoughtfully discuss topics" (Graves, 2009, p. 14). Small-group and whole-class discussions on subject topics help students more deeply understand vocabulary and, thus, content.

   - Give students time to write about new concepts and incorporate the words they have learned, as Caroline did in her lesson on the alimentary canal.

2. Teach individual words [related to disciplinary topics]

   - Base instruction on both student-friendly definitions and contextual information.

   - Use word parts (prefixes, suffixes, and roots) to help students understand meanings, especially in science and world language classes.

   - Show students how to use context to figure out word meanings, especially in social studies and ELA.

   - Reinforce meanings and show word connections by using and having students use words multiple times before, during, and after a specific unit, especially in real-world, relevant situations.

3. Teach word learning strategies [that support discipline-specific vocabulary]

   - Encourage students to create their own associations or connections to help them remember word meanings. Show them how experts in the field learn to make connections.

Sixth-grade students draw a nonlinguistic representation of vocabulary words in social studies.

- Show students how to use a dictionary, hyperlinks, and other discipline-specific resources.
- Foster the use of nonlinguistic representations such as diagrams, sketchnotes (see page 104), drawings, or concept maps.
- Have students work together to adapt or create concept maps to help them conceptualize meanings and find relationships among words.

4. Foster word consciousness (an awareness of and interest in words and their meanings—especially as related to specific content areas) (Graves, 2006, p. 7)

- Give students multiple opportunities to encounter and use words, especially in discussions or problem-solving scenarios.
- Have students create interactive word walls with topic-specific vocabulary surrounded by synonyms, antonyms, examples, illustrations, and so forth.
- Show students why certain words are used differently in various disciplines and how writers in specific content areas uniquely use words.

Brain Connection

HOW DO WORDS GO FROM SHORT-TERM TO LONG-TERM MEMORY?

Willis (2008) writes about the importance of the repetitive use of newly learned vocabulary so the knowledge can go from short-term or working memory to long-term memory storage. Once in long-term memory, vocabulary can be readily accessed for future use. "These rehearsals need to be sustained over time so consistent patterns of neuronal activation occur repetitively, strengthening the networks that link vocabulary in brain storage centers to the processing centers of higher cognition" (p. 83). Once vocabulary knowledge is internalized, students are better able to devote energy to more complex cognitive tasks.

- Allow students to explore words and the concepts they represent through infographics, illustrations, concept maps, Ted Talks, or news articles.

- Read aloud passages to students that introduce new words, especially those that require extended conceptual understandings for content area learning.

- Share your curiosity and enthusiasm about words and how they specifically relate to your discipline.

Students connect science vocabulary to something in their life. This "Science Selfie" shows how inertia, motivation, gravity, force and motion, and velocity apply to this student's love of track and running.

Figure 3.5 offers more ideas for changing the way your students encounter, absorb, and activate new vocabulary.

Figure 3.5

Try This: Disciplinary Vocabulary

Instead of . . .	Try . . .
Giving vocabulary tests	Creating vocabulary activities where students use words to demonstrate their understanding
Approaching all words as equally important	Working with other teachers in your content to target key vocabulary your students must understand to unlock content
Assigning lists of words to be defined	Having students group words or organize them into categories as experts might when addressing a problem
Having students complete worksheets or word puzzles games that elude deep understanding	Having students experiment with words as they use them in real-world situations
Teaching all words the same way	Varying ways of helping students understand words based on the content

We have highlighted only a few examples of ways to support students in reading widely, frequently, and deeply in all disciplines. Your literacy leadership team or content area group will undoubtedly come up with many more ideas that can be more customized to your school population. In any case, remember that anything you can do to get kids reading will result in higher performance in all subject areas. That's a guarantee.

Fostering Disciplinary Literacy Dialogue

1. How would you describe yourself as a reader? What, how, and when do you read? If you were once a reader but now read very little, how could you fit in more reading so you are able to share disciplinary texts with your students?

2. Look again at the tips for implementing independent reading on pages 69–72. How could you make these tips more specific to your discipline?

3. In what ways could you encourage a schoolwide culture of literacy? A disciplinary culture of literacy?

4. Read again Caroline's science lesson on the alimentary canal (pages 84–86). What made this lesson especially effective regarding vocabulary study? In what way could you adapt a lesson you currently teach to encourage students to use words instead of merely memorizing them?

5. Choose the appendix (pages 271–324, available on the companion website) that matches your discipline. What more would you add to the lists of ways that students read in your discipline? How will you help students learn these skills?

Notes:

Resources for Continued Learning

Allen, J. (2002). *Inside words: Tools for teaching academic vocabulary grades 4–12*. Portland, ME: Stenhouse Publishers.

Beers, K., & Probst, R. (2016). *Reading nonfiction: Notice & note*. Portsmouth, NH: Heinemann.

Chick, N. (n.d.). Metacognition. Nashville, TN: Vanderbilt University. Retrieved from https://cft.vanderbilt.edu/guides-sub-pages/metacognition/

Cobb, C., & Blachowicz, C. (2014). *No more "look up the list" vocabulary instruction*. Portsmouth, NH: Heinemann.

Gordon, B. (2017). *No more fake reading: Merging the classics with independent reading to create joyful, lifelong readers*. Thousand Oaks, CA: Corwin.

Kittle, P. (2013). *Book love: Developing depth, stamina, and passion in adolescent reading*. Portsmouth, NH: Heinemann.

Robb, L. (2014). *Vocabulary is comprehension: Getting to the root of text complexity*. Thousand Oaks, CA: Corwin.

Serravallo, J. (2017, May). Dropping Everything to Read? How about picking some things up! *Voices from the Middle*, 24(4), 24–27. Retrieved from http://www.ncte.org/library/NCTEFiles/Resources/Journals/VM/0244-may2017/VM0244Dropping.pdf

Wilhelm, J., & Smith, M. W. (2017). *Diving deep into nonfiction, grades 6–12: Transferable tools for reading ANY nonfiction text*. Thousand Oaks, CA: Corwin.

4

CREATING A SCHOOL-WIDE CULTURE OF DISCIPLINARY WRITING

Writing is how students connect the dots in their knowledge.

National Commission on Writing (2003)

The National Commission on Writing in America's Schools and Colleges created a report in 2003 titled *The Neglected R: The Need for a Writing Revolution* in which it warned that the teaching and practice of writing are shortchanged in schools. Unfortunately, even with the strong emphasis on writing in schools and the inclusion of writing in standards, this aspect of literacy continues to be neglected (or only used for assessment purposes) in most content areas. The Commission's

(2003) recommendations were targeted and urgent—and are still relevant today (see Figure 4.1 on page 98 for several of its recommendations), but the directive that struck us as most pertinent is contained in a single sentence: "Writing should be taught in all subjects and at all grade levels." The creators of the report didn't specifically use the term *disciplinary literacy*, but they do describe how writers in various disciplines have changed not only our individual lives but also society at large:

> At its best, writing has helped transform the world. Revolutions have been started by it. Oppression has been toppled by it. And it has enlightened the human condition. American life has been richer because people like Rachel Carson, Cesar Chavez, Thomas Jefferson, and Martin Luther King Jr. have given voice to the aspirations of the nation and its people. And it has become fuller because writers like James Baldwin, William Faulkner, Toni Morrison, and Edith Wharton have explored the range of human misery and joy. (p. 10)

Exploring Disciplinary Writing

Unfortunately, school writing is often reduced to a dry treatise that asks the writer to restate previous learning with the goal of gaining points for a grade instead of as a powerful instrument of knowledge, analysis, communication, reflection, or creativity. Such an ambitious application of writing, however, can only be developed through practice, modeling, and instruction in the disciplines—which requires expertise on the part of content teachers. They must understand, identify, and teach the literacy practices and discourses (written or spoken communication) specific to their discipline (Moje, 2008), which include knowing what genres experts in the field use as well as *how* they write in that genre. For instance, a law studies teacher could show students how someone in the criminal justice field might write about surveillance in *Popular Mechanics* magazine, or a science teacher might explain how a scientist might research and write an article for a journal or even a science fiction novel. The National Commission on Writing (2003) gives the example of fields like engineering where employees must write proposals as well as interim and final reports, "essential by-products of technical work" (p. 11).

Looking In

Looking in on Marge Ackert, physical education teacher, who regularly infuses real-life reading and writing into her curriculum in the following ways:

- Students journal about their outside physical activities including goals and accomplishments. At the end of the year, students write reflections regarding their experiences in her class.

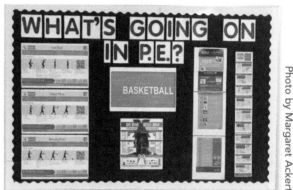

Marge creates bulletin boards that show how writing is used to convey meaning in physical education.

- Text sets are created by Marge to kick off each unit. By collaborating with the reading specialist, she is able to collect a variety of articles and readings relevant to the unit so that all students, regardless of reading skills, can be successful. Merging Marge's disciplinary knowledge with the reading specialist's literacy knowledge makes this process extremely effective.

- Students are given opportunities to "dig a little deeper" into topics. For instance, when learning about heart rate, students use simple math equations to determine their resting, maximum, and target heart rate zones. Marge includes multimodal literacy resources such as videos, infographics, and articles to prompt discussions and written reflections about the movement of blood and how it impacts physical activity.

- Marge maintains a sports bulletin board in the hallway outside the gym. Picture books, novels, magazine articles, infographics, and information books are regularly featured to highlight the craft of sports authors. As students line up before and after class, they become aware of how professional authors and journalists write about sports.

- A "PE in the News" folder is kept up-to-date and made accessible as an online resource for students. They are able to read and informally discuss current events topics related to sports and other concepts in the physical education curriculum. In addition, students are exposed to the writing of experts in the field.

Quoteworthy

"I've been lucky to have been able to merge my love of music with my love for writing. In truth, they are simply different expressions of the same creative force."

Jim Reilly (2015), musician and
author of *Stick Man: The Story of Emmett
Chapman and the Instrument He Created*

High school students write about their observations while engaging in a science experiment.

When students are shown how to write in discipline-specific ways in each class, they are better prepared to become proficient writers in each content area as well as overall. That means that every teacher has a responsibility to understand fully what writing in his or her discipline looks like *and* how to teach students to become competent writers in that discipline. It also means that general writing strategies aren't enough to ensure that students have a broad range of writing experience.

While such disciplinary writing instruction might sound daunting, the good news is that content teachers should not

Quoteworthy

"Writing extends far beyond mastering grammar and punctuation. The ability to diagram a sentence does not make a good writer. There are many students capable of identifying every part of speech who are barely able to produce a piece of prose. While exercises in descriptive, creative, and narrative writing help develop students' skills, writing is best understood as a complex intellectual activity that requires students to stretch their minds, sharpen their analytical capabilities, and make valid and accurate distinctions" (National Commission on Writing in America's Schools and Colleges, 2003, p. 13).

try to become clones of ELA teachers; they should simply teach writing as it relates to their discipline. Writing skills in most content areas are identified in this book's Appendices. We suggest that teachers use these lists as springboards for creating full descriptions of what writing looks like in their own content areas.

Writing to Learn in the Discipline Areas

Many content teachers may not have written anything substantive in years and might feel unsure about their abilities as writers or as teachers of writing, even in their disciplines. It's true that writing can be intimidating, even for those who practice often. That's why it is so important for teachers to work together in learning communities to hone their own skills as subject-area writers and to learn how best to help their students learn to write. A good place to begin is to explore with colleagues what and how students should be writing, and this means going beyond textbook prompts or short-answer test questions. The following sections on writing will help facilitate individual reflection and group dialogue about disciplinary writing.

Figure 4.1

Sample Recommendations for Writing Instruction in Schools, Districts, and the Nation

The National Commission on Writing in America's Schools and Colleges makes the following recommendations regarding writing. See the entire list of recommendations on pages 3–5 in its online report. Note the number of recommendations that address disciplinary writing.

- Every state should revisit its education standards to make sure they include a comprehensive writing policy. That policy should aim to double the amount of time most students spend writing, require a writing plan in every school district, and insist that writing be taught in all subjects and at all grade levels.

- All prospective teachers, no matter their disciplines, should be provided with courses in how to teach writing.

- Writing should be assigned across the disciplines.

- More out-of-school time should be used to encourage writing, and parents should review students' writing with them.

- Assessments of student writing must go beyond multiple-choice, machine-scorable items. Assessments should provide students with adequate time to write and should require students to actually create a piece of prose.

- Writing is everybody's business, and state and local curriculum guidelines should require writing in every curriculum and at all grade levels.

- Common expectations about writing should be developed across [and we would add *within*] disciplines through workshops designed to help teachers understand good writing and develop as writers themselves.

- Teachers need to understand writing as a complex form of learning and discovery both for themselves and for their students. Faculty in all disciplines should have access to professional development opportunities to help them improve student writing.

Listening In

Listening in to a student in the class of our team's social studies teacher, Kathleen Duffy:

"We write a lot in my Social Studies class. Usually it's after we watch a documentary, listen to a speaker, read an article, or argue our point in a seminar. It's just a chance to get our thoughts on paper. Ms. Duffy is always saying, 'Your voice matters,' and for me it's easier to write than talk. I have time to think it through and explain my opinion. We have lots of discussions in class, and kids really get heated about some of the topics. But after we've argued and disagreed with each other, it's nice to be able to stop and write. We can think about where we really stand and get it down in writing while it's fresh on our minds."

WRITING: A TOOL FOR THINKING

When we ask teachers why kids should write, they usually take their time in answering. We often hear "to communicate," followed by "to reflect" or "to explain," and then they list various skills such as to analyze, summarize, persuade, or create. We compile their answers under a graphic of an umbrella with a bright yellow heading that says *Writing Is Thinking*.

When students write without investing in thinking, such as when copying notes, filling in memorized answers on a test, or engaging in formulaic writing where someone else has done the thinking for them, writing becomes a rote activity instead of an active learning process that expands learning. In Applebee and Langer's (2013) research regarding the act of composing, they make the point that one of writing's most important functions is to help students "clarify understanding of the subject," that is, to comprehend content topics more deeply. Similarly, research regarding writing in math has shown that writing can improve students' understanding of mathematical concepts (Cross, 2009), make

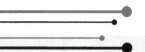

Brain Connection

HOW DOES WRITING REFINE THINKING?

Patricia Wolf (2001) writes about how brain research can translate into classroom practice. She explains that procedural memory is for learning and remembering how to do something, such as playing the flute or formulaic writing, and requires rote memory. Semantic memory, on the other hand, requires elaborative rehearsal. Writing activities fit in the latter category because they challenge students to clarify, organize and express what they are learning. In other words, writing, a method of elaborative rehearsal, is a tool for refining thinking (pp. 170–171).

One of writing's most important functions is to help students "clarify understanding of the subject."

math more meaningful for students (Porter & Masingila, 2000), and promote student engagement (Applebee & Langer, 2013). In science, research points to advantages in understanding scientific concepts through writing—specifically writing to learn rather than traditional science writing, such as formulaic lab reports. The authors of another study present more general benefits of thoughtful writing as students "re-represent" their knowledge in different forms, which serves to create even greater learning opportunities (Gunel, Hand, & Prain, 2007).

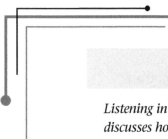

Listening In

Listening in to Amanda Cavicchioni, middle school math teacher, as she discusses how her students use writing as a way to deepen learning:

"The 'Snapshot of Algebra' project, which asks students to reflect on what they know and where they are confused, provides a valuable opportunity for learning. Rather than my telling them whether or not they have grasped the math concepts we have studied, they gain information about their own learning through writing—while sharpening their analytical skills in the process. They learn that a mistake is not a statement about their math abilities, but a way to clarify their thinking. It really forces them to use their metacognitive skills and think about their thinking—where it is accurate and where it went wrong.

"I start by giving my class a handout that instructs them to go to certain pages in their textbook and do specific problems from each chapter. Once they have completed every problem, they check their answers and then reflect in writing on their strengths and areas needing improvement for the year. The 'Snapshot of Algebra' activity is a way to celebrate their hard work and progress."

Listening In

Listening in to Katelyn Noelle, Amanda's eighth-grade student, describe how writing in math helps her understand more about her abilities in this discipline:

"After reviewing, I realized that there were a lot of problems that I forgot how to do. But there were some that I had a good handle on. For example, I had a great handle on finding consecutive numbers and finding the slope and y-intercept. I also did a good job on simplifying expressions like in Problem #2. Some of the areas I need improvement on are finding the wind and airspeed like in Problem #14. I wanted to distribute when you had to divide the distances by the time. I also had trouble finding "k" in Problem #3. I kept multiplying by the reciprocal when you had to multiply by just 12.

One last thing I had trouble on was finding the width and length like in Problem #11. I didn't know how to start the problem, but once I did, it was easy the rest of the way. Overall, even though I struggled on some questions, I think I have a pretty good handle on it. I was definitely surprised that I knew as much as I did and was able to solve the problems I did."

Traditional, often simplistic writing instruction and assignments will not offer students the "thinking" advantages that are created through good disciplinary writing instruction. Teachers must work with others in their field to learn about and plan writing activities that will help students with the messy process of deep learning through writing.

Traditional, often simplistic writing instruction and assignments will not offer students the "thinking" advantages that are created through good disciplinary writing instruction.

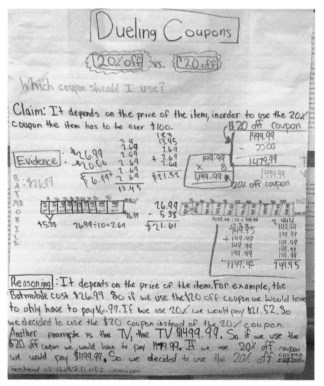

This is an example of writing-to-learn from a student in Miguel Ortega's sixth-grade math class at Lakeside Middle School in California.

Quoteworthy

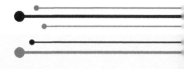

"The writing process provides discipline and focus, and is thus integral to conducting . . . research. Writing is part of the expedition, not a report on it, because it helps expose flaws in logic, gaps in the evidence, and missing links in the chain or argument: 'What do I really mean here? This doesn't follow or feel quite right. How can I account for X? Might there be data on that?'" (Linda Gottfredson, 2010, p. 30).

TIPS FOR WRITING TO LEARN IN THE DISCIPLINE AREAS

- Incorporate some type of writing for students every day that goes beyond their copying notes or providing short answers to questions. Learning logs, either digital or print, are good ways to keep students engaged in writing as well as helping teachers know if students are "getting it." See Figure 4.2 for prompts that encourage writing to learn.

- Share examples of professional content area writing, called *mentor texts*, with students. See pages 112–113 for tips regarding how to find and use mentor texts.

- Allow students to work together in composing essays, reports, blogs, stories, poetry, cartoons, reflections, analyses, or opinion pieces.

- Give students opportunities to write for an authentic audience and purpose; practice for the types of writing they will need in the workplace.

- Allow choice in writing assignments. Provide an overall topic based on a unit of study—for example, the civil rights movement, poets of Harlem, or the solar system—and then support students as they decide what they want to research and how they want to frame their new understandings in writing. Students may also keep lists of questions or confusions they have about topics and then choose one of their questions to explore in writing.

- Ask students to help develop a rubric for grading final writing projects so they can set goals, assume ownership, and understand what is expected from a particular piece of writing.

- Show students processes for writing: various ways of pre-writing such as lists, charts, graphs, and concept maps; how to compose as experts in the field; ways to revise; and suggestions for how to get help from others when they become stuck.

- Develop patience for the messy process of writing to learn that allows your students to reap the rewards of newfound knowledge, independence, and self-efficacy.

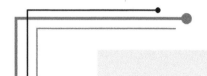

Listening In

Listening in to Mary Stec, technology coach, who discusses a different type of writing to learn–sketchnoting:

"Sketchnoting requires students to use higher level thinking skills when creating a visual representation of ideas and how they are related. The visuals trigger students' recall and their deeper analysis of an author's craft and text structure, often becoming a greater support for many students compared to other forms of notetaking."

A middle school social studies student creates a sketchnote that demonstrates evidence of thinking.

Figure 4.2

Sample Prompts for Writing to Learn in the Content Areas

- What do you think . . .?

- Why did this event, result, problem, or solution occur?

- What would happen if . . .?

- How do you know . . .?

- In what way is this new information important? If you don't believe it is important, explain your thinking.

- What is the significance of this report, document, lab, finding, event, hypothesis, or problem?

- What is most important in what you read or learned today? Why?

- What do you question about what you learned today?

- How would you consolidate (or synthesize) . . .?

- What argument would you make about . . .?

- How would you change . . .?

- Do you agree or disagree with . . .? Why?

Take a look at Figure 4.3 to see an example of writing to learn in science. Notice that this middle school student, Melissa Flores, from Lakeside Middle School, keeps her notes in electronic format, inserting photographs to support her statements. She is learning to write in an observant manner with precise details. Her teacher is helping her learn to think as a scientist by asking questions and then having her note how she might find the answers.

Figure 4.4 provides suggestions for assigning and assessing writing across content areas.

Figure 4.3

Writing to Learn in Science

DATA COLLECTED *(should include QUANT & QUAL, may be bullets, may include pictures of data)*

- 1 leaf has fallen and is dried
- About 11 inches of Elodea
- Water is looking the same its clean
- #1 snail is at the very top of the bottle under the cap
- #2 snail is a little above the water
- #3 snail is almost above the water but still not quite
- Water is still 8.9 inches in height
- There is circular object in my bottle
- There are no more air bubbles in my bottle anymore

THINGS I OBSERVED *(include any pictures you might have related to your observations)*

One of my leaves have fallen and has now become the microorganisms and bacteria's food source. The Elodea plant has grown about 1 inch. The water has not quite changed since the last observation it is still clear. Snail #1 is at the top of the bottle under the cap but has no water. Snail #2 is half in the water and the other half is out of the water. I am not sure if it is ok if the snails are not entirely in the water. Snail #3 is toward the top of the bottle but still in the water. The water has not changed; it is 8.9 inches. I have observed a circular object; it sort of looks like the texture is a jelly surface. It is a dark brown color. It blends in the rocks but I noticed it because I was moving the bottle a little bit, and I see it floating and I was wondering where it could have come from. The object/thing was not in there when I assembled it or in my last observations. I am not sure if it was there for a while because it does blend in with the rocks but I have not seen it in my bottle until today. There is completely no more air bubbles at the top of the bottle anymore. In my last observations I have inferred that it was because of the change in temperature but they are all gone. I do not see them at night or the morning.

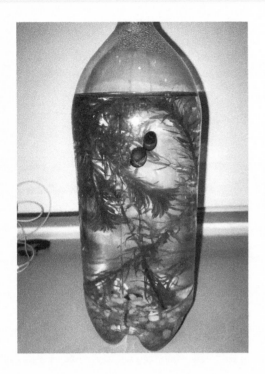 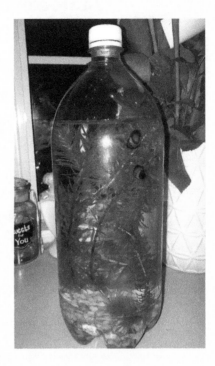

QUESTIONS I HAVE *(include ways you plan to answer these questions)*

- What exactly is that circular thing in my ecosystem?

I will keep a close eye on it to see if any more appear.

- Did the thing come from the snail?

This is a possibility. I will do some research on it to see if it can affect my ecosystem.

CLOSING THOUGHTS *(may include any concerns, overall condition of your ecosystem, next steps)*

My ecosystem remains healthy and strong. My concern is that the circular object appeared, and I am worried that it might affect the ecosystem. I am also concerned about the air bubbles because all of them disappeared and none are present. I do think that snails suck the bubbles because they have been toward the top and maybe as they were slithering they sucked up the bubbles.

Quoteworthy

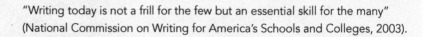

"Writing today is not a frill for the few but an essential skill for the many" (National Commission on Writing for America's Schools and Colleges, 2003).

Figure 4.4

Try This: Disciplinary Assignments and Assessments

Instead of . . .	Try . . .
Assigning writing where students recite information	Providing opportunities for students to use writing in ways that experts use it: to create, understand, transfer, or apply learning to a new situation or problem
Grading all writing	Thinking of assessing writing according to categories: • Reflections or responses that help students understand their thinking and learning: completion grade or no grade • Shorter pieces that show understanding or construction of learning: holistic grade • Essays or project-based writing that demonstrates learning: major grade based on rubric that students help create
Creating one whole-class writing assignment for all students	Offering a variety of writing options that encourage choice, ownership, and individual exploration
Placing an inordinate amount of emphasis on grammar, punctuation, and spelling	Placing an emphasis on content first and allowing students the freedom to explore their thinking and learning without worrying about conventions; that can come later, depending on the audience
Making you (the teacher) the audience for all your students' writing	Creating authentic audiences—other students, blogs, booklets, or presentations

For the Curious

WHAT TYPE OF WRITING IS MOST VALUED IN THE WORKPLACE?

- Writing that is clear, concise, accurate, and often brief
- Writing with a real purpose and audience for the purpose of communication or publication
- Writing that is collaborative
- Specialized writing such as reports, narratives, letters, instructions, or filling in of forms
- Writing that is persuasive, which involves
  - **"Purpose** (why the document is being written, the goals of the document)
  - **Audience** (who will read the document, includes shadow readers—unintended audiences who might read your work)
  - **Stakeholders** (who may be affected by the document or project)
  - **Context** (the background of and situation in which the document is created)" (Purdue Online Writing Lab, n.d.; http://owl.english.purdue.edu/owl/resource/624/01/)

Following the Pros: Disciplinary Mentor Texts

Most students experience content writing through textbooks in which publishers have hired teachers or scholars in the field to write about curricular topics. In recent years, more emphasis has been placed on helping students read such texts through the generic strategies we mentioned earlier, but many teachers don't show students how to pay attention to disciplinary writing. For the most part, students learn to write in ELA classes and then write *about* the subject as directed by their teachers. Teaching writing by immersing students in the writing of experts in the field, in whatever form that may take, is where disciplinary literacy really shines. In English, for example, writing abounds in the form of essays, novels, short stories, op-ed pieces, or poetry. Good ELA teachers not only have students read such texts but also show them how writers craft argument, use voice, employ figurative language, and utilize dialogue.

Teaching writing by immersing students in the writing of experts in the field, in whatever form that may take, is where disciplinary literacy really shines.

But what about in science, social studies, math, or other content areas? Showing students how Nobel Prize–winning author Toni Morrison utilizes repetition for effect in a novel will not help them become better writers in science. What *will* help is asking them to read an article by Ewen Callawy (2018), "Geneticists Unravel Secrets of Super-Invasive Crayfish," in *Nature* magazine about a highly invasive species of crayfish that can reproduce without mating and pointing out how the author explains the phenomenon and uses scientific language while interspersing credible quotes. Mentor texts are used not only to introduce students to real-world writing in the field but also to help students emulate such writing when they compose in various disciplines. Figure 4.5 provides a number of ideas for incorporating mentor texts within disciplines.

Teachers must carefully choose mentor texts to demonstrate to students what it is they want them to understand about how writers organize information, make a point, choose vocabulary, or utilize figurative

Figure 4.5

Try This: Disciplinary Mentor Texts

Instead of . . .	Try . . .
Using the textbook as a mentor text	Using a wide variety of texts such as blogs, articles, op-ed or op doc pieces, videos, websites, and books, such as *The Best American Science and Nature Writing 2017* or other content-specific fiction and nonfiction
Expecting that students will write like experts even after having been immersed in the study of many mentor texts	Thinking of writing as a process and celebrating all thoughtful writing
Looking for long mentor texts that demonstrate several writing skills	Providing short pieces such as tweets, quotes, statistics, maps, charts, infographics, or sections of article or books
Assessing students on their ability to recognize good mentor texts	Using mentor texts as tools to hone disciplinary writing

language, for example. They must be explicit in how the use of graphs, illustrations, or photographs help writers effectively communicate what they want to say. Each discipline will look different regarding the types of texts and skills used, whether analyzing data manuals and design sketches in a career and technical class or evaluating a play script and visualizing the set design in a theatre class.

Kelly Gallagher (2014), author of several books on writing instruction, makes the point well when he says, "If we want our students to write persuasive arguments, interesting explanatory pieces, or captivating narratives, we need to have them read, analyze, and emulate persuasive arguments, interesting explanatory pieces, and captivating narratives" (para. 4).

Teachers must carefully choose mentor texts to demonstrate to students what it is they want them to understand about how writers organize information, make a point, choose vocabulary, or utilize figurative language.

A simple activity that can help students understand how writers may approach text differently in various content areas is to find a compelling article about a topic that could cross content areas, such as volcanic eruptions, climate change, the Zika (or another) virus, the changing roles of robots, or the Holocaust. Each content area teacher on a team or grade level will have students in his or her class read the same article and show them how the article could be read from the point of view of that particular discipline. Then teachers will show how an expert in the field would write about the topic and whether or not the sample article meets the writing standards of such an expert. For example,

In science:

- Is the information based on objective, scientific principles?

- Are there other studies that support the author's findings?

- Are there data that support the conclusion?

- Is the article written in a concise manner without flowery language?

In math:

- Has the author written with sound mathematical reasoning?

- Have numbers or mathematical principles been woven into the text to support the writer's point and show real-world connections?

- Are there graphs or charts that validate the point?

In ELA:

- Has the writer demonstrated logical thinking in the text?

- Does his or her voice and vocabulary support the message?

- Do the organization and transitions make the piece easy to read?

- Is there a narrative that helps create and sustain interest?

- Is the writing engaging?

In history:

- Has the writer created a historical connection, if there is one?

- Does he or she compare sources or perspectives?

- Has he or she clearly articulated arguments from different sides?

- Is there sufficient and credible evidence to support the author's conclusion?

TIPS FOR USING MENTOR TEXTS IN THE DISCIPLINE AREAS

- It isn't necessary to have students read an entire article to expose them to quality writing. Show students a sentence, paragraph, or section to help them identify the characteristics of specific disciplinary writing.

- Provide students with disciplinary texts and ask them to evaluate the writing based on a rubric you have developed together.

- Choose articles that aren't too difficult for students to comprehend or too perfectly written to avoid discouraging them in their own attempts at writing.

- Share your own writing with students, even essays from college courses if that's all you have. Show them your own struggles as you learned how to write in ways that demonstrate disciplinary writing and point out how such writing may not fit the ELA mold.

- Ask students to bring in texts related to your subject and share in small groups why they think the writing is noteworthy or not especially good.

- Share good student writing with the class and point out what makes it exemplary in your discipline.

- Remember that humor and interest count when trying to engage students in mentor texts; otherwise, they may think writing in a particular field must be boring or filled with "just the facts."

- Provide an explicit reason for why you chose the mentor text.

- In ELA, where mentor texts are used extensively, create mini-lessons that highlight pieces of mentor texts to help students become better writers during all aspects of the writing process.

Middle school library information teacher Laura Winter previews content-related books in an effort to help teachers find quality mentor texts.

- Consider using picture books as mentor texts. Ask a library information teacher to find several related to your topic of choice and show students how the author organizes information, utilizes pictures to extend meaning, or engages readers in scientific concepts, for example. This book's companion website features a downloadable list of discipline-specific picture books that may serve as mentor texts in various content areas.

Listening In

Listening in to Robert Seidel and Kurt Weisenburger, high school AP history teachers, as they describe how they use Twitter to help students find and share texts about history from professional writers:

"As part of participation for our course, we encourage our students to research articles related to material from class and share them to our course hashtag on Twitter, #APUSH220. These articles can provide alternative viewpoints, explore topics not covered in class, or connect material to modern day. In essence, anything connected to our course material in some way is allowed, as long as it comes from a reputable source. This allows us to teach about assessing sources and digital citizenship in addition to providing our students with an endless stream of mentor texts.

"We recognize students who share particularly good mentor texts by retweeting them, giving them a shout-out at the beginning of class, and featuring them in our weekly online newsletter. In some instances, the article shared is also utilized in class. We also try to facilitate some discussion on Twitter regarding really stellar texts. These steps encourage students who have found and shared good mentor texts to continue to share, while also modeling for other students the attributes of good historical writing.

This screenshot shows articles students shared on their class hashtag.

"With each student sharing articles, our hashtag becomes a menu from which students can pick to read and comment. This menu is filled with a wide variety of topics and arguments, and students have a great deal of choice in deciding which of these mentor texts they are going to read.

"Our goal is to help students become habitual consumers of nonfiction. By participating on our course hashtag, students become accustomed to reading and thinking about secondary sources."

Feedback: From Master to Apprentice

While mentor texts provide the working model that informs students' writing, feedback provides the scaffolding that guides them as they compose. Before examining the qualities of good feedback, let's look at what feedback is *not*.

Teacher makes an assignment, provides a rubric, and posts a due date. Students write required essay at home, possibly on the night before the assignment is due . . . maybe after the assignment is due. Teacher spends next 2 weekends grading papers. Essays are returned to students who look at grade on top of paper and complain or smile depending on grade. Student may or may not glance briefly at teacher's thoughtful comments before trashing paper at earliest opportunity.

If this scenario is played out in most content classes, students are missing valuable opportunities to learn how to write—and teachers are missing valuable opportunities to engage in real-time feedback in the disciplines. Feedback is no small thing, either, which is why it shows up in the top 10 factors that influence achievement according to John Hattie (2012) and has one of the highest effects on student learning. Hattie suggests the following ways to make feedback effective:

- Begin with these questions:
  - Where is the student going?
  - Where am I going?
  - Where to next?
- Clarify the goal
- Ensure that students understand the feedback
- Seek feedback from students

Quoteworthy

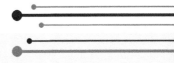

"Four ways to offer feedback that really make a difference: (1) Supply *information* about what the learner is doing rather than simply praise or criticism, (2) [t]ake care in how you present feedback, (3) [o]rient feedback around goals, (4) [u]se feedback to build metacognitive skills" (Annie Murphy Paul, 2013; emphasis in original).

Effective feedback that increases student learning occurs as students are composing, which might entail creating in art, solving in math, or making observational notes in science. Art and music teachers understand this concept well since much of their actual instruction is done through feedback. Feedback that happens during the act of writing, or learning overall, needs to occur when there is sufficient time for the student to receive the feedback, process it, and then act on it. Grant Wiggins (2012) notes that feedback after the fact is not really feedback at all, since we need information about how we are doing in our efforts to reach a goal. Feedback should be timely, specific, understandable to the learner, and actionable.

Feedback that happens during the act of writing, or learning overall, needs to occur when there is sufficient time for the student to receive the feedback, process it, and then act on it.

Quoteworthy

Feedback "*[r]equires more work from the recipient than from the giver. If feedback highlights everything that is wrong in a piece of work, there is nothing left for the recipient to do. If a student has solved a number of equations, some correctly and some incorrectly, the teacher could say, 'Five of these are incorrect. Your challenge is to find them and fix them.' For students who have solved all of the equations correctly, the teacher could say, 'Make up three questions for others to solve; one harder, one at about the same level, and one easier than the ones you've just solved'*" (William, 2012, p. 34; emphasis in original).

PROVIDING DIFFERENTIATED DISCIPLINARY FEEDBACK

While the most effective feedback occurs when teachers are able to conference one-on-one with students about their writing and learning, this model is not feasible in many classes other than ELA, where conferring should be a regular part of writing instruction. Whenever possible, content teachers should walk around the room while students are writing and offer feedback, especially if students ask for specific help. Remember that in some content areas the writing may be in formats other than sentences and paragraphs. In math, for example, students may be composing an informational analysis of a problem, a reflection on how they solved a problem, or a problem itself.

In an excellent article titled "Those Who Can Coach Can Teach," the authors offer the suggestion that disciplinary teachers and coaches both must "meet the demands of many students at diverse skill levels, each of whom would benefit from calibrated feedback" (Ehrenworth et al., 2015). Specifically, they say that the qualities of coaching feedback include the following:

- It happens in the moment.

- It is specific and calibrated.

- It is focused and honest.

- It offers one or two practical strategies/tips.

- It lays out a plan for follow-up.

- It demands a high level of agency from the student.

- It acts as a model for other players/students. (p. 9)

Let's listen in to a social studies teacher who demonstrates these elements in a conference he is having with a student.

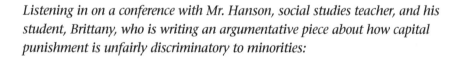

Listening In

Listening in on a conference with Mr. Hanson, social studies teacher, and his student, Brittany, who is writing an argumentative piece about how capital punishment is unfairly discriminatory to minorities:

Mr. Hanson: Let me take a look at how your writing is progressing.

Brittany: I have a lot of cases about people found innocent after being on death row but when I start writing about them, I think I might be writing too much about the case. Maybe because I started caring too much about the people I'm writing about and then I get off topic or put too much in?

Mr. Hanson:	What is the purpose of your essay?
Brittany:	To show that lots of times minorities can be sentenced to a death penalty when they didn't even commit the crime.
Mr. Hanson:	Can you find some similarities in the cases that you could target instead of looking at each individually?
Brittany:	Umm. I don't know. They are all different.
Mr. Hanson:	Maybe you could make a chart of the cases you have and see if you can't find some common thread and then use more statistics and facts instead of coming at this through the human interest side of it?
Brittany:	But I want to show how this affects them as people and how wrong it is that they sometimes don't get a fair shot at justice just because they are poor or part of a minority group or at the wrong place at the wrong time.
Mr. Hanson:	Okay. Do you think you could do that by taking a few cases that really resonate with you and showing why the injustice happened in each case? You might be able to use your examples to make an overall point about capital punishment and its inequalities?
Brittany:	How do I start?
Mr. Hanson:	How do you think you should start? What's most important?
Brittany:	Okay, I'll start with a chart and see if I can get my research organized and then maybe narrowed down to a few cases, but I still want to show how it hurts these people and their families. They aren't just statistics.
Mr. Hanson:	Why don't you ask Shauna to help you create some categories for your chart? She's pretty good at getting to the bare bones of things.

Notice that, in this conference, the teacher showed the student a technique to help her narrow her focus. The tone was one of suggestion: "Can you? Maybe you could? Do you think?" Also, the student was encouraged to think out loud and voice her doubts or confusion so the teacher could offer guidance for next steps. Eventually she came to believe she was capable of using the feedback. If the student had written and turned in her paper without her teacher's feedback, she would have missed a chance to learn how nonfiction writers organize research to best make their point. Figure 4.6 provides suggestions for rethinking feedback on student writing.

If the student had written and turned in her paper without her teacher's feedback, she would have missed a chance to learn how nonfiction writers organize research to best make their point.

TIPS FOR OFFERING EFFECTIVE FEEDBACK

- Offer suggestions to help students gain improvement based on the intended purpose of the writing.

- Look at what students are doing right to support suggestions for improvement.

Figure 4.6

Try This: Feedback for Disciplinary Writing

Instead of . . .	Try . . .
Giving students one shot at writing	Allowing revisions, especially after students have learned new skills
Placing a numerical grade on a piece of writing	Grading holistically with a focus on progress rather than only on product
Using conferences to focus primarily on grammar and punctuation (even in ELA)	Using conferences to help students improve the content
Addressing every error	Choosing only significant problem areas to address
Providing the feedback yourself	Encouraging self-reflection and allowing opportunities for peer feedback

For the Curious

Butler and Winne's (1995) research review showed that both external feedback (such as teacher feedback) and internal feedback (such as student self-evaluation) affect student knowledge and beliefs. Both (especially when used together) can help students with self-regulation: deciding on their next learning goals, devising tactics and strategies to reach them, and producing work (Brookhart, 2017).

Nick offers feedback and support to a student who has been working on an essay.

Peer editing can produce valuable input. In this ELA class, students read their stories aloud while others in the group listen so they can give feedback: what they liked, where they were confused, or a question they had, for example.

- Ask students to come to you with specific questions about their writing. (*Note*: "Is this okay?" is not a specific question.)

- Promote self-reflection so that students begin to take ownership of their progress. After conferring, ask students to think about their next steps.

- Devote at least one class period for conferring with students when they are writing major pieces. Choose one area of focus so students don't become overwhelmed.

- Make specific comments that students can act on immediately.

- Have students engage in peer revision where they read each other's pieces and offer feedback. They may be accustomed to this practice from their ELA classes.

- Use whole class feedback only if most students need instruction in one area. Otherwise, try to individualize feedback as much as possible.

- Consider taking up students' writing in progress, not for the purpose of grading, but for formative assessment purposes—to find out who needs additional help or how to pair students most effectively during peer revision.

- Frame your feedback within the context of how experts write in your discipline. See Appendices 271–324.

- Delineate between the words "assessment" and "feedback" when talking with students so they understand the difference.

Alexandra Stevenson provides feedback to a high school student as they discuss his art work.

Quoteworthy

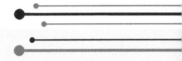

"The 'snapshot view' means looking at the feedback as an episode of learning, as if a camera were taking a snapshot of the learning. In the snapshot view, we ask two questions:

1. What did the teacher learn from the feedback episode? and

2. What did the student learn from it?" (Susan Brookhart, 2017, p. 4)

Writing can become a powerful tool in all disciplines if teachers take the time to incorporate writing as a necessary function of learning. We have found that structuring time for teachers to collaborate is essential as they reflect on what good writing looks like in their discipline, talk through the qualities of writing they want to share with students, and find mentor texts that illustrate ways to embed these writing skills into their content teaching.

Fostering Disciplinary Literacy Dialogue

1. Discuss your own skills, experience, and challenges with writing now or when you were a student.

2. What is the purpose of writing in your discipline?

3. What challenges do your students have when they write to learn in your discipline?

4. What type of feedback is most important for helping your students write as experts in your discipline?

5. Choose the appendix (pages 271–324, available on the companion website) that matches your discipline. What more would you add to the lists of ways students write in your discipline? How will you help students learn these skills?

Notes:

Resources for Continued Learning

Applebee, A., & Langer, J. (2013). *Writing instruction that works: Proven methods for middle and high school classrooms.* New York, NY: Teachers College Press.

Bernabei, G., & Reimer, J. (2013). *Fun-size academic writing for serious learning: 101 lessons & mentor texts.* Thousand Oaks, CA: Corwin.

Brookhart, S. (2017). *How to give effective feedback to your students* (2nd ed.). Alexandria: VA: ASCD.

Lent, R. C. (2012). *Overcoming textbook fatigue: 21st century tools to revitalize teaching and learning.* Alexandria, VA: ASCD.

Marchetti, A., & O'Dell, R. (2015). *Writing with mentors: How to reach every writer in the room using current engaging mentor texts.* Portsmouth, NH: Heinemann.

Rothstein, A., Rothstein, E., & Lauber, E. (2007). *Write for mathematics* (2nd ed.). Thousand Oaks, CA: Corwin.

CREATING A SCHOOL-WIDE CULTURE OF DISCIPLINARY THINKING

A culture of thinking produces the feelings, energy, and even joy that can propel learning forward and motivate us to do what at times can be hard and challenging mental work

Ron Ritchhart (2015, p. 5.)

Aaron Gardner taught economics to seniors for many years. His curriculum looked pretty much the same year after year: a unit on supply and demand, a unit on interest rates and income, a unit on trade—you get the picture. Most of his students read the assigned text, wrote essays as required, and seemed relatively interested in the content. Aaron was satisfied if his students passed the end-of-term exam and remembered some of what he had taught them. As he saw it, he was definitely the "insider" and most of his students were "outsiders" with whom he shared his insider knowledge, similar to kids who are required to play soccer in PE but never really saw themselves as soccer players unless they joined the team. Then Aaron attended a disciplinary literacy workshop and began to consider how to help his students *think* like economists.

On June 2, 2017, he read an article in the *New York Times,* economics pages titled "We May Be Closer to Full Employment Than It Seemed: That's Bad News" (Irwin, 2007). On June 1, the quarterly unemployment rate had been announced at 4.3 percent, the lowest in sixteen years, and Aaron had mentioned it in class as he always did when the jobs report came out. On June 2, however, after seeing the headline about full employment being bad news, he decided to give his students a chance to think like economists instead of merely being told how economists think. He wrote the headline on the board and asked his students to talk in small groups about why this author's supposition might be true. For those who had no idea, he offered a clue: What if the unemployment rate dropped for the wrong reasons? Students quickly reasoned that fewer people had been seeking jobs so they weren't counted in the numbers of the unemployed. He then gave them the article and asked if the reasoning of the author was valid based on what they knew of economics. This activity marked a shift in how Aaron taught economics the following year.

He decided to give his students a chance to think like economists instead of merely being told how economists think.

Brain Connection

HOW DO EXPERTS THINK?

According to researchers Bransford, Brown, and Cocking (2000), experts do not simply store knowledge as "a list of facts and formulas." Instead, "their knowledge is organized around core concepts or 'big ideas' that guide their thinking about their domains" (p. 36). When attempting to solve a problem, they do not search through everything in their brains to find what is important, but they can efficiently retrieve what is relevant to a particular task. They have more conceptual chunks in memory, more features defining each chunk, and more interrelations among the chunks. Teaching novices how to organize their knowledge helps them to become "insiders" and better problem solvers in the discipline (Bransford et al., 2000).

Learning to Think in Disciplinary Ways

Disciplinary literacy is not only about subject-specific reading, writing, and communicating; it is also about thinking in ways that are relevant and unique to each content area. Such thinking is the antithesis of finding the "right" answer or merely engaging in a strategy to comprehend the text.

William Gormley (2017) lists several hallmarks of critical thinking that might help us as we consider how to engage students deeply in our disciplines:

- Willingness to challenge conventional wisdom
- An inclination to reconsider your own cherished beliefs
- A relentless search for good evidence
- An ability to draw appropriate inferences from good evidence
- Respect for competing points of view
- Persistence when answers to important questions seem elusive (p. 2)

The expression of these skills will look different depending upon the discipline in which they are employed, but the essence of the skills, respecting competing points of views, for example, remain relatively similar across content areas.

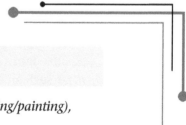

Listening In

Listening in to Alexandra Stevenson, studio arts class (drawing/painting), as she discusses how she teaches students to think in art:

"By starting with observation and description, then moving to analysis, and finally to interpretation and evaluation, students learn to investigate *how* a painting or drawing works, which is helpful

Students in an art class consider how one artist's work differs from another.

for both artist and viewer. Holding interpretation and judgment at bay is crucial.

"For example, initial questions I ask students in a critique require observation and description. What do you see? Students might describe subject matter, materials, or techniques. Asking students to chart the path their eyes travel as they look at the artwork can move them from description to analysis as they explain why they think their eye traveled a particular route. This question helps students think about composition and structure in artwork. After spending time looking at and analyzing what they see, students move to interpretive questions, describing what the artwork communicates to them as viewers. Last, we focus on evaluation, and at this point students talk about the most successful aspects of the artwork and areas that need further development."

Disciplinary literacy is an exciting approach because as students learn to think in critical ways within the disciplines, they are better able to navigate across subjects and, as Moje and Sutherland (2003) posit, also better able to construct a "just and democratic world" (p. 149). Is it possible that a change in the way literacy is taught in content areas can make such an enormous difference in students' lives? Many experts think so. Gormley (2017) says that one reason to focus on critical thinking is that "[i]t is a potential cure for some of the biggest problems we face as a nation" (Intro, p. 2).

Rainey and Moje (2012) explain that disciplinary literacy requires that students learn how to interact with a variety of disciplinary texts and move among them fluidly and, in thinking as specialists in the field, learn when and how to "produce (and challenge) knowledge within various fields of study" (p. 77).

Immersing students in disciplinary thinking gives them the practice they need to engage in a deeper type of learning, one that leads to doing, instead of reading about doing. It follows that students need many opportunities to practice such skills in various ways every day in every discipline, schoolwide, to help them prepare for a future that is in all ways uncertain. In the sections that follow, we show specific examples of how content area teachers have shifted their instruction to support students' thinking. Keep in mind, these are but a few examples—there are many more possibilities, and we encourage you to explore more ideas with your colleagues.

Immersing students in disciplinary thinking gives them the practice they need to engage in a deeper type of learning, one that leads to doing, instead of reading about doing.

Quoteworthy

"Mrs. Turton says when something happens that no one can explain, it means you have bumped up against the edge of human knowledge. And that is when you need science. Science is the process for finding the explanations that no one else can give you."

From *The Thing About Jellyfish*,
a middle school novel by
Ali Benjamin, 2015, p. 45

THINKING LIKE A SCIENTIST

In an article published in *Psychology Today* titled "How to Think Like a Scientist" (2013), author Jonathan Wai summarized the thinking of Linda Gottfredson (2010), author of an intriguing piece titled "Pursuing Patterns, Puzzles, and Paradoxes," about how "scientifically important a knotty puzzle or seeming paradox can be" (p. 26). Her insights are listed below:

1. Pursue what appears to be a paradox. It will force you to reexamine the full body of evidence with new eyes.

2. Spot contradictions and novel patterns by going on cross-disciplinary research expeditions.

3. Focus on data and methods. Ignore the author's conclusions.

4. Don't rely on fancy statistics or mathematical modeling: They can obscure the structure of evidence.

5. There is no single formula for doing good science. Be open to having your basic presumptions shattered. (Wai, 2013)

In concert with your team, develop some principles of scientific thinking that are important for your students to consider as they begin moving as insiders in the scientific world.

If you are a science teacher then you may, or may not, agree with Goffredson's conclusions. What's important is that you consider how scientists *do* think and, in concert with your team, develop some principles of scientific thinking that are important for your students to consider as they begin moving as insiders in the scientific world.

High school chemistry teacher Jessica Royal, a member of a disciplinary literacy cohort, wanted her students to begin to think like scientists as she engaged them in an inquiry project based on nuclear technology. She explains that she had already helped her students build background knowledge so they had a reference point. They understood nuclear equations as well as the energy input and output process of a nuclear reaction. Now they were ready to explore nuclear technology. She told her students they could choose an area to research among categories she provided, such as nuclear-powered ships, food safety and preservation, or nuclear waste disposal. They could also come up with another topic as long as it was approved by Jessica.

After researching their topic, students had to design an infographic that presented accurate information, include a brief description of nuclear technology and how it worked, and provide real-life examples of where the technology was used or could be used. "Before students began, I used a model to facilitate a class discussion about the qualities of an effective infographic to ensure their posters met the scientific criteria we agreed upon as a class. I wanted them to organize their information as real scientists would," Jessica said.

She provided several "must haves" for the infographics such as a clear representation of the energy input and output of each system, but Jessica also gave students options from which to choose, including an "other" for anything they deemed interesting about their topic, to encourage ownership.

Once students finished their infographics, they were ready to present their research findings. They hung their posters on walls throughout the classroom and participated in a gallery walk—taking notes as they walked so they could better understand each other's findings on the different topics of nuclear chemistry. Jessica asked students to keep in mind two questions during their walk:

- How is nuclear chemistry used in society?
- How does nuclear technology impact society?

Figure 5.1 shows an example of one student's infographic.

Jessica wanted students to practice speaking as experts might about their research in the project, so the next day she facilitated a seminar. "First, I had students reflect on the project, and then they debated which nuclear technologies positively and negatively impacted society. They used their gallery walk notes to offer evidence to support their opinions," Jessica explained. Jessica asked a student to map the flow of the discussion in a spaghetti graph (see Figure 5.2) so she could encourage those students who were hesitant to participate. "I wanted this seminar to become a sort of scientific think tank," she said.

As Jessica reflected on the project, she noted that students were enthusiastic about the learning although the content was difficult. "They were invested in the topics they had chosen and researched. Rather than my giving them the information, they were curious enough to research it on their own and then use it to create their projects. During the gallery walk, students took pride in displaying their research findings and were interested in learning from others. The discussion was lively and informed by evidence. As students presented their viewpoints, it was obvious that they were thinking beyond a surface level. I felt like my class had the opportunity to experience what it is really like to research a topic that they were interested in, share

Jessica, center, facilitates a seminar with students who have researched nuclear technology.

Figure 5.1

Science Student's Infographic on Nuclear Accidents

 Nuclear Accidents

"The unleashed power of the atom has changed everything, save our modes of thinking and we thus drift toward unparalleled catastrophe."

–Albert Einstein

Nuclear power plants began sprouting up in the 1950's and 1960's. At the time they were said to be a safe and clean alternative energy source.

The amount of energy produced by the fission of a single uranium atom is 10 million times the energy produced by the combustion of a singel coal atom

$$^{235}_{92}U + ^{1}_{0}n \rightarrow ^{90}_{32}Kr + ^{143}_{56}Ba + ^{1}_{0}n + ^{1}_{0}n + ^{1}_{0}n$$

Chernobyl, Ukraine (1986)

–result of flawed reactor design that was operated by inadequately trained personnel

–explosion and fire of a reactor sent radioisotopes into the atmosphere and downwind

–Two plant workers died on the night of the accident, and a further 28 people died within a few weeks of acute radiation poisoning.

–Total of 350,000 people have been relocated

Fukushima, Japan (2011)

– Massive 9.0 earthquake triggered a tsunami that hit the northern part of japan. Including the Fukushima Dai-ichi Nuclear power plant

– Facilities for external and backup power were destroyed, causing 3 nuclear reactors to meltdown

–Damaged reactors started leaking radioactive water and air that contaminated everything within a 20k range

–160,000 people fled their homes to escape radioactive contamination

To this day the world is still learning more about nuclear energy and how to harness the immense power. These accidents teach scientists more and more about how to make it safe and clean for the environment.

After Chernobyl, nuclear power was researched to prevent an event like that from ever happening again. Reactors were greatly improved along with the training of personnel that operated them. Unfortunately, due to poor location and an unpredictable natural disaster Fukushima experienced an event very much like Chernobyl.

Nuclear power is the future of energy. It is incredibly powerful and much more beneficial to the world. Although it can be extremely dangerous, people everyday are working to improve it.

Figure 5.2

Spaghetti Chart of Student Interaction During a Seminar

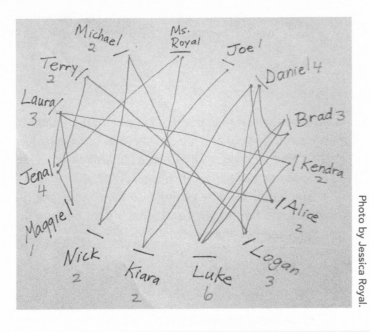

Photo by Jessica Royal.

findings in a succinct, graphic format with data and charts, and think like scientists with hard evidence and facts to back up their opinions."

The method of inquiry that Jessica used in her class is identified by Jeff Wilhelm (2016) as a "rigorous cognitive apprenticeship into disciplinary expertise and meaning-making" (p. 58). He cites a study conducted by Fred Newman involving 23 schools and more than 2,300 students, where learners were found to have "significantly higher engagement and achievement on challenging tasks when they learned with an inquiry environment" (Newman & Associates, 1996; Newman & Wehlage, 1995, as cited in Wilhelm, 2016). Our observations confirm this research; inquiry requires content area thinking and doing that is at the core of disciplinary literacy.

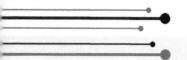

Quoteworthy

"Like works of literature, mathematical ideas help expand our circle of empathy, liberating us from the tyranny of a singular, parochial point of view. Numbers, properly considered, make us better people."

From *Thinking in Numbers: On Life, Love, Meaning and Math*, a nonfiction book by Daniel Tammet, 2012, p. 10

THINKING LIKE A MATHEMATICIAN

We will be the first to admit that we are not mathematicians. That's why we were intrigued to find a clearly written booklet by Kevin Houston (2010) titled *10 Ways to Think Like a Mathematician*. If only it were so easy. Mathematicians sometimes don't realize that the rest of us may have a difficult time getting into their world, but Houston seems to understand this problem and offers advice through the following principles and questions:

1. Question everything.

2. Write in sentences.

3. What about the converse?

4. Use the contrapositive.

5. Consider extreme examples.

6. Create your own examples.

7. Where are your assumptions used?

8. Start with the complicated side.

9. Ask "What happens if?"

10. Communicate.

We are not suggesting that teachers should follow these ten "rules" when showing students how to think like mathematicians, but we offer them as a sort of mentor text for you to consider when creating your own guidelines for helping your students learn how mathematicians do think.

Consider other models as well, such as one offered by Conrad Wolfram, director of one of the most important mathematical companies in the world. He says that a "chasm has opened up between the subject of math in education and math outside" and provides four steps for learning math:

1. Posing the right questions

2. Real world –> math formulation

3. Computation

4. Math formulation –> real world, verification

"In education," he says, "we spend perhaps 80 percent of the time on step 3 by hand, yet it's rarely used outside above the most basic arithmetic. Computers (and don't forget phones, iPods and iPads) do that bit—and usually much better than any human could" (Rivero, 2010).

Jo Boaler authored an excellent book that imbues the principles of disciplinary literacy, *Mathematical Mindsets: Unleashing Students' Potential Through Creative Math, Inspiring Messages, and Innovative Teaching* (2016). In it, she endorses a project-based approach to math, contending that students "achieved at significantly higher levels in mathematics, both in standardized tests (Boaler, 1998) and later in life (Boaler, 2005)" (pp. 66–67) when learning in such a way. See pages 134–142 in *This Is Disciplinary Literacy* for examples of project-based learning as well as templates to help students get started. For those who want to know more about this type of learning, go to The Buck Institute's website at www.bie.org. You might also check out DoSomething.org, a website that offers ideas for projects in all disciplines and also connects students to other students engaged in the same type of project.

Middle school math teacher Tina Reckamp doesn't follow a formula for

Middle school math students use words, symbols, and diagrams to explain their answers.

helping students think as mathematicians, but she does employ inquiry every day in her lessons.

"I have my students think about math as a story and a mystery to solve. Every time the students encounter a math problem, I encourage them to ask, 'Who is in this story?' and 'What is this story about?' Math becomes a way of thinking about situations that happen in real life," she says.

She also uses debate to immerse her students into mathematical thinking. They share their ideas with partners or in small groups and challenge each other's reasoning. Tina says that activities such as this help her students see math as more than just numbers and procedures. "I want them to know that math is a subject where they have to reason logically, make inferences, and explain their thinking."

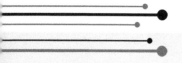

Quoteworthy

"History is the business of identifying momentous events from the comfort of a high-back chair. With the benefit of time, the historian looks back and points to a date in the manner of a gray-haired field marshal pointing to a bend in a river on a map: *There it was*, he says. *The turning point. The decisive factor. The fateful day that fundamentally altered all that was to follow.*"

From *A Gentleman in Moscow*,
a novel by Amor Towles, 2016,
p. 173; emphasis in original

THINKING LIKE A HISTORIAN

The Stanford History Education Group (n.d.) offers a historical thinking chart with which most social studies teachers are familiar. The skills it endorses are

- Sourcing
- Contextualization
- Corroboration
- Close reading

But what if these skills are only the beginning? They may support students in reading as historians, but how do students learn to *think* in ways that require more than answering questions about texts? Acting as a historian requires students to be able to engage in cause-and-effect thinking, understand how story creates meaning, and make arguments to support theories, according to Kim Kutzh, historian at Kahn Academy. Content instruction in the past has told students what they need to do (read closely or consider sourcing for example), but have we taught them how to *think* in ways that utilize these skills? And what, actually, does it mean to teach students to think as a historian or social scientist? It may begin with students pondering the following questions:

How do students learn to think in ways that require more than answering questions about texts?

- When you read a statement in a primary or secondary source, do you consider the social and political environment and how that might affect the communication of the writer?

- Do you think about events in the past as a pattern that may predict events in the present?

- Do you look for subtle (or not-so-subtle) underlying messages intended to influence the reader or viewer?

- Do you broaden your view of a historical time period to include its art, music, or literature?

- Do you always consider the source to and determine its credibility?

- Do you think about other pieces of evidence when drawing conclusions about an event, occurrence, or pattern?

- Do you seek various perspectives and consider how and why each might be biased?

Kathleen Duffy, our team's social studies teacher, relies on questions such as those above as she moves her students deeply within her content, offering a variety of texts for students to utilize as they expand their thinking. "Too often, we, as educators, are guilty of teaching the same content over and over each year. People argue that in social studies, keeping the same content is fine because the history itself isn't changing. But that couldn't be further from the truth." She contends that historians have been finding new information from diaries, journals, and artifacts, and scientists have been unearthing new skeletons and fossils, all that literally change history. As an example, she points to the diaries of Holocaust victims and survivors that have recently emerged as well as stories of females outside the normal scope of domestic roles such as abolitionists, World War II spies, or NASA scientists.

"So," she says, "one of the thinking skills important in a history class is for students to learn to modify their knowledge base and reconsider their beliefs as they incorporate new information. I also want my students to be cognizant of different perspectives and how that plays into interpretations." How does she do that? By offering different points of view and new information about "heroes" such as Christopher Columbus or Robert E. Lee. She also has students examine motives and moral characters of figures from the past, studying accomplishments as well as mistakes. "Humans are inherently flawed and, in my courses, we look to understand, not to judge, in order to gain a wider perspective," she says.

When her students study figures like Elizabeth Cady Stanton, Emmeline Pankhurst, and Margaret Sanger, for example, all of whom have paved the way for women's progress, she also asks them to consider how their flaws (racism, classism, etc.) divided their movements and hindered their progress. "I don't want my students to repeat incomplete histories; I want them to look at how to include more: more people, more diversity, more perspectives, more heroic acts, more flaws, and more humanity."

One of the thinking skills important in a history class is for students to learn to modify their knowledge base and reconsider their beliefs as they incorporate new information.

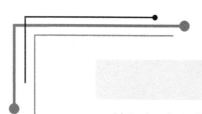

Listening In

Listening in to Kathleen Romero, a student in Luana Byte's band class, as she reflects on writing after a performance. Notice how her thinking mirrors that of professional musicians.

"The piece 'Falling Leaves' was my favorite piece that we played because of its craft, its meaning, and because this piece described, for me, death. It appeared in my head when I heard this piece, but for me death symbolizes that it is the end of your time to learn and go where you belong.

"I did feel like something changed about the way we played this piece in the gym—or it might've just been that the gym was bigger, so there was a greater sound bouncing off the walls. Anyway, in this piece there was a huge amount of passion. There was a smooth, dark, and hollow entrance, where only the clarinets had the melody, which was followed up by all the other instruments to create a great force of satisfaction. This led to Sophia to start playing her part, introducing the fragile, high and soft melody. Then the rest of the band had their part to haunt the beauty, to make it stronger.

"Overall, this piece was just hauntingly beautiful and represented how, when leaves fall off a tree, they leave their family. This is terrifying for most, but I also see it can be a huge amount of pride and beauty about your life and who you are. I feel like this piece was the most compassionate."

Work by Katherine Romero and Luana Byte.

Middle school students in Luana Byte's band class learn to think as musicians such as when they pay attention to the most challenging of the eighth- and sixteenth-note rhythm combinations while rehearsing "Swamp Rabbit Stomp" by Michael Sweeney.

- Show students how experts in the field think by modeling the ways specialists reason through problems, participate in a task, or ask questions when discussing a complex issue or text.

- Engage students in role playing where they actually "become" an expert and answer questions, demonstrate skills, or construct new knowledge or products.

- Point out to students the difference between acting as an "insider" in your discipline and following directions as an "outsider" might.

- Invite guest speakers in your discipline to talk with students about their thought processes as they perform their work.

- Ask students to reflect on their thinking (in writing or with a learning partner) after working on a topic, problem, or performance. Point out student examples that emulate the thinking and reasoning of experts in your discipline.

Curiosity Drives Disciplinary Thinking

In disciplinary literacy instruction, curiosity is at the forefront as students seek ways to increase, evaluate, internalize, and apply what they have learned. Contrast this approach to traditional instruction where the teacher either creates or is given the content to be covered and then transfers that information to students who must gain sufficient understanding to pass a test. The two approaches are fundamentally different, and research indicates that the former results in deeper learning and longer-lasting benefits. A recent meta-analysis, for example, concluded that effort and curiosity have as much influence on student success as intelligence does (Von Stumm, Hell, & Chamorro-Premuzic, 2011, as cited in Bryan Goodwin, 2014, September, p. 74). Other studies have linked curiosity to better job performance (Reio & Wiswell, 2000), greater life satisfaction (Kashdan & Steger, 2007), and even longer lives (Swan & Carmelli, 1996).

A recent theme of the Learning and the Brain conference centered on curiosity, marking a shift from many conferences that offer sessions on how to "teach" students rather than how to develop instructional practices that switch on their "need to know." A major take-away from the conference was that curiosity is far more complex than kindergarteners wondering why the sky is blue. "Curiosity may put the brain in a state that allows it to learn and retain any kind of information, like a vortex that sucks in what you are motivated to learn and also everything around it," explains Dr. M. J. Gruber (2014).

With the infusion of research-based strategies and a focus on "covering the curriculum," educators sometimes dismiss "soft" skills such as curiosity, mindset, and habits of mind. Fortunately, researchers and scholars have now placed these characteristics back in the spotlight. Wendy Ostroff, cognitive psychologist and author of *Cultivating Curiosity in K–12 Classrooms* (2016), begins her book by offering research that supports the three significant advantages of fostering curiosity in students:

1. "Curiosity jump-starts and sustains intrinsic motivation, allowing deep learning to happen with ease" (p. 4). When students' curiosity was sparked in one study, they spent more time (even their own time) on new learning, which increased depth of learning and helped them understand complex concepts and then remember content later.

2. Curiosity releases dopamine, a neurotransmitter that helps improve observation while increasing attention and remembering as well as fostering pleasure in the experience. It is so important that it actually entices students, pulling them into a form of learning that sticks and often expands.

3. "Curious people exhibit enhanced cognitive skills," (p. 5) which means they "learn more and learn better"—and the effects are longer lasting. There is even some research that suggests that curiosity could ward off Alzheimer's.

Curiosity is an essential characteristic for students to develop if teachers want to adopt a disciplinary literacy approach, one that relies heavily on inquiry, problem solving, and critical thinking.

Quoteworthy

"The meaning of 'knowing' has shifted from being able to remember and repeat information to being able to find and use it."

Nobel laureate Herbert Simon (1996, as cited in Salen, 2008)

An ELA teacher in California, Nancy Florez-Muro, wanted her students to think critically about how to approach a biographical figure. She knew that one way she could accomplish that would be to ignite their curiosity about a biographical subject she would use as a model for their own research later. Interestingly, she tapped into the ways experts in several disciplines think as she facilitated an engaging activity. Her subject? The artist Georgia O'Keeffe.

First she used a video with accompanying music and taught students how to watch and listen. During a second viewing, she asked students to engage in a literacy skill used by artists, careful observation, and by musicians, careful listening. Students made notes about what they saw and heard. She then asked students to go back and write about what they had been thinking when they made their notations, after which they would create five questions they had about what they had experienced. "Finally, I asked students to connect the sights, thoughts and questions in any way they liked. This immersion got the students ready to analyze Georgia O'Keeffe from a biographical viewpoint, much as real biographers might." (See Figure 5.3 for an example of the graphic organizer she used to help students organize their thoughts.)

The activity didn't end there, however. Students were given several quotes from O'Keeffe and asked to choose one that "spoke" to them. They wrote about the quote based on what they knew of O'Keeffe. Figure 5.3 shows how one student responded to the assignment. The O'Keeffe quote she chose to respond to was "Someone else's vision will never be as good as your own vision for yourself. Live and die with it because in the end it's all you have. Lose it and you lose yourself and everything else. I should have listened to myself."

Just as Nancy had utilized disciplinary skills outside her subject area—art and music—others are also using specific disciplinary skills as a

Figure 5.3

I See, I Think, I Wonder, I Connect Graphic Organizer

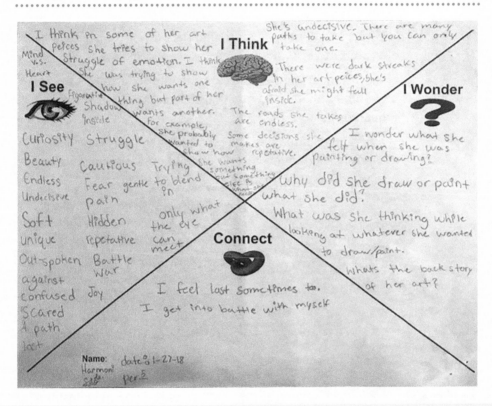

way to deepen learning. A collaborative in New York City's high schools wanted to help students with skills such as close reading and argumentation across the disciplines so they taught students to "analyze athletic competitions, to compose sports arguments, and to transfer and apply these skills to academic subjects" (Ehrenworth et al., 2015, para. 1). It seems that disciplinary thinking can be used in a variety of ways by teachers who understand how to integrate content area skills.

TIPS FOR INCREASING
CURIOSITY IN THE DISCIPLINES

- Begin each class with a question that tugs at curiosity, even one tangentially related to your content. See pages 124–134 in *This Is Disciplinary Literacy* for more suggestions on how to infuse lessons with curiosity.

- Instead of asking students to find the answer, ask them how many answers can be found.

- Show students how to fold curiosity into solid, academic questions and how then to find credible, valid answers to questions.

- Model critical thinking and problem solving based on your own curiosity about topics in your discipline. Show students how experts in your field display curiosity.

As Alexandra Stevenson provides instruction to her art students, she encourages both curiosity and perseverance, two qualities that Mihaly Csikszentmihalyi (1996) found in creative individuals.

- Resist providing answers unless they are for surface knowledge that students need. Counter students' questions with your own questions, such as "How could you find out?" "What do you think?" or "Why do you want to know?" to help them become cognitively aware of their own curiosity.

- Engage the class (or small groups) often in brainstorming (which employs divergent thinking) to "turn on" thinking, encourage curiosity, and stimulate ideas.

- Encourage students to challenge the thinking of others by asking what more the creator or author could have included.

- Allow students the time and space to ask and investigate their own discipline-specific queries. Keep a question board in your class and have students keep a question page in their learning logs.

- Encourage students to satisfy their curiosity outside of class instead of only answering school-related questions.

For the Curious

HOW DO YOU KNOW IF YOU ARE A GENIUS?

Michael Michalko (2001) found in his research that a key characteristic of all geniuses is their intense childlike curiosity and a high degree of inquiry. For instance, Leonardo da Vinci wrote questions to himself in his notebooks. Tesla imagined whole new worlds and then wondered how to make them manifest. Einstein spent his life asking questions about why objects behave the way they do, and what would happen if rules were altered. In fact, Einstein once said that the ordinary person could learn all the physics he or she will ever need to learn if the person could assume the willingness to ask childlike questions.

Students and Teachers: Thinking Like Insiders Together

We continue to return to the idea of insiders and outsiders in disciplinary learning and thinking because it is an important distinction between traditional content area instruction and a disciplinary literacy approach. Many teachers have been insiders to their content for a long time, perhaps beginning as early as elementary or middle school. They continued the insiders' journey through high school, college, or their careers, increasing knowledge in their chosen fields along the way. As such, they became immersed in the thinking habits of experts—often becoming experts themselves. As Rainey and Moje (2012) point out, such teachers "hold deep understandings of the ways that knowledge is produced and communicated in the discipline, the types of arguments that are valued, and the types of evidence and warrant that are acceptable" (p. 76). Disciplinary literacy asks teachers to invite students into their club by showing them how experts in their content think instead of welcoming students as visitors to the subject.

Disciplinary literacy asks teachers to invite students into their club by showing them how experts in their content think instead of welcoming students as visitors to the subject.

Photo by Kathleen Duffy.

Students are engaged in a nonverbal activity to simulate the encounter of the Spanish Explorers meeting Natives in the Americas. They were not permitted to speak and had to demonstrate how they would acquire valuables, host a welcome dinner with all parties sitting, and convert the Natives to Christianity. During the wrap-up and reflection activity, students expressed frustration due to misconceptions and miscommunications and were thus able to connect their experiences to that of the Explorers and Natives.

INSIDER PROBLEM SOLVING IN SCIENCE

Lauren Pennock, high school science teacher, inadvertently discovered how being on the inside makes all the difference in content area learning. It began when some of her science equipment malfunctioned. At a lab station, she had three glass tubes of colored water that bubbled simultaneously, all connected by rubber hoses. Suddenly, the bubbling stopped. She was discouraged because she couldn't manage to get all of the tubes working at once. "Just as I got one to bubble, two more stopped—so I realized it was going to take a lot of perseverance and problem solving to fix this seemingly small problem," she said.

The next day in class, she presented the challenge of the unbubbling tubes to two boys who had not seemed particularly interested in science but who did seem attracted to the tubes and other lab equipment. She was surprised when they offered to come in during their lunch period to help her fix the tubes and then began coming in after school to work on the project. They continued to show up each day, one of them even telling Lauren that he was getting all his homework done in other classes so he could be released during his study period to work on the tubes. She observed these two boys transition from rather disengaged students to focused scientists, trying first one thing and then another in an effort to figure out how they could solve the problem.

"They told me initially that they thought there was a hole in one of the hoses that was causing the leak and it took some time and experimentation to discover that wasn't the case. They finally announced that it wasn't a hole but that they thought a hose was imperceptibly leaking at one of the ends. They asked if I had a wider hose. I gave them a box of hoses of various sizes, they found one that fit and, suddenly, all of the tubes bubbled."

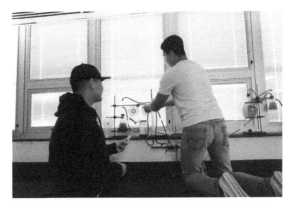

Students learn how to think like scientists by solving real-world problems.

Lauren explained that these students received no extra credit or points for this time-consuming work. They responded to a scientific challenge, and Lauren treated them as if they were associates or apprentices as they solved the problem. "It was amazing to see how invested they were without any external motivators," she commented. Lauren is now thinking about how she can transfer what she has learned from these two students into her curriculum in the form of fewer "lessons" and more inquiry with the goal of allowing students to think and act as scientists. Figure 5.5 provides some ideas for shifting your instruction to help students think more like insiders.

Quoteworthy

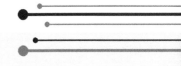

"What if, instead of having you look closely at the poem itself, I present you a statement about 'the meaning of the poem'? There's no way you can connect with that—it's too closed, too fixed.

"This is what happens when everything we want kids to learn is fixed, finished, done. One kid explained this, talking about his science class. 'The trouble is, everything's all figured out. So there's no place for me. They figured everything out already so why should I? Where's *my* place?' On the other hand, if we recognize knowledge as being partial, tentative, a matter of human construction, then every learner has a place" (Meek, 1991, p. 31).

TIPS FOR TURNING STUDENTS INTO DISCIPLINARY INSIDERS

- As much as possible, provide students with autonomy and encourage ownership in projects, questions, texts, and ways of working with the content.

- Provide relevant, real-world texts rather than textbook chapters and questions.

- Allow students to share insights from their reading, problem solving, or investigation and have other students ask questions or contribute to the discussion.

- Bring in (or have students bring in) current events or news articles related to the latest findings in your discipline. See an activity called "Current Events Short Takes" on pages 33–37 of *This Is Disciplinary Literacy*.

- Flip your classroom with students watching videos at home and then applying their new knowledge in class the next day with the teacher as a facilitator.

- Create a problem-based classroom where students do the work of the discipline rather than learning about the subject.

- Provide opportunities for service learning where students act as practitioners in the field with the added advantages that come with altruism.

- Treat students more like colleagues than subordinates, respecting their processes and abilities. Use feedback to guide their learning. See pages 119–121 regarding tips on incorporating feedback.

- Encourage intellectual risk taking. Provide opportunities for self-regulation as students wrestle with various perspectives, new findings, and complex issues.

- Whenever possible, reduce the emphasis on grades and create opportunities for intrinsic rewards.

- Show students the "habits of mind" that experts in your field must develop to become successful and expect them to model such habits.

- Have students set their own goals for learning and participation.

For the Curious

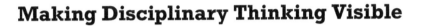

WHAT IS *THE* MOST IMPORTANT SKILL FOR NEW HIRES IN THE WORKPLACE?

A survey of 343 executives of U.S. companies found that the skill deemed most important for new hires was "critical thinking and problem-solving (identified by 72% of executives), followed by collaboration and teamwork (63%), and communication (54%)" (Goodwin & Hein, 2016/2017, p. 84).

Making Disciplinary Thinking Visible

Critical thinking has been a goal in education for decades but such *thinking* is only one part of the disciplinary literacy model. Roberts and Billings (2012), in their book on how seminars increase critical thinking, contend that learning to think is a "process of successfully explaining and *manipulating* increasingly complex texts"—and they make clear that when they say "texts" they mean "a set of interrelated ideas often represented in a human artifact" (2012, p. 1). We like this definition for many reasons but especially because Roberts and Billings use the word "manipulating," which we italicized in their quote, as a critical component of thinking. The manipulation of knowledge is the *doing* that disciplinary literacy requires, which also shows students' thinking.

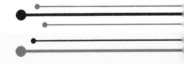

The manipulation of knowledge is the doing that disciplinary literacy requires, which also shows students' thinking.

How is thinking made visible? Through experimental inquiry in science, interpretation and communication of multiple artifacts in history, critique of literature in English, and rational, evidence-based argumentation in all subjects. Without such doing, thinking may become stagnant or passive, resulting in a sort of educational game that favors extrinsic rewards.

Quoteworthy

"The role of education is no longer to teach content, but to help our children learn—in a world that rewards the innovative and punishes the formulaic" (Wagner & Dintersmith, 2015, p. 197).

MAKING THINKING VISIBLE IN MATH

Let's take an example from math to make our point. An important study (Schwartz & Bransford, 1998, as cited in Boaler, 2016) compared three ways of teaching mathematics:

1. The teacher shows the methods; students solve problems using the methods they have been shown.

2. Students discover methods through exploration.

3. Students are given problems to work on (though they had not been taught the methods for solving them); they were then shown methods for solving.

How is thinking made visible? Through experimental inquiry in science, interpretation and communication of multiple artifacts in history, critique of literature in English, and rational, evidence-based argumentation in all subjects.

When students were divided into groups and each group was taught according to one of the techniques described above, guess which one led to significantly higher learning? You might think the best approach is Number 2 based on our discussion about "doing," but inquiry relies on students having some surface knowledge about the topic or content; exploration is venturing into unknown areas with little background. According to the researchers involved in this study, the instruction in Number 3 was most effective. Presenting the problem first and allowing students to wrestle with it created curiosity. When students were then shown various methods for solving it, they were eager to learn the methods. We are most intrigued by the fact that they were allowed to think through and then manipulate the texts, *do* something with the texts, before being shown the mathematical thinking necessary to solve the problem. Astute teachers might look in on students' thinking as they try to solve the problem and then assess their ability to use disciplinary thinking once they had been shown it. Figure 5.4 provides some ways to shift traditional instruction to allow students space to make disciplinary thinking visible.

With the risk of overplaying our point, we offer Wendy Ostroff's (2016) perspective once again: Just providing factual material rarely corresponds to deep understanding. Although some content is important, we must remember that the human brain is less detail oriented and more process oriented. Students think through and, thus, remember actions and things they manipulate, interact with, and do—the core of disciplinary literacy.

TIPS FOR MAKING DISCIPLINARY THINKING VISIBLE

- Give students opportunities to solve or think through a text or problem before offering advice or a method for solving.

- Allow students to work with partners or in small groups as often as possible and teach them how to talk with each other about problems or texts. Starting with prompts may help at first, but relinquish prompts as soon as possible to encourage meaningful discussions that demonstrate thinking.

- Offer performance assessments and have students include in their presentation how their thinking demonstrates the reasoning of experts in your discipline.

- Ask students to tackle topics with alternative points of view, sometimes allowing them to choose the side they want to defend and other times having them assume the opposite side of an argument. As they research a topic, encourage them to reconsider their opinions and respect a competing point of view. Websites such as procon.org feature articles with opposing views.

- Commit to engaging students in at least one seminar, debate, or discussion forum per grading period. It takes a bit of planning up front but students quickly learn to become independent thinkers from such experiences. See Resources for Continued Learning at the end of the chapter for more information on how to conduct seminars.

Chris Hawkins's physics students are demonstrating scientific thinking when they create a Rube Goldberg device that has five different energy transfers and ten different steps.

- Keep track of how much classroom time is spent with the teacher talking (demonstrating his or her thinking) and how much time students are demonstrating their thinking through talking. If necessary, readjust the equation.

- Show videos or interviews of experts speaking about topics related to your discipline or ask expert guests to come into your classroom to discuss a topic. Have students become aware of how thinking is made visible through speaking. You may want to use the form in Figure 5.4 to help students with this endeavor.

The real measure of disciplinary thinking is when students begin to act as insiders, participating in the discipline by exhibiting curiosity, accepting challenges, and demonstrating thinking that takes on the habits of those in the field. This shift may require a restructuring of classroom practices and relinquishing beliefs in how things have always been done. The best way to accomplish this fundamental change is within a community of colleagues that is provided the time, resources, and support to engage in its own transformative thinking. The next section of this book shows you how to make that happen.

Figure 5.4

Evaluation of a Speaker's Thinking Process

Speaker:

Topic:

1. What is the purpose of the talk or interview?

2. Why was this speaker chosen to speak on the topic?

    • What are his or her credentials?

    • In what way is he or she an expert in the field?

3. How did this speaker's thoughts differ from others who speak on the same topic?

4. How did the speaker make key points? (For example, did he or she tell a story, show graphs or charts, use persuasion or emotion, use facts and figures, or employ humor?)

5. What question(s) would you like to ask the speaker about his or her thoughts on the subject?

6. What do you think the speaker's notes looked like as he or she was preparing the talk or presentation?

7. Did the speaker leave out something you feel was important to include?

8. Write an analysis of this speakers' thoughts using examples from the talk to substantiate your thoughts.

    • In what ways are your thoughts different or similar to the thoughts of the speaker?

    • How might the speaker have made his or her thinking more clear?

9. In what way did the speaker demonstrate the thinking of experts in his or her field?

Fostering Disciplinary Literacy Dialogue

1. Recount a time when you felt like an outsider in your discipline. What does it mean to be an insider?

2. What could you do, specifically, to elicit students' curiosity in your content?

3. Have you ever engaged your students in a seminar or project-based learning? If so, what did you observe about students' learning? If not, what topic might fit well into the seminar or project-based format?

4. What does it mean for students to participate in your discipline?

5. Choose the appendix (271–374, available on the companion website) that matches your discipline. What more would you add to the lists of ways that students think in your discipline? How will you help students learn these skills?

Notes:

Resources for Continued Learning

Armstrong, T. (2016). *The power of the adolescent brain: Strategies for teaching middle and high school students.* Alexandria, VA: ASCD.

Bean, T. W., & Dunkerly-Bean, J. (2016). At the intersection of creativity and civic engagement: Adolescents' literacies in action. *Journal of Adolescent & Adult Literacy, 60*(3), 247–253.

Boaler, J. (2016). *Mathematical mindsets: Unleashing students' potential through creative math, inspiring messages and innovative teaching.* San Francisco, CA: Jossey-Bass.

City, E. A. (2014). Talking to learn: Talking, listening, and thinking are a potent combination—each strengthens the other. *Educational Leadership, 72*(3), 10–17.

Cunny, C. (2014). What is the value of life? . . . and other Socratic questions: Four steps to planning insightful seminars. *Educational Leadership, 72*(3), 54–58.

Daniels H., & Ahmed, S. K. (2015). *Upstanders: How to engage middle school hearts and minds with inquiry.* Portsmouth, NH: Heinemann.

Larmer, J., Mergendoller, J., & Boss, S. (2015). *Setting the standard for project-based learning: A proven approach to rigorous classroom instruction.* Alexandria, VA: ASCD.

Mandell, N., & Malone, B. (2008). *Thinking like a historian: Rethinking history instruction.* Madison: Wisconsin Historical Society Press.

Ritchhart, R. (2015). *Creating cultures of thinking: The 8 forces we must master to truly transform our schools.* New York, NY: John Wiley & Sons.

Roberts, T., & Billings, L. (2012). *Teaching critical thinking: Using seminars for 21st century literacy.* New York, NY: Routledge.

Wilhelm, J. D., Douglas, W., & Fry, S. W. (2014). *The activist learner: Inquiry, literacy, and service to make learning matter.* New York, NY: Teachers College Press.

Creating a culture of disciplinary literacy schoolwide is obviously the first step in reaping the substantial benefits of this approach. But its creation may turn out to be the easy part. Sustaining any initiative in an exceedingly complex, multitasking school environment can sometimes seem impossible, and this important shift in instruction is no exception. It will take a concerted effort on the part of teachers, instructional coaches, teacher leaders, as well as district and school adminstrators to maintain an unrelenting focus on what matters most, increased student learning, through the vehicle that we know works: ongoing, collaborative professional learning, reflection, and action—all driven by disciplinary literacy instruction. As the graphic below shows, when all these components are in place—occuring simultaneously or recursively according to the unique circumstances of each school—the process becomes an active embodiment of *sustained* change that positively impacts both students and teachers.

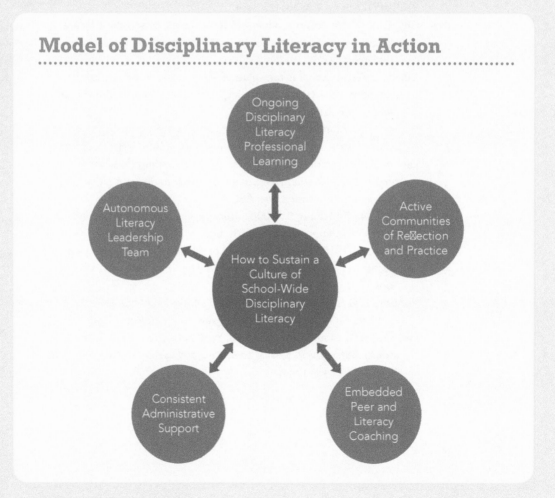

Model of Disciplinary Literacy in Action

- Ongoing Disciplinary Literacy Professional Learning
- Active Communities of Reflection and Practice
- Embedded Peer and Literacy Coaching
- Consistent Administrative Support
- Autonomous Literacy Leadership Team

How to Sustain a Culture of School-Wide Disciplinary Literacy

6

BUILDING DISCIPLINARY LITERACY (DL) LEARNING COMMUNITIES

Community, not curriculum, is where many of our improvement efforts now need to be focused.

Andy Hargreaves (Hargreaves, Earl, & Ryan, 2003)

There is little doubt based on a variety of studies that professional learning communities (PLCs) have the capacity to increase student learning by improving teaching practice (Vescio, Ross, & Adams, 2008). It gets a little sticky after this broad statement, however, as most teachers and administrators who have tried to sustain effective PLCs know. Even Rick DuFour (2004) admitted that the acronym *PLC* had been used to describe almost any combination of individuals associated with schools. He feared the term could lose all meaning unless educators focused exclusively on embedding student learning and teacher collaboration into the culture of schools.

The Problem With PLCs

Several "real-school" scenarios come to mind when thinking about PLCs that have been less than successful. In one large high school, for example, every teacher had to choose from a list of PLC topics and then sign up for membership in a yearlong study. The administration was trying to increase buy-in through autonomy. Unfortunately, all autonomy ceased with the sign-up sheets. Members were given the protocol, told what to read and discuss, and assigned tasks by which their participation could be evaluated for professional development points. Not surprisingly, when teachers are denied the opportunity to reflect on their practice or discuss common learning issues, the value of the experience decreases. In this case, teachers took comp time, scheduled parent conferences, or found other opportunities to miss meetings because they saw them as a waste of time. Since these were "in-name-only" PLCs created to meet required professional development mandates, everyone acquiesced to their dysfunction.

In another school, PLC meetings had devolved into checklists of things to accomplish, often with members dividing up the tasks as students might when a collaborative activity in the classroom goes awry. Still another school tasked their PLCs with drafting sample writing mission statements that would be considered when creating the school's official mission statement. This process took almost a semester because PLC meetings were often canceled for other, "more important" initiatives. Still another school decided to use the PLC format to discuss how to increase test scores, and the outcome was more test prep. Most often, we have seen PLCs formed for the express purpose of having teachers analyze data, despite a number of studies that demonstrate little instructional change when teachers engage in analysis of assessment data (Datnow & Hubbard, 2016). We all have our own experiences or examples from colleagues that confirm the fact that somewhere along the way PLCs often stopped functioning as they were intended.

We want to make clear that we are not pointing fingers. Schooling is an extremely complex, time-consuming, often emotional endeavor with too many critically important issues that need attention—all at once. It's understandable that in such an environment the calm retreat of a PLC is at odds with the lure of seemingly quick fixes.

In a review of the research on the impact of professional learning by Vescio et al. (2008), the authors found that learning communities are grounded in two assumptions:

Figure 6.1

Why Haven't PLCs Been Successful?

Too Little	Too Many
Autonomy	Instructions
Inquiry	Predetermined outcomes
Dialogue and reflection	Tasks
Attention to student learning	Objectives unrelated to student learning
Sharing of student work	Data-driven activities
Content area learning	Generic teaching practices or strategies
Risk taking	Routines
Peer coaching	Silos
Feedback	Evaluations
Time	Initiatives
Collaboration	Meetings
Professional learning	Professional development in-services
Ownership	Mandates
Ongoing learning	Quick fixes

When learning communities work well, they create both the energy and the synergy that fuels teachers' impact.

1. "Knowledge is situated in the 'day-to-day' lived experiences of teachers and best understood through critical reflection with others who share the same experience (Buysse, Sparkman, & Wesley, 2003)" (p. 81) and

2. Teachers' professional knowledge should increase—leading to enhanced student learning (p. 81).

Most PLCs are formed based on the above expectations but, as we noted in the beginning of this chapter, the actions necessary to fulfill such statements can be difficult to sustain. Sometimes the "learning" is incrementally dropped from PLCs in favor of more urgent matters, or it may become challenging to schedule teachers "who share the same experience." Then there is the myth that teachers must always produce something (lesson plans, common assessments, pacing guides, for example) for the purpose of accountability, an attitude that undermines trust and genuine learning. Perhaps most frequently, authentic communities based on communication, reflection, collaboration, and trust are simply not afforded the time to develop.

Fixing the Problem Through DL Learning Communities

Dennis Sparks (2002) makes a good argument for teachers to engage in PLCs when he writes about a study conducted by Lee, Smith, and Croninger (1995):

> In a study of 820 secondary schools . . . schools characterized as learning communities . . . [members] did indeed hold collective responsibility for the learning of students, worked together and changed their teaching. As a result, students had greater academic gains in science, math, history, and reading than those in traditionally organized schools. According to the researchers, teachers in these schools also reported more satisfaction in their work, had higher morale, and were absent less often (p. 57)

How do we attain these advantages without falling into a dysfunctional PLC trap? We contend that disciplinary literacy provides the foundation on which relevant learning communities can be formed and, what's more, sustained. Let's return to a brief definition of disciplinary literacy: the ability to read, write, speak, reason, and perform in discipline-specific ways. Moje reminds us that learning in content areas requires understanding not only the practices specific to a discipline but also its discourse (Luke, p. xii, 2001; cf. O'Brien, Moje, & Stewart, 2001, as cited in Moje, 2008). These two important factors provide a compelling *purpose* for the learning community, one that is not artificially imposed by federal, state, or local mandates, and one that does not rely on "check-off" or "next-task" thinking. By its very nature, a disciplinary literacy approach engages teachers in collaborative learning with others who share the same challenges and interests. Like any type of club or group where people meet with a common goal, this learning community provides an opportunity for members to solve problems and discuss the most important challenges and successes that occur in their classroom lives. When learning communities work well, they create both the energy and the synergy that fuels teachers' impact.

Listening In

Listening in to Nick Yeager, ELA teacher on our team, as he reflects on how an interdisciplinary literacy cohort improved his teaching:

"Working within the cohort—having the opportunity to truly collaborate and share with colleagues, especially those from other disciplines—has been refreshing and eye opening. Being able to present my own ideas, knowing that I will get uncensored and honest feedback, along with constructive suggestions for how to potentially expand my original thinking leaves me feeling comforted and energized to try new things in my classroom. Furthermore, hearing ideas from others and having the opportunity to spin them around in my mind and think about how I might be able to implement them has helped me stretch and grow professionally. The disciplinary literacy cohort is easily the best professional development that I've experienced in my 15-plus years of education."

Hearing ideas from others and having the opportunity to spin them around in my mind and think about how I might be able to implement them has helped me stretch and grow professionally.

Janet, our library information teacher, and Kathleen, our social studies teacher, are joined with teachers from science and English language arts to talk about ways to sustain a culture of deeper disciplinary learning.

In talking with teachers who are members of strong disciplinary learning communities, they tell us they look forward to returning to their team—and will find ways of doing so even without scheduled meetings because they experience significant intrinsic rewards. In one district where funds for such professional learning were cut, several members met on their own after school. They also met with their principals and contacted district administrators to let them know how important the meetings were for their professional growth, asking pointedly that they be reinstated. The district decided, instead, to use what funds were available to send a few teachers to national conferences and bring back what they learned, an ill-advised decision. Without a strong, embedded community to reinforce new learning, teachers reported a decline in collective efficacy, morale, and literacy learning for both students and faculty.

Our experiences have been confirmed through a recent report from The Learning Policy Institute, whose authors defined seven characteristics of effective professional learning. Their research indicated that the following were essential.

1. A focuses on content

2. The incorporation of active learning that utilizes adult learning theory

3. Collaboration, typically in job-embedded contexts

4. The use of models and modeling of effective practice

5. Coaching and expert support

6. Opportunities for feedback and reflection

7. Duration that is sustained (Darling-Hammond, Hyler, Gardener, & Espinoza, 2017, pp. v–vi)

These components taken together create a picture of the type of DL learning communities that we are illustrating in this section of the book. We also

Without a strong, embedded community to reinforce new learning, teachers reported a decline in collective efficacy, morale, and literacy learning for both students and faculty.

adhere to the principles cited in the report that encourage a job-embedded approach so that teachers have opportunities to try out new practices, examine students' work, test out new curriculum, or "study a particular element of pedagogy or student learning in the content area" (p. 5).

ELA teachers from Rocky View Schools in Calgary, Alberta, collaborate on how to use infographics with their students.

As we discussed in the introduction, we spent the past several years facilitating just such professional learning with eight cohorts of teachers across one district. Because we believe strongly that no one person or group has *the* answer regarding how to help diverse, differentiated students with challenges that often vary from subject to subject or even day to day, we have discontinued the search for one-size-fits-all solutions. They simply do not exist. Instead, we slowed down the frenetic pace to which we have become accustomed and gave teachers the time to learn with and from each other as they shared and refined practices based on their own curriculum and students. What might that look like? We offer two different configurations of such learning communities—interdisciplinary literacy learning communities and common subject literacy learning communities—as catalysts for your own thinking about how to create effective disciplinary literacy professional learning in your district or school.

Tips for Creating Interdisciplinary Literacy Learning Communities

While it may seem counter intuitive to focus on disciplinary literacy through interdisciplinary teams, this type of community can actually work very well as long as more than one member of a discipline is included on the team. Many schools have found success with grade-level teams, for example. Such a structure ensures that there is both disciplinary dialogue and interdisciplinary collaboration, which leads to a stronger whole overall.

GETTING STARTED

In the large high school where we began our work together, we started with one cohort of twenty-two teachers who shared a common challenge: How to improve the reading skills of struggling students. Within this cohort at least two teachers from each of the following disciplines were represented: ELA, math, social studies, science, world language, health, and specific learning disability (SLD). The teachers were recommended by department heads, the reading coach, and the principal as those who demonstrated a willingness to learn and take risks, those who were seen as leaders in their departments and, importantly, those who demonstrated a can-do attitude. They were invited by the principal to join the group and asked to commit to a year of professional learning within a small community. When the group first met with us for a full-day's workshop, they were less than enthusiastic despite their reputation for being can-doers. We heard "one more thing" whispers, "we're not reading teachers" warnings, and "why are we here?" confusion.

Instead of traditional norm-setting activities, we began with an open discussion and answered questions as best we could. We assured teachers that this was not just another generic reading strategy workshop; they had been asked to come together based on their strengths. We talked about our vision of a genuine learning community, where we value each other's expertise, try out new practices, reflect on what works and what doesn't, and then try again in our effort to improve our practice and students' learning.

The principal, Steve McWilliams, understood the pitfalls of moving too quickly and not allowing teachers the space they needed to assimilate new information. He pointed this out to us on the first day. "Be sure and give the teachers time to explore and process what is important in terms of new learning, new approaches, and a new philosophy." He reminded us that just as our students need to be able to explore deeply rather than experience speedy surface coverage, our teachers deserve the same.

We invited teachers to talk honestly about the literacy challenges they faced with their students, and Marsha took impeccable notes throughout so we could utilize this formative assessment to plan for future workshops in ways that best met teachers' goals. We then

Just as our students need to be able to explore deeply rather than experience speedy surface coverage, our teachers deserve the same.

moved into the learning part of the day. ReLeah began, as always, with book talks—a preview of books that could be used to engage students in reading in various disciplines. She discussed shifts in 21st-century learning, specifically how effective teachers were moving away from so much lecturing and were, instead, facilitating learning *within* the disciplines as students engaged in *doing* the work instead of passively listening to or reading about it. She asked teachers to dialogue in small groups about what engagement looked like in their content areas before providing them with research and another book talk—this time on Daniel Pink's *Drive: The Surprising Truth About What Motivates Us* (2012). Teachers were then offered a choice of news articles and participated in a collaborative activity focused on how to read and evaluate subject-specific informational text in small groups. Figure 6.2, Collaborative Evaluation of Informational Text, provides instructions for the activity.

Figure 6.2

Collaborative Evaluation of Informational Text

Title of Article:

Author/source:

Write the name of the group member who will take on each role below.

Facilitator _____

Recorder _____

Reporter _____

Each group member will read the article silently. When everyone is finished reading, the **facilitator** will lead the group through each of the questions. He or she will make sure everyone participates. Everyone in the group will then work together to come up with an answer to the question that will be written on chart paper by the **recorder.** The **reporter** will share the group's work with the rest of the class.

(Continued)

(Continued)

Choose four questions to answer.

1. Write a new a new headline and subhead for this article.

2. Briefly summarize the article as if you were telling someone you know about the article. Use only one sentence.

3. Find one phrase, statement, or assumption in the article that you might question because of its accuracy or reasonableness. Write it on your chart and be prepared to explain why you chose this statement.

4. What information did the writer leave out that you think should have been included?

5. What one sentence or phrase is written as a scientist, mathematician, historian, or novelist might write it? Read it aloud to the class and explain why you chose it.

6. Write a question you would like to ask the author.

Teachers from West Island College in Calgary, Alberta, collaborate during the first day of a disciplinary literacy workshop.

"TRYING OUT" DISCIPLINARY LITERACY ACTIVITIES

During each phase of the workshop, we encouraged teachers to speak up with adaptations of the practices or activities that would work better for the students in their disciplines and to speak out if they had questions, concerns, or doubts about the effectiveness of any suggested activity. We wanted teachers to become completely involved, to actually experience for themselves what a particular approach felt like as ReLeah modeled and they participated in the activity. As Marsha assumed her role of note-taker in chief, jotting down activities, discussion points, ideas, materials, and resources, teachers were able to concentrate on being fully present during the workshop.

At the end of that first day, Marsha had listed on chart paper twenty ideas that had come up, and we asked teachers to commit to trying two or three new classroom practices or approaches to student learning during the upcoming weeks. This "try something new" list became a staple for each workshop, and Marsha eventually created a sort of newsletter containing a smorgasbord of ideas for teachers to think about and experiment with during the upcoming weeks. She sent out the newsletter to teachers soon after each workshop to remind them of things they could do in the classroom to effect change. Teachers could choose any activity or new practice they would like to try or adapt, but we did ask them to engage in a bit of risk taking as a way of encouraging them to move out of their comfort zones. Figure 6.3 shows an example of a "Try Something New" bulletin Marsha created after each workshop to remind teachers of their new learning and offer choices in what they could try in the classrooms.

Figure 6.3

Example of a "Try Something New" Bulletin

Try Something New

Be sure to adapt, modify, and tweak to fit your students' needs.

Bell Ringer With Question

ReLeah posted the question "What do labs and rats have in common?" as an example of an article and associated question (along with a visual) that could be used in science.

- Ask bell-ringer questions related to your discipline to encourage students to think like a scientist, historian, mathematician, and so on.
- Find compelling visual images or infographics to increase motivation.
- Follow up with a read aloud, turn and talk, or quick write.

(Continued)

(Continued)

- You might provide a link for students who want to read more or provide a choice of articles related to the topic. Remember that we also did this with the article about robots ReLeah provided.

- Eventually students can sign up to bring in bell ringers as they learn to be "text scavengers."

Article a Week

Adapt Kelly Gallagher's idea of an article a week (or month). ReLeah suggested we create a student literacy team to help find articles or ask different departments to be in charge of finding articles. Remember that articles are a great way to build schoolwide background knowledge or use as mentor texts.

- When choosing articles, the more relevant to students' lives, the better.

- Justin shared how he has been using an article a day related to science in the news. He gives his students a three-minute free write, answering a prompt such as: How does this impact life or science? Or he asks them to choose one side of this issue and defend it. See Justin for more ideas.

- Janet said she can help with databases that would support your subject area if you want to do an article a week in your class.

Independent Reading

ReLeah shared a review of research from *School Library Media Research* titled "Independent Reading and School Achievement." (The article is in the Google Community.)

- During independent reading time, rotate among students and have mini-conferences with them to increase motivation and content learning. This practice is a key difference between sustained silent reading and independent reading.

- We talked about grants through the PTO for starting classroom libraries as well as titles for various contents.

- Dave told us about a discount bookstore and will post information in Google Community.

- Check out pages 24–25 in *This Is Disciplinary Literacy* for ideas about other texts to use in content areas.

Influential Teachers and Successful Students

Look in the Google Community for the Harvard research article we discussed by Tony Wagner.

- Reflect on your skills as a teacher to see if you want to improve a particular area such as team collaboration, risk taking, creating learning as opposed to consuming knowledge, or cultivating intrinsic motivation in students.

- Examine the traits of successful lifelong learners to see if you can help students build some of the skills Wagner talks about in his study.

- Consider working with a learning partner for this endeavor.

Deep Understanding Through Multiple Resources

ReLeah talked about 21st-century lessons. The point is to combine engaging activities and multiple sources to help students develop deep understanding. In the workshop we experienced this approach with ReLeah's lesson on immigration. Her lesson included a visual text, choice of articles, active reading with annotation, group discussion, and completion of a Collaborative Group Evaluation of Informational Text. This was followed by a choice of readings (fiction and information articles) and ended with an analysis of an infographic.

- Think about working with other teachers in your discipline to create a multi-resourced lesson along with a text set. Marsha will help you develop active reading strategies that fit your discipline. Janet volunteered to work with you in locating resources.

In later workshops, teachers began looking at specific skills required for students to read, write, reason, and participate in various content areas. This comparing and contrasting of disciplinary skills led to a more cohesive understanding of literacy within and across content areas as well as providing the groundwork for the creation of a schoolwide culture of disciplinary literacy.

HOW TO CREATE INTERDISCIPLINARY LITERACY LEARNING COMMUNITIES

1. Invite a specific number of teachers to join an initial interdisciplinary literacy cohort, or form more than one to encompass a larger number of teachers. In a small school, all faculty members can join learning communities based on disciplinary literacy.

2. If at all possible, provide quarterly full- or half-day meetings with a knowledgeable consultant or coach to allow cohorts to develop relationships and engage in deep, collaborative inquiry and learning. It is best not to have an administrator act as facilitator. Stress that this type of learning community encourages ownership and does not adhere to a formula or preset tasks. After this initial gathering, chairs or co-chairs can be responsible for the logistics of future meetings.

3. Determine an area of disciplinary concern to drive new learning based on qualitative as well as quantitative data, dialogue, and teacher/administrative observations. By including a variety of data sources (student work, teacher observations, and formative as well as

Stress risk taking as a necessary step for growth and view mistakes as learning opportunities, not as failures.

summative assessments), adjustments can be made before standardized test results are available. You will probably find, as we did, that initial areas of concern diminish during the process and others surface as teachers begin to use new practices and experience shifts in instruction.

4. Understand and articulate the power of collective efficacy (see pages 21–24). Do everything possible to support its development.

5. Provide targeted, *collaborative* professional learning with a consultant, coach, book study, or knowledgeable staff or district member. All activities, such as the Collaborative Evaluation of Informational Text in Figure 6.2 (page 165), should be adaptable to all content areas. In addition, make sure teacher learning

   • is active and ongoing;

   • includes modeling, practice, and feedback; and

   • leaves time for questions and reflection.

6. Give members opportunities to create, revise, or improve lessons with support from colleagues and leaders. Stress risk taking as a necessary step for growth and view mistakes as learning opportunities, not as failures. Ask members from each discipline to share how they will use such an activity in their curriculum.

A middle school reading coach, social studies teacher, and special educator offer their perspectives for a disciplinary literacy lesson.

7. At subsequent workshops, provide time for sharing student work, new or adapted practices, reflections, and informal data. The use of videoed lessons can spur conversation and deepen understanding of effective instruction.

8. Encourage co-teaching, peer coaching, and teachers observing other teachers and their students during lessons to encourage transfer of new learning.

9. Provide consistent support from a coach or teacher leader as an important support for busy teachers. This component also sustains the momentum and synergy of the group overall.

10. Create a location for housing resources and lesson ideas. We have seen teachers effectively use a Google Community for this purpose.

Listening In

Listening in to Tracy Kalas, ELA teacher, as she discusses how her interdisciplinary literacy community created strong teacher bonds that ultimately increased student learning:

"Within the cohort workshop walls, the energy was electric. It felt like we were plugged in and had exploded into another world. We were reading, debating, creating, and getting to know each other on a deeper level in natural ways through our shared experience of disciplinary literacy. I did not know Katie (history) had a creative flair, and Paul (Latin) was a hilarious comedian. One of my colleagues, Josephine (math), and I (English) discussed how I could support her class through a story writing activity using math vocabulary. Suddenly, the disciplines did not divide us—literacy unified us as we discussed our content. I now know what a strong community of literacy learners is all about.

Tracy Kalas, ELA teacher, has students assume the personalities and backgrounds of characters in a novel while their classmates pose questions—an idea she gained through collaborative professional learning.

"By being part of a learning community, I have become a better teacher. I have learned multiple ways to help students understand literacy, which has brought tremendous variety to my teaching. My students are so much more engaged and are actually learning more from the new activities. Most important, I model ReLeah and Marsha's approach in my class so students have become a community of literacy learners just as the adults in our cohort have.

"The real test of a successful cohort is continued interest in literacy. It has been about a year since the official cohort met but the teachers are still meeting and expanding on what we learned."

Common Subject
Literacy Learning Communities

In a common subject literacy learning community, teachers gather from the same subject areas or grade levels with goals that are similar to those of an interdisciplinary learning community. Clearly, the work in these teams can be much more targeted to discipline-specific skills, with teachers spending extended time steeped in their content by using their subject topics as an authentic backdrop to literacy. Literacy learning increases, as does content knowledge, when teachers share learning with others who may teach different courses in the same discipline or grade level. In addition, book studies can be targeted to the subject area, learning to read as a historian, for example, or using interactive notebooks to write in science. It is important to have a literacy expert work with the group, such as an instructional coach or consultant, to keep teachers' attention on how to infuse literacy into instruction. This will keep the group from becoming so laser-focused on content that they forget the goal of their own learning: to make their content accessible to students through the tools of reading, writing, speaking, reasoning, and participating.

ReLeah has been working over a period of time with an English department whose goals are to shift from whole-class traditional instruction to a reading and writing workshop approach. Obviously, it would not be feasible to create an interdisciplinary cohort for such a specific endeavor. The purpose of the DL learning, then, is key in determining the make-up, size, and content areas of the literacy team.

CONSIDERATIONS FOR CREATING
COMMON SUBJECT LEARNING COMMUNITIES

While there are definite advantages to common subject communities, there are a few reasons to think twice about this configuration for general DL learning. Content teachers working exclusively together can effectively develop and revise quality lessons, but it is sometimes more challenging for them to think in innovative ways because they have spent so much time with the same colleagues and curriculum. For example, science teachers in an interdisciplinary team showed social studies teachers how they could use the scientific method to have students analyze primary documents.

It is unlikely that social studies teachers would have come upon this idea while working only with each other.

We have also found that a "this is the way we have always done things" attitude can develop more quickly among same subject-area teams, especially in established content-area departments, often fostering a reluctance to engage in risk taking. And while it's true that a department or discipline does have the advantage of a common purpose (and content), it is sometimes hard for such groups to leave logistical disciplinary tasks (such as creating a common assessment or reviewing textbooks) behind and move into the distinctly different work of a DL learning community.

In addition, relationships within content areas may be complicated, especially if teachers have worked together for many years. Cliques exist, grievances are remembered, resentments may not have dissipated, or, in contrast, a few teachers may be close friends socially. Strong emotions and interactions can interfere with the objective work of a PLC such as some not wanting others in their department to observe a lesson or feeling they are being criticized by a colleague who teaches the same material and offers a suggestion for change.

Finally, as a cautionary note, sometimes one subject area may take the lead in disciplinary literacy teaching and learning—which at first may appear to be a good thing. Just remember that the goal is to build a *schoolwide* culture of disciplinary literacy so students learn how to employ literacy tools appropriately and flexibly in all disciplines. As a lead teacher in a content-area team said, "We don't want to lead this initiative. We want to be a part of the initiative."

Looking In

Looking in on West Island College, a school for Grades 7–12 in Calgary, Alberta, as it works in interdisciplinary and same-subject PLCs.

The entire staff of this school was seated in small groups, with the first day of the workshop devoted to helping teachers understand not only the concept of disciplinary literacy but also the shifts that would need to take place in implementing this approach. Teachers engaged in activities that could be adapted to various disciplines, enjoyed plenty of time for dialogue, and were immersed in content area reading, writing, thinking, and doing.

As is common in groups that tap into the "wisdom of the crowd," ideas began to percolate, thinking began to expand, and collective efficacy began to emerge. By midmorning of the second day, teachers were ready to separate into content area PLCs to take what they had learned and decide together on at least one new activity that they would try in their disciplines. They would then reunite with the entire group to share.

As we sat in on the various content-area meetings, we heard energetic discussions:

- The middle school science team talked about how their students would "act as scientists" through an interdisciplinary project based on how the world could produce and sustain enough food in the future.

- Math teachers looked at how to have students reflect more of their thinking through writing.

- World language teachers went deep into a discussion about vocabulary, excited about how they could reinforce it through visual texts.

Social studies teachers from West Island College create a disciplinary literacy plan that they will share with the entire faculty.

- In PE/Health, we witnessed a bit of cognitive dissonance as teachers productively struggled to determine how they would incorporate literacy practices through a wide variety of texts.

- Social studies teachers tossed around ideas about how content-based reading could be increased during class time as well as the creation of a digital social studies library.

When the faculty came back together, there was a sense of curiosity and comradery as the group asked questions and then applauded after each content area shared. One teacher commented that she appreciated being given time to "listen to other departments so we can better help each other."

The All-Important First Meeting

Whether you opt for an interdisciplinary literacy learning community or one with same subject-area teachers, the first meeting is critical in establishing an atmosphere of trust and respect as well as developing a common understanding of disciplinary literacy. Chapter 8 offers other suggestions for getting off on the right foot, but for now, consider some of the following activities to ensure a productive first meeting, whether as an entire faculty, an interdisciplinary team, or a common subject community.

KEEP READING AT THE FOREFRONT

Begin by reading aloud from a book or an article, one that might be especially thought-provoking or complex, and explain how you might use it to help students become more literacy proficient in that discipline. (See lists of texts for various disciplines in the appendices and companion website.) Then ask teachers to share at their tables books or other texts they could use in their subject areas. Encourage teachers to bring a title of a book or text to the next workshop to share with their group.

ENGAGE TEACHERS IN A COLLABORATIVE LITERACY ACTIVITY

Engage teachers in a literacy activity that can be adapted to various disciplines such as the activity in Figure 6.2 regarding reading informational text or choose a lesson from *Diving Deep Into Nonfiction: Transferable Tools for Reading Any Nonfiction Text* (Wilhelm & Smith, 2017). *This Is Disciplinary Literacy* (Lent, 2016) also provides a variety of discipline-specific practices and activities. Participation in such lessons shows teachers how to make important shifts in their teaching practices while also allowing them to begin to know each other better. Give plenty of time for sharing and honor divergent views of the activity. Ask teachers to return to the next workshop with notes about how the activity (or an adaptation of the activity) worked with their students.

IDENTIFY DISCIPLINE-SPECIFIC LITERACY SKILLS

This is an important activity for all teachers and administrators. With participants in content areas, ask them to respond to the following

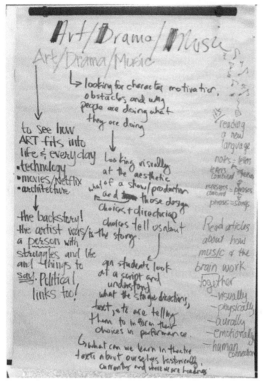

At one small school the art, drama, and music teachers worked together to determine how students read in their disciplines.

Teachers in one of our cohorts offer a disciplinary perspective on a workshop activity.

questions by brainstorming on chart paper: What skills do students need to read in your discipline? How do experts in your discipline read? If all teachers are from the same content, have them engage in this activity in groups of two or three. When they finish, ask each discipline to share with the entire group and discuss similarities and differences. Teachers can then compare their lists to those in Appendices A–I. Encourage teachers to post the skills on their classroom wall as a reminder for students. Continue this activity in future meetings for writing and thinking (which can include reasoning, speaking, and participating).

IDENTIFY DISCIPLINE-SPECIFIC LITERACY CHALLENGES

Begin by having teachers engage in a quick-write response to the following question: What literacy challenges do you find most difficult to overcome in your discipline? Make sure teachers understand that literacy is *not* simply reading and writing but that it encompasses all the skills experts need to do their jobs in specific fields. You will find that challenges frequently span the disciplines, though solutions for the challenges are more discipline specific.

Then, place teachers in common subject areas and ask them to arrange their challenges on a continuum from most important to least important. Compare responses from the groups. Ask teachers to bring back to the next meeting some sort of data (such as student comments or work samples, formative assessment notes, or testing data) to confirm their responses. Make sure the facilitator distinguishes between literacy strategies and discipline-specific literacy tools (see Chapter 3).

For the Curious

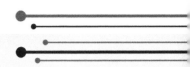

WILL THIS APPROACH WORK IN ELEMENTARY SCHOOLS?

Although our middle and high school examples might imply that this initiative is only for secondary schools, ReLeah has worked with many elementary schools in districts across the nation and the process is much the same, though leaders there sometimes prefer whole-faculty disciplinary literacy initiatives rather than one-cohort-at-a-time learning, especially in smaller schools. As one district coordinator noted, "It is important for students to understand in early grades that literacy looks different in each content area."

Supporting DL Learning Communities

One of the most important aspects of our professional learning with teachers was that Marsha, acting as a district literacy coach, returned periodically to meet with teachers in small groups (interdisciplinary or common subject) to encourage and support them, field questions, and provide additional resources to extend new learning *before* the next whole-group meeting. She also kept ReLeah apprised of progress and stumbling blocks so that the next workshop would be customized to meet teachers' needs and requests. Although the focus was always within the framework of DL learning, topics varied depending on specific challenges and teachers' self-reflections.

It is difficult to overstate the importance of this follow-up support regarding maintaining a cycle of continuous learning as well as the development of individual and collective efficacy. Teachers who might be reluctant to speak out in cohort meetings felt comfortable exploring new ideas in a small group while others simply needed additional encouragement, suggestions, or resources. Often, Marsha acted as a facilitator for small-group book study meetings or to reflect on student work as a peer coach. She found it interesting that each small group developed its own unique personality and, because she wasn't tasked with other school-related "duties," she had the time to devote to this critical aspect of the initiative.

What this support amounts to is what is commonly called *capacity building*, "the capability of the individual or organization to make the changes required and involves the development of knowledge, skills, and commitments" (Fullan & Quinn, 2016, pp. 56–57). Read more about building capacity in Chapter 9, pages 254–259.

Listen in to what teachers wrote in their reflections about the power of these coaching meetings with Marsha and their colleagues.

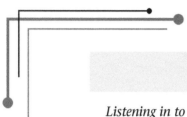

Listening In

Listening in to cohort teachers discuss the power of follow-up coaching meetings:

- "For me, the follow-up meetings with Marsha were a confirmation that I was on the right track. I regained my confidence about what I believed was good teaching. I could give some of the newer teachers in our group tips and suggestions, and they shared ideas that I hadn't thought of before. It was a win-win."

- "It was so nice to have the expertise of each other all in one place at one time. I felt like my voice mattered and I could talk about what I wanted my students to be able to do. Janet (our team's library information teacher) helped with technology or databases. Marsha gave us ideas about literacy strategies that fit our discipline and often brought in additional professional resources. Everyone gave input and pooled their ideas. It was the interplay of each individual—teachers, literacy coach, and library information teacher—that created the value. It's not often that we can we take advantage of different areas of expertise all in one setting."

- "The best part of the coaching meetings was that we supported each other and nobody thought they had to pretend to be perfect. We all shared frustrations and lessons that bombed. But the cool thing was that it didn't turn into a gripe session. One time I was having trouble with trying to use inquiry circles in science. Everyone helped with ideas on how to modify the approach. We trusted each other. It wasn't about competition."

- "In one of our follow-up meetings, I brought in work from some of my struggling students and the group brainstormed with me ways to work with them. In fact, the most help came from a history teacher, and I teach science! Then other people started bringing in work samples—from both successful and struggling students. We don't usually have time in our day for this type of collaboration."

- "It was during these small-group meetings that we had our best professional conversations. One time we talked about how much autonomy is too much and another time about how to educate parents about why we might use a picture book to introduce a concept or why we give kids time to read in class. So often school meetings are about deadlines and grades and test preparation. It is rare that we get time to talk about what is important."

- "I have one thing to say about the meetings and that is the power of professional relationships! With only four of us, it made it possible to get close to a small group of teachers we could count on. As a new teacher, I really appreciated these friendships."

- "I liked being able to talk through a problem with the others in my group. For instance, I was stuck on a way to assess my students that would tap into a more authentic application and not just memorization. We came up with a great project that put the kids into the mindset of a detective solving a crime rather than the traditional unit test I gave last year."

- "One of the best things that came out of these meetings was that Marsha knew another teacher in the district who was working on the same thing as I was. We connected and started sharing ideas. Eventually our classes became pen pals and our students gave each other feedback."

Listening In

Listening in to Janet Anderson, our team's library information teacher, as she discusses the value of Google Community in supporting ongoing, embedded collaborative learning:

This is a screen shot of one of our cohort's Google Communities.

"Our cohort quickly realized that we needed a place to share our new learning, so we chose Google Communities. We invited our team members to be in our community where we could load ReLeah's PowerPoint, lesson ideas, and book recommendations. Then we had teachers share their success stories within the community. Marsha posted additional resources that supported topics we had discussed at our workshops as well as our group's 'Try Something New' bulletins. We now had an organized, searchable, user-friendly home for our work."

Moving Toward Collective Efficacy

An environment of sharing, encouragement, supportive feedback, creativity, and confidence emerged among teachers.

As we mentioned earlier, we began to see a significant increase in both individual and collective efficacy (see pages 21–24) as well as the development of a culture of peer coaching as the comments from teachers in Marsha's small-group follow-up demonstrate. An environment of sharing, encouragement, supportive feedback, creativity, and confidence emerged among teachers.

The magic that produced such powerful efficacy inevitably appeared at the beginning of each workshop. Teachers brought in student work and with little urging began sharing in earnest. For example, a science

For the Curious

WHAT IS PEER COACHING, AND WHAT EFFECT DOES IT HAVE ON STUDENT LEARNING?

Peer coaching, simply put, is when colleagues pair up to support each other in trying out new ideas, activities, and practices in the classroom. This might entail planning and revising lessons collaboratively, observing lessons in action, reflecting on the effectiveness of lessons, or engaging in further learning or problem solving together. The coaching part of "peer coaching" is not well defined, however, because neither partner (or member of a small group) is by definition a coach, but they can engage in positive coaching habits, such as providing encouragement or ideas to deepen a lesson. Just having a colleague with whom to share concerns, ideas, successes, and frustrations makes a huge difference with teachers who take risks in their instruction.

Joyce and Showers (2002, as cited in Goodwin, 2014, May) identify four common components of effective professional learning in a workshop-type setting.

1. Presentation of information about the topic

2. Demonstration of new skills and teaching methods

3. Opportunities to practice the new skills and methods

4. Peer coaching on the new skills and methods

The first three components increased teachers' knowledge of the targeted professional learning but, surprisingly, showed a negligible effect on teachers' application of this knowledge to classroom instruction. When peer coaching was added, however, an estimated 95 percent of teachers transferred the new knowledge to their classrooms (pp. 80–82).

teacher had found various articles that addressed her current topic, and she talked about how she had asked students to approach the articles as scientists who were tasked with evaluating their accuracy for inclusion in a journal. She reported that students had, indeed, begun to view the articles from the lens of scientists. A discussion ensued about how the activity could be adapted for other disciplines.

These teachers from across College Station Independent School District attended the Heart of Texas Writing Project Summer Institute and formed a learning community that collaborates regularly. Here, they are looking at nonfiction books from Jackie Shoemake's classroom library to discuss how they might be used in an independent study project. Pictured, left to right: Aaron Hogan (ELA district coordinator), Marina Rodriguez, Grace Stanford, Jackie Shoemake, Amanda Simmons, and Kiesha Shepard.

Sustaining DL Learning Communities

The initial burst of energy when teachers begin authentically working together is always hopeful and often gives a much-needed shot in the arm to groups within the school or even to the entire faculty. The real challenge, of course, is in sustaining the enthusiasm, ongoing learning, and initiative as a whole. As we noted in Chapter 2, PLCs are difficult to maintain for a variety of reasons, but we have seen an increased commitment to and sustainability of DL Learning Communities as opposed to traditional PLCs because the day-to-day, real work of teachers is embedded in their content. Much like disciplinary literacy instruction within the classroom, this isn't an "add on" to teachers' duties; it is, rather, an integral part of their jobs, a support for what they must do anyway: lesson planning, inquiry, reflection, and ongoing content learning.

As we described earlier, the longest running initiative with which we were continuously involved lasted 4 years in one school district. We began with one cohort of twenty-two high school teachers from various content areas (what we called the Year 1 cohort), added another high school cohort and a middle-school cohort in Year 2, and in each additional year (Years 3 & 4) created still other high school and middle school cohorts of various content area teachers—as well as an administrative cohort during our final year.

Initially, each new cohort attended a full day's workshop four times a year, and in subsequent years, they met quarterly for a half-day workshop with us. All received follow-up with Marsha, and we created opportunities for cross-cohort sharing. This district had the significant benefit of a grant to help fund all aspects of the professional learning, including providing substitutes for teachers to attend workshops.

The members of the first cohort were invited by the principal, but all other cohorts were created on a voluntary basis. Interestingly, there was no lack of interest in literacy professional learning; in fact, the district curriculum director told us that there was an "overflow" list of teachers who wanted to join a cohort based on the feedback from their colleagues.

Many said they had never been involved in professional learning that was energizing instead of draining. When teachers are given the autonomy to learn, to adapt, and, especially, to engage professionally with an enthusiastic group of colleagues, they *want* the momentum to continue. The relationship building that began in each workshop continued during the school day, often in hall discussions during change of class, or through impromptu sharing on planning periods. In the high school, we began to see teachers leaving their own department workrooms to go into other departments to find members of their cohort with whom to discuss an idea that had come up in the workshop. This initiative became self-sustaining as capacity was built, one cohort after another, primarily as members developed into literacy leaders and mentors to other teachers.

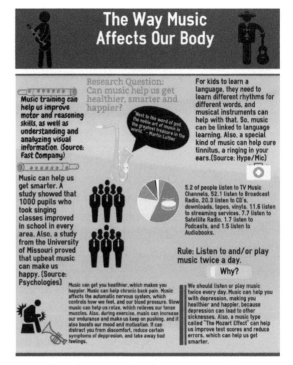

At Little Lake City School District in California, teachers returned to their third disciplinary DL workshop with examples of student work that demonstrated disciplinary literacy. Laura Garcia from Lakeside Middle brought infographics that each student had created on www.easel-ly.com after researching a question of his or her choice, determining that the source was credible, and summarizing their findings. Diego Coronado's is pictured here.

As for administrators, a few individually joined the teacher cohorts, but we found that, for the most part, teachers' literacy learning quickly outpaced administrators' knowledge in key areas, leading to issues with teacher evaluations. As a result of this challenge, an administrative DL Learning Community was also created. The focus of this cohort was somewhat different, because we discussed issues related to teacher

support, but we also asked administrators to participate in many of the same activities we had presented to teachers so they could understand the research and practices surrounding disciplinary literacy. In Chapter 9 we delve into the reasons that administrative support and learning is absolutely key in creating and sustaining disciplinary literacy instruction.

TIPS FOR MEETING CHALLENGES TO SUSTAINABILITY

Despite the overall success, there were times when teachers in some cohorts felt discouraged, and we were concerned that the forward momentum might be waning. As we reflected on these circumstances, we identified several factors that might serve as channel markers to others who are embarking on such a journey.

1. When teachers are excited about their new learning and accomplishments in the classroom, they need to be able to share with others in their building or in some way *do something* with their experience. We found that if teachers were not provided time to meet or opportunities to engage in ongoing professional learning and sharing, discouragement often set in. To avoid stagnation and that detrimental silo effect, keep disciplinary literacy as a major focus and feed it through faculty meeting presentations, summer institutes where teachers present, and DL Professional Learning Communities.

Ana Gutierrez, principal of Lakeside Middle School in California (left), collaborates with Susan Reinoso, an ELA teacher, at a disciplinary literacy workshop.

2. Don't make the mistake of thinking that once teachers are "trained" in disciplinary literacy instruction, it's finished, like handing out some sort of certification and then moving on to a new initiative. Disciplinary literacy instruction is a process that must be continually reinforced.

3. Professional learning that reverts back to "mandatory" professional development where everyone is required to attend cohort meetings or, worse, become "trained" in disciplinary literacy instruction can set up a paradigm

for resistance. The hallmark of a disciplinary literacy initiative is ownership, efficacy, and a desire for new learning. The stragglers will come along—or they may not—but we found that when administrators forced compliance, they often received noncompliance in return. That's not to say there should be no expectations for teachers' instruction and practice, but helping teachers develop a mindset for such a broad initiative is key by providing as much choice and autonomy as possible.

Sustainability means just that: Keep the initiative viable to continue gaining the benefits.

4. If resources or funding are diminished, those in charge should reach out to teachers right away and gain their input regarding how to sustain the initiative in whatever way possible. Look for creative supports, such as grants, rearrangement of schedules, or comp time to keep the communities intact and productive. From the beginning we faced skepticism because teachers felt this was one more thing that would disappear with the advent of the next best thing. Sustainability means just that: Keep the initiative viable to continue gaining the benefits.

5. Beware of sabotaging disciplinary literacy instruction, which relies on teachers' increasing expertise in both literacy and content, by buying into mandatory quick fixes. As our cohorts began working toward autonomy and creating new ways of infusing learning in their classes, a new district level supervisor suddenly brought on a packaged literacy program without consulting the teachers in the cohorts. Teachers felt that just as they were moving into a new level of instruction through a cycle of lesson planning, classroom action, reflection, and revision of lessons, this program stopped them in their tracks. We saw widespread discouragement and a marked decrease in efficacy.

There are as many configurations of DL Learning Communities as there are schools, and we suggest that you don't try to make a predetermined model fit your unique circumstances. Look at your own goals as well as the strengths and challenges of your teachers and students. Consider the resources you have or those you can obtain and how you can leverage them to make the most impact. Read Chapter 7 to ensure the most important components are at the forefront: collective inquiry, autonomy, collaboration, and a laser focus on learning. Then trust teachers to bring their disciplinary knowledge to the team; you can expect a joyfully productive struggle as they learn to blend literacy with content.

Fostering Disciplinary Literacy Dialogue

1. Discuss the experiences you have had with PLCs. What worked? What didn't?

2. One of the goals of a learning community is for members to critically reflect on their day-to-day lived experiences. This seems especially difficult for busy teachers and may be perceived by some as a waste of valuable time. How might this important element be encouraged in your school or district?

3. One of the principals with whom we worked warned against going too quickly. How can you slow down professional learning so that it, like student learning, is deep and meaningful instead of quick and superficial?

4. On pages 175–177, we provide suggested activities for a full day of disciplinary literacy collaborative learning. Read through these pages again and discuss how you might customize the day to fit the needs of your teachers and students.

5. What topics in your content would you like to know more about? For example, reading like a scientist, writing in mathematics, inquiry in ELA?

Notes:

Resources for Continued Learning

DuFour, R. (2014). Harnessing the power of PLCs. *Educational Leadership*, 71(8), 30–35.

Hargreaves, A., & Fullan, M. (2012). *Professional capital: Transforming teaching in every school.* New York, NY: Teachers College Press.

Lent, R. (2007). *Literacy learning communities: A guide for creating sustainable change in secondary schools.* Portsmouth, NH: Heinemann.

Perkins, D. N., & Reese, J. D. (2014). When change has legs: Four key factors help determine whether change efforts will be sustained over time. *Educational Leadership*, 71(8), 42–47.

Searle, M., & Swartz, M. (2015). *Teacher teamwork: How do we make it work?* Alexandria, VA: ASCD.

WHAT MATTERS MOST IN A DISCIPLINARY LITERACY (DL) LEARNING COMMUNITY

In a time when so much of what we know is subject to revision or obsolescence, the comfortable expert must go back to being a restless learner.

Warren Berger (2014)

In Union County, a district near Charlotte, North Carolina, the opening on the first day of preplanning for teachers included an address from a yoga teacher who described the effects of stress as he led teachers through some breathing exercises. His sessions on mindfulness and ways to reduce stress were listed as choices for teachers alongside a variety of academic topics including writing, vocabulary, mathematics, close reading, and classroom management. When the superintendent, Dr. Hoolahan, took the microphone, he talked about the importance of teachers taking care of themselves—reminding them why flight attendants say adults should place the oxygen mask on themselves first in case of an air emergency. "If they don't," he said, "they will be unable to help those seated beside them who might need help."

Similarly, learning communities must attend to the needs of their collective well-being first before delving into the business at hand. A learning community isn't a product; it is a process, and all processes take time to develop, to grow, and to become fully functional. They must be nourished from both the outside and the inside—with time synonymous with the oxygen in the mask that Dr. Hoolahan referenced.

What other important components should we become aware of if we want to develop vibrant, thriving learning communities? While there are certainly many aspects of successful learning communities that have been described in the literature about professional learning communities (PLCs), our experience with *disciplinary literacy* learning communities has helped us identify three essential characteristics:

1. Collective inquiry
2. Autonomy and authority
3. Collaboration

We delve into these components in the following sections, focusing specifically on how they support schoolwide disciplinary literacy.

Collective Inquiry

Virtually all teachers would say that one of their major instructional goals is to engage students in deep thinking but, paradoxically, teachers are seldom allowed the opportunity to participate in the very type of thinking they are asking of students. The notion of collective inquiry in learning communities, one advocated by most educational thought leaders, has the "potential to transform education systems," says Jenni

A learning community isn't a product; it is a process, and all processes take time to develop, to grow, and to become fully functional.

Donohoo (2017). "The process necessitates the reconstruction of beliefs about the nature of learning, leading, and teaching" (2017, p. 1). Disciplinary literacy (DL) learning communities provide a common purpose for the reconstruction of beliefs *and* practice. Within such a context, teachers grapple with subject-area questions, seek and analyze evidence related to their content, take part in dialogue with others, and create a plan of action, all while practicing skills they want students to hone: listening, speaking, evaluating, and compromising.

WORKING FROM A QUESTIONING STANCE

In the past, teaching was driven by the notion that we, educators, had all the answers and our job was to make sure students knew those answers. We assumed that if students passed a test they understood the material, and we could then move on to inculcating the next set of answers. And today? With questions seeming to swirl around us from all directions, we have come to realize that not only are answers often elusive, but the questions may be as well.

An English teacher recently asked us, "If I don't teach *Mockingbird*, who will? How will students know about this great text?" Perhaps she was asking the wrong questions. This mindset reverts to the "coverage" model predominant in the 20th century instead of the "thinking" model that is indicative of skills needed in the 21st century. The proliferation of "fake news" is one of the most obvious examples. It is no longer enough to read something and assume you have the answer. You must read, consider the author's purpose and motive, evaluate the evidence, ask questions, think critically about the content, and then compare that content to other sources in an effort to ferret out accurate information. Questions drive such thinking, forcing us to deal with complexity, ambiguity, various perspectives, and bias. Instead of asking "How will students know this great work?" perhaps we might do better to wrestle with these questions:

Questions drive thinking, forcing us to deal with complexity, ambiguity, various perspectives, and bias.

- What will students learn by studying this single text?
- How will this text meet the goals of my discipline?
- How might students' learning be deepened through multiple texts?
- Will the time spent on this text best help students learn the skills they will need to enter college and pursue a career?

Teachers in a disciplinary literacy workshop question if and how they could use picture books to build background in their content areas.

- Are all students equipped to read this text?

- And, most important: How do we work together to find the answers to these and other disciplinary questions?

Questions beget questions but, unfortunately, teachers are rarely given the time to work through some of the most important queries of their teaching lives.

We encourage questions in all our workshops and subsequent coaching sessions, believing that the process of inquiry revolves around intellectual curiosity. It is no surprise, then, that all our cohorts deal in inquiry, many resulting from questions similar to those in Figure 7.1.

DISCIPLINARY QUESTIONS LEAD TO COLLECTIVE INQUIRY

We encourage questions in all our workshops and subsequent coaching sessions, believing that the process of inquiry revolves around intellectual curiosity.

ReLeah was working recently with a group of social studies teachers who were directed by their district to make some changes in their teaching practices. A few of the teachers resisted, saying that what they had been doing was working well for their students and, thus, they had no reason or desire to change. These teachers needed time to become immersed in collective inquiry to find out if, indeed, what they had been doing *was* working. Because they had the advantage of collaborating for an entire day, their discussion eventually led to the following questions:

- What is the best way to provide the foundational knowledge students need to engage in deeper learning?

- What should we have students do after providing foundational knowledge?

- How effective is lecturing in providing foundational knowledge?

Figure 7.1

Questions That Drive Deep Disciplinary Professional Learning

- What teaching practices work best in my discipline?
- How can I transition from traditional writing assignments to having students write in the way experts in my field write?
- Why did this practice work with one class and not with another?
- How can I help students learn to think as experts in my discipline through discussion and argumentative reasoning?
- What are some ways students can present their findings that mimic those of experts?
- How can I create a safe environment where students feel free to engage in risk taking with new learning?
- How do I teach students to evaluate disciplinary sources?
- How can I make my content engaging for students?
- What does formative assessment look like in my discipline?
- How do I help students learn to ask questions that are at the core of content leaning?
- How can I incorporate project-based learning so that it deepens students understanding of my content?
- How do I ensure that students find relevance in the content?
- How do I support students in reading challenging text and still maintain a focus on my content instead of on reading skills?
- How can I move students from passive observers of my teaching to active participants in my discipline?
- How can I help my students think as historians, scientists, mathematicians, artists, musicians, athletes, readers, or writers?

- How often do students go "off task" when learning in small groups? When listening to lectures? Watching PowerPoint presentations and taking notes?
- What does "off task" mean?

- What can be done to keep students engaged and on task?
- What is the most effective way for students to deeply learn key vocabulary specific to our discipline?
- What is the best way to prepare students for end-of-course exams or standardized tests?
- Is expecting students to participate as experts in the discipline going overboard?

Quoteworthy

"Regardless of their educational path, students moving into adulthood today need more than anything else to be voracious, passionate learners, adept at creating their own personal learning curriculum, finding their own teachers to mentor and guide them in their efforts, and connecting with other learners with whom they can collaborate and create." (Richardson, 2016/2017, p. 26).

The process of collective inquiry has a measurable effect on increased student achievement.

Some administrators might have told these teachers that changes were going to happen, like it or not. Fortunately, school leaders wanted lasting change, and they knew that such transformation comes when teachers engage in a process of inquiry. In fact, the process of collective inquiry has a measurable effect on increased student achievement (Reeves, 2010). While the brainstormed list of questions the teachers created was too broad for a focused inquiry, it was a first step in considering how their practice might be more effective.

ReLeah then asked individual teachers to choose one area of inquiry on which they wanted to focus, and she adapted Donohoo's (2017) four stages of collaborative inquiry to help them create a more targeted approach:

Stage 1—Problem Framing
- Example: Is lecture a more effective way for students to gain content knowledge than students participating in small groups?
- Even if student learning increases, is it worth the time it takes to engage students in collaborative learning?

Stage 2—Collecting Evidence

- What type of data will we collect (e.g., observational notes, student work, student surveys, test scores from traditional classes and collaboratively grouped classes)?
- How will we collect the data, and who will collect it?

Stage 3—Analyzing Evidence

- When and how will we meet to make meaning of the data we have collected?
- What conclusions will we draw, and what will we do with those conclusions?

Stage 4—Donohoo (2017) calls this stage *celebrating and sharing*. We renamed the stage "sharing and action."

- Based on our shared findings, how will we change practices?

A different group of teachers, this time from the ELA department, also were required to engage in the sometimes uncomfortable process of change. They were moving from a textbook-based curriculum to a multi-modal textset approach, one that utilized multiple resources for thematic reading and writing. Their intensity (and, let's face it, frustration) was evident. "Where do we begin?" They asked since it seemed an overwhelming task to flesh out ideas, determine the types of texts that would support essential questions, actually use some of the texts in classroom lessons, and then evaluate the results. Once they got their minds around the idea of collective inquiry, however, something they were accustomed to facilitating with their students, productive energy began to emerge.

Brain Connection

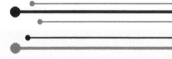

WHY DO WE WANT TO ENCOURAGE DIVERGENT THINKING?

What do we know about divergent thinking? According to Berger (2014), we know "that it mostly happens in the more creative right hemisphere of the brain; that it taps into imagination and often triggers random association of ideas (which

(Continued)

is a primary source of creativity); and that it can be intellectually stimulating and rewarding. So to the extent that questioning triggers divergent thinking, it's not surprising that it can have a kind of mind-opening effect" on the learner. (p. 18)

Teachers work collaboratively to create discussion questions for deeper student learning.

Professional learning in the past for both these groups had been a top-down approach, and suddenly they were being asked to find ways of creating deeper learning for their students through unfamiliar techniques and practices. It was quite a shift, but one that better prepared them to engage in their content. Because these were common-subject DL learning communities, they would meet often to assess lessons, texts, practices, and student learning. They knew their first efforts may be far from perfect but they were already beginning to exhibit collective efficacy and, if John Hattie's (2016) research is accurate, they were on their way to making a positive impact in their classrooms.

Quoteworthy

"When educators reflect on their theories, collaborate, and develop solutions to address their problems of practice, efficacy increases. John Hattie's (2016) research indicates that collective teacher efficacy is the number one factor that impacts student achievement" (Donohoo, 2017, p. xv).

COLLECTIVE INQUIRY LEADS TO ACTION

As we saw with our cohorts, self-directed, participatory professional learning encouraged teachers to take ownership of their efforts, become more willing to engage in reflection, and, in turn, improve their teaching practices based on what they have learned. See Figure 7.2 as a model of

Figure 7.2

Graphic of Disciplinary Literacy Participatory Learning

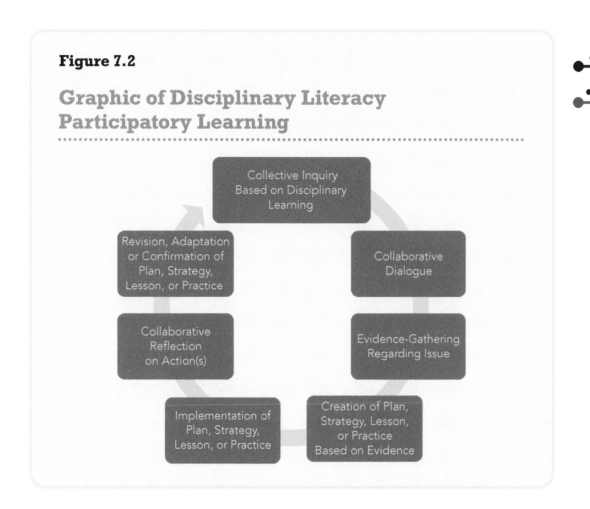

how such targeted, recursive actions can lead a community of teachers to effective instruction.

It may not be clear from Figure 7.2 that each teacher in the learning community does not necessarily need to take the exact same action, and teachers can engage in more than one cycle at a time if they desire. One of the cohorts with whom we worked, for example, found through quantitative as well as qualitative data that students were not reading enough in the disciplines and their professional inquiry initially revolved around how to increase content area reading. They knew from their own experiences that students avoided reading whenever possible, leading teachers to "deliver" content. As they collaboratively engaged in activities modeled in our workshops and read research on the importance of students engaging in wide and content-relevant reading, teachers or teams of teachers took different actions based on their subject areas, but all fully participated in the cycle shown in Figure 7.2.

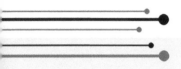

Quoteworthy

"'[C]ollaborative inquiry . . . engages educators in self-directed' and participatory learning, moving beyond collective passive learning to learning with and from colleagues through action and reflection. In the supportive content of collaborative inquiry, participants explore agreements and disagreements about learning and teaching, uncover tacit knowledge, and come to individual and shared understandings of how, why, and under what conditions instruction and leadership yield positive student results" (Palmisano, 2012).

As an example of the power of collaborative inquiry, two AP history teachers decided to have students read content texts and then tweet about their findings with a class hashtag (see pages 113–114 for more information about their project). Through reflection, discussion, problem solving, and a bit of risk taking, they have continued to improve the process over the years. Similarly, middle school ELA teachers began changing their practices to utilize small-group reading of texts with associated small-group activities. By trying first one configuration and then another, seeking engaging texts, and revising their plans based on what worked and what didn't, teachers made substantial changes in their instruction.

Autonomy and Authority

Daniel Pink (2012) minces no words when discussing autonomy, stating, "According to a cluster of recent behavioral science studies, autonomous motivation promotes greater conceptual understanding, better grades, enhanced persistence at school . . . higher productivity, less burnout, and greater levels of psychological well-being" (pp. 88–89). He goes on to cite a study at Cornell University that involved "320 small businesses, half of which granted workers autonomy, the other half relying on top-down direction. The businesses that offered autonomy grew at four times the rate of the control-oriented firms and had one-third the turnover" (p. 89).

As an outgrowth of her work with the DeKalb County School District Literacy Learning Community, academic coach Marcia Wingfield formed a Literacy Learning Community within her high school that consisted of teachers from multiple content areas. This group developed and implemented several disciplinary literacy practices by following the process depicted in Figure 7.2.

Why would we think that such a powerful motivator would only apply to businesses that want to increase their profit margin? The notion of autonomy is a potent factor in all human undertakings, and the best teachers and administrators understand its positive impact in all areas of education.

IMPORTANCE OF PROFESSIONAL AUTONOMY

Despite an OECD (2011) report that shows better student performance when teachers have greater professional autonomy, this important component is often ignored in teacher learning communities—either because those at the top can't release autonomy to communities or because the idea of teacher autonomy has been so overlooked in professional learning that it is difficult to conceptualize it at all in this context. We contend that this lack of autonomy may well be one reason for the discouraging results from PLCs. Teachers who are told what and how to learn in predetermined time slots—often with associated but irrelevant tasks—simply don't become invested.

The notion of autonomy is a potent factor in all human undertakings.

What most *are* invested in is their content, their students, and their lessons. They are invested in the daily workings of their classes, the many unpredictable challenges that arise and the glimmering successes that stay with them long after they have gone home for the day. They talk with colleagues about these investments when they can spare a few minutes between classes or at lunch and try to find time to reflect and make sense of the thousands of unpredictable moments that define their school day. That's why a DL learning community, if given time, support, and autonomy, can become one of the most powerful forms of professional learning.

We will say again what we've emphasized throughout this book: Teachers in DL learning communities are not being "trained" on how to use a program, textbook, or technique; they are utilizing their content area expertise to create classroom practices by melding their content knowledge with content-specific literacy practices. Successful communities of learning around disciplinary literacy can't exist if teachers are not afforded the autonomy to engage in innovative work.

Successful communities of learning around disciplinary literacy can't exist if teachers are not afforded the autonomy to engage in innovative work.

One middle school cohort with whom we worked was so enthusiastic that teachers' energy spilled out the door each time we met with them. They wanted us to visit their classes to observe and even participate in their lessons. It seems that whatever we suggested or modeled—using news articles for scaffolding content literacy skills, for example, or creating writing practices specifically tailored to their disciplines—they were on it. It helped that the library information teachers and technology coaches were at cohort meetings to support teachers' ideas with resources. In this case, autonomy actually seemed to produce individual and collective efficacy, specifically in teachers' ability to teach writing and facilitate their students' growth as writers. They were eager to learn more about effective practices in writing and began sharing with each other in ways that we had rarely seen before—such as inviting each other in to observe lessons and asking for feedback from their peers.

It remains a mystery to us, then, why the district decided to "supplement" their professional learning with a mandated program for writing. Perhaps instructional leaders felt they were not doing their job unless they sought out and implemented what they deemed the best available programs, those that are often marketed with promotional accolades and promises. It's not that some programs can't be extremely helpful if used as a resource along with teacher expertise, but the developers of programs or curriculum guides don't know your students, your community, or your teachers' differentiated strengths and challenges. When teachers are afforded the autonomy to engage in true professional learning, the results can exceed any program used in isolation, especially when it is expected that teachers will use it with "fidelity." We have come to believe that fidelity to a program often supplants fidelity to our students' learning.

We have come to believe that fidelity to a program often supplants fidelity to our students' learning.

Pink (2012) calls for a "renaissance of self-direction" as opposed to "better management." That makes sense, especially in leaning communities where teachers should be engaging in habits they want to instill in their students: productive struggle; dialogue with others about complex challenges; collaborative inquiry; the ability to create, carry out, and evaluate solutions; and in the process become, as Pink terms it, "happily interdependent" with others.

For the Curious

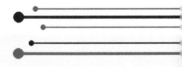

HOW MUCH AUTONOMY DO TEACHERS HAVE IN FINLAND?

"Teachers in Finland [one of the highest achieving nations in the world] are given a great deal of responsibility and are allowed unfettered flexibility in what and how they teach. Performance isn't observed and graded. Instead, annual development discussions with school leaders provide feedback on a teacher's own assessment of their strengths and weaknesses. Detailed plans are not expected, either. The notion that a teacher should provide evidence to prove what they've done is ludicrous. Each teacher marks work when it benefits them or the student, but not for anyone else's sake." (Hart, 2017, para. 8)

Finding new ways to support students or just figuring out a piece of the puzzle turns into a barren intellectual exercise without the ability to put new knowledge to work.

FROM AUTONOMY TO AUTHORITY

Autonomy's partner, authority, can also contribute to the success of disciplinary literacy learning communities. Finding new ways to support students or just figuring out a piece of the puzzle turns into a barren intellectual exercise without the ability to put new knowledge to work. When teachers feel they have the authority to implement new learning, they become more engaged in the process as a whole, allowing that all-important transfer to the classroom. Authority also contributes to collective efficacy and creates a cycle of confidence that, combined with the freedom to learn from mistakes, can create transformational changes. The next section lists ways of extending autonomy and authority to DL learning communities.

TIPS FOR BUILDING AUTONOMOUS DL LEARNING COMMUNITIES

- Make time during faculty meetings, department meetings, or grade-level meetings for disciplinary literacy cohorts or teams to share new practices and reflect on how content-specific practices are impacting student learning. Such sharing, especially when teachers open up their classrooms for peer observations, can create strong professional relationships and important peer coaching opportunities.

- Provide resources that teachers may need to extend their learning or improve their teaching, such as professional books, classroom texts, or opportunities for extended learning, such as allowing members to take turns attending conferences (or, even better, attending as a team). When they return, often with renewed passion and enthusiasm, find opportunities for teachers to share new ideas with colleagues.

- Plan a school or district conference where teachers lead sessions. Not only do teachers learn from each other, but they also form interdisciplinary bonds as they discover how other content areas engage in literacy.

- Honor teachers' commitment to meet after school or during the summer by offering compensatory time or stipends.

- Consult with teachers in learning communities before making decisions involving literacy. Ask for their input and listen to their suggestions.

- Be aware that different learning communities may pursue different priorities under the common goal of creating a schoolwide culture of disciplinary literacy. Follow the principle that student learning drives priorities, recognizing that teachers know best their students and what they need.

Meaningful Collaboration

Just as students engage in "fake reading," a compliant behavior where they pretend to read, teachers sometimes engage in "fake collaboration": They appear to be working together in a PLC, yet they are talking but not engaging in productive dialogue, identifying problems but not solving them, or interacting on a surface level but not involved in the messy give-and-take that undergirds true collaboration.

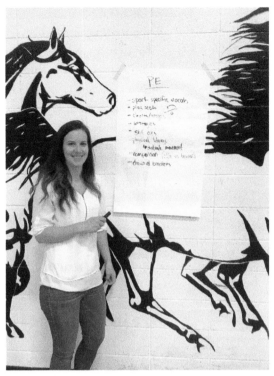

Jacqueline Toane, teacher and athletic director at George McDougall High School in Alberta, leads the faculty in understanding how literacy can be incorporated into physical education.

For the Curious

HOW DOES PARALLEL COLLABORATION DIFFER FROM AUTHENTIC COLLABORATION?

Anthony Tjan (2017), business owner, advisor, and author, writes about the power of groups that truly collaborate rather than work in parallel, where they sequentially assign jobs to achieve a singular goal. For instance, he suggests, "[D]on't ask the businessperson to write the business case, then pass that to the engineer for the technical specifications, and then pass this to a designer instructed to 'make it look pretty.'" He claims that in the very best products, all disciplines are synchronized and working toward the same goal collaboratively (pp. 180–181).

While listing characteristics of collaboration might be as useless as mandating it, there are conditions that can support meaningful collaboration. Nurturing these conditions is far more effective than finding ways of ensuring that teachers are "accountable." Keith Sawyer, author of *Group Genius* (2017), spent years studying collaboration in an effort to discover key characteristics of effective creative teams in order to find out which characteristics translated from a single person's creativity into group genius. We have adapted some of his findings in the following sections to our work on collaboration for disciplinary literacy instruction, including the following:

- Deep listening invites collaboration
- Sharing ideas builds collaboration
- Risk-taking results from collaboration

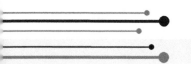

Brain Connection

HOW DOES COLLABORATION LEAD TO GROUP GENIUS?

Keith Sawyer (2017), in writing about creativity, reminds us that "collaboration makes the mind more creative because working with others gives you new and unexpected concepts and makes it more likely that your mind will engage in the most creative types of conceptual creativity—combining distant concepts, elaborating concepts by modifying their core features, and creating new concepts. Collaboration makes each individual more creative, and most important of all, the emergent results of group genius are greater than those any one individual could think of alone." (p. 147)

DEEP LISTENING INVITES COLLABORATION

Attentive listening may be the most important characteristic that emerged in the strongest cohorts with whom we worked. Less effective cohorts (defined as those whose members acted as individuals or where a majority of members remained fixated on a problem, often assessing it as insoluble) would engage in "sidebar" talk or wait impatiently for someone to finish speaking so they could speak, sometimes without addressing the comments of the previous speaker. In place of collaborative dialogue, conversations dominated, often those that involved proving a point rather than moving forward with an idea. These behaviors translated into a less cohesive group overall with fewer innovative ideas.

Conversely, some of the most effective cohorts would sometimes sit in silence as they thought through another's comment. On one occasion, Nick brought his students in to discuss with teachers how independent reading had transformed their academic lives. In one particularly collaborative cohort, the teachers listened especially intently and asked thoughtful questions of the students, showing the same respect and curiosity they exhibited toward each other.

Attentive listening may be the most important characteristic that emerged in the strongest cohorts with whom we worked.

SHARING IDEAS BUILDS COLLABORATION

There is really no way to explain how the act of sharing and building on others' ideas leads to a strong collaborative bond unless you have experienced it, as most people certainly have at one point or another in their professional lives. ReLeah began her career as an ELA teacher in a middle school and was fortunate enough to have been hired into a department of teachers whose collaboration about their content and students created an environment that ultimately won the department a national award of educational excellence. How did it happen? Were all these teachers individually exceptional? No. The secret lay in the collective excellence that emerged when teachers interacted, learning with and from each other. These teachers even spent a weekend together in a retreat in an effort to improve their ability to teach writing. When they collaborated, the ideas glided around the room and back again: building, almost spinning from the realistic to the impossible, and finally settling into something actionable.

For the Curious

HOW IMPORTANT IS COLLABORATION IN THE CORPORATE WORLD?

In 2016, the *New York Times* (Sawyer, 2017) wrote that teams are the fundamental unit of organizations. Today, most businesses understand the value of collaboration and its relationship to innovation as the article indicated:

- "After 10 years [of] building a collaborative future, Proctor and Gamble more than tripled its innovation success rate."
- "Whole Foods Market attributes its success to its use of self-managed teams, which it calls the 'Whole People' philosophy" (Sawyer, 2017, p. 15).
- Verizon advocates what it calls "co-opetition."
- "The pharmaceutical companies Lilly, GlaxoSmithKline, and Pfizer are now using collaborations with universities and even competitors to develop life-saving drugs more rapidly" (Sawyer, 2017, p. 15).

Science teachers Lauren Pennock and Colleen Zenner work closely together for planning, teaching, and follow-up with students.

RISK-TAKING RESULTS FROM COLLABORATION

Risk taking is an important component of our work with teachers because we view mistakes as essential to the process of learning and change. Of course some ideas turn out not to be the best, but they often provide opportunities for laughter and a reminder of the value of humility. Brian Cambourne (1988), a well-known Australian researcher who developed Conditions for Learning, termed what we call risk taking as "approximation" or "giving it a go." Feeling safe to try and sometimes fail requires a great deal of trust on the part of teachers and administrators, a process that begins with collaboration. Chapter 8 delves deeper into the importance of trust.

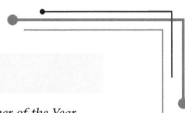

Listening In

Listening in to Sydney Chaffee (2017), 2017 National Teacher of the Year, on the beauty of messing up—and learning:

"As teachers, we sometimes fall victim to the myth of the perfect classroom, the perfect students, the perfect lesson. We feel the need to perpetuate this myth, to pretend that we have it all figured out. We feel vulnerable without it, worried that we will be identified as frauds or imposters." (para. 6)

"We must reject the 'super teacher' myth and be brave enough to advocate for what we know to be true about learning: Real learning takes time. It is not always linear. And sometimes, the best learning happens when things don't go perfectly." (para. 11)

Risk taking is an important component of our work with teachers because we view mistakes as essential to the process of learning and change.

Taking risks is not easy under most circumstances but it can be especially difficult when there are consequences if the risk fails to produce results. When teachers in the cohorts felt they would be "marked down" on evaluations or even in walk-throughs if they engaged in an innovative lesson or practice that might not go as planned, they were reluctant to venture beyond where they felt safe, and this sometimes led to more traditional and often less effective teaching, particularly during evaluations.

Interestingly, teachers in highly collaborative cohorts would support each other in astounding ways, such as offering to co-teach if a teacher felt unsure about trying something new. In Chapter 8 we describe how Caroline, our team's science teacher, actually challenged her administrator to take a risk in engaging students in a seminar. Innovation in teaching often means continuing to hone a lesson even if it has fallen flat the first time around, something that is easier to do when a caring colleague is available to offer support.

Listening In

Listening in to Kathleen Duffy, our social studies team member, as she discusses the value of trial and error:

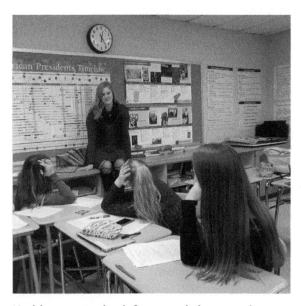

Kathleen came back from workshops and told her students, "I'm trying something new I learned with my literacy group. Let's see how it works." Her students became invested in the process and came to understand that continuous learning was a natural part of a professional life.

"The best part of the cohort was the collaboration and discussion between educators. It was a place to engage in untested lesson plans, expand upon failures and successes, pass along and build upon others' lessons, and share ways to spread literacy (all types) to other colleagues and students. Our quarterly meetings were a time of expression, guidance, and reinvigoration of literacy across disciplines. Being the lone social studies teacher involved in my cohort, I was able to learn from all the other disciplines without a second thought or preconceived bias. I felt secure when expressing failed lessons without the pressure of being perfect for administrative evaluation purposes, which allowed me to grow from my mistakes. The cohort became a place where I felt comfortable and gained confidence from this "trial and error" setup.

For the Curious

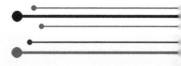

WHAT HAPPENS TO CREATIVITY WHEN MAKING MISTAKES IS SEEN AS A NEGATIVE EXPERIENCE?

Beghetto (2016) noted that creativity has been described as a 21st-century thinking skill. If we want schools where both students and teachers can be creative, we will become familiar with the kinds of environmental pressures that tend to undermine the motivation necessary for creative expression. A focus on making mistakes is one of those constraints, as well as competition, surveillance, and comparisons.

TRUST CEMENTS COLLABORATION

It will come as no surprise that our most successful cohorts not only exhibited a high level of trust but also a strong sense of loyalty. Their feedback was honest yet caring, and they were quick to reassure each other when a member expressed discouragement. The longer they met together, the greater this commitment appeared to be—almost becoming a club or team mentality, perhaps the "insider" sense that we discussed in Chapter 2 when students are welcomed as insiders to a discipline instead of as outsiders. Perhaps because they were from different disciplines, the competition that we sometimes see in content-area departments was absent, replaced with the comradery of a true community. This level of trust isn't just a nicety in learning organizations, either. In a study by the Consortium on Chicago School Research (Barlin, 2016), researchers found that in schools with flat or declining student test scores, faculty members are more likely to say that they do not trust one another. Conversely, "in schools where teachers report strong trust and cooperation among adults, students said they felt safe and cared for, as well as more academically challenged. And stronger student test scores often bear this out" (Barlin, 2016). In addition, once distrust begins to form, teachers are less likely to take risks or try new practices. Scapegoating can even occur as a means of self-preservation.

In schools where teachers report strong trust and cooperation among adults, students said they felt safe and cared for, as well as more academically challenged.

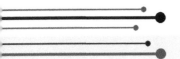

For the Curious

WHAT'S THE BEST WAY TO KILL COLLABORATION?

"By trying to enforce and police everything, you stifle collaboration within your organization. Some best practices and guidelines are fine to have but let your employees do what they need to do," says Jacob Morgan, author of *12 Habits of Highly Collaborative Organizations* (2013, para. 9).

Learning communities don't always come together in a beautifully harmonious way; some take a lot of time and effort, and others seem never to quite gel. In one case, we had to divide a large cohort into two smaller ones to find the right chemistry for collaboration as well as to allow opportunities for everyone to actively participate. When groups are too large or an unbalanced mix of talkers and quiet thinkers exists, a sort of disequilibrium can result.

Knowing what is important from the start, however, and setting goals for working together in ways that target disciplinary learning can make a substantive difference. Equally important is understanding how to foster inquiry, autonomy, supported risk taking, and meaningful collaboration within and across disciplines if our goal is sustainable change through professional learning.

Fostering Disciplinary Literacy Dialogue

1. We discussed a teacher at the beginning of this chapter who made the point that if she did not teach a particular great work of fiction, who would? What part of the curriculum might be hardest for teachers to release "teaching" in favor of broadening their perspective through essential disciplinary questions and resources other than the textbook?

2. The three components most essential to success, according to research and our experience, are (1) collective inquiry, (2) autonomy and authority, and (3) meaningful collaboration. Discuss which of these is most important to the teachers in your school or district. Are there other components that you would add?

3. Who is a good listener in your school or district? How do you know? Why is listening such a difficult skill to master?

4. To what extent does your school or district have a tolerance for risk taking? How could it be realistically and productively encouraged? Read and discuss the feature on page 201 about how much autonomy teachers in Finland have. Could a system such as that in Finland be feasible in your school? What would need to change?

5. How much room for "messing up" is allotted to teachers in your school or district?

Notes:

Resources for Continued Learning

Beghetto, R. A. (2016). *Big wins, small steps: How to lead for and with creativity*. Thousand Oaks, CA: Corwin.

Donohoo, J. (2013). *Collaborative inquiry for educators: A facilitator's guide to school improvement*. Thousand Oaks, CA: Corwin.

Donohoo, J., & Velasco, M. (2016). *The transformative power of collaborative inquiry: Realizing change in schools and classrooms*. Thousand Oaks, CA: Corwin.

Lamb-Sinclair, A. (2017). Why teachers need their freedom. Retrieved from https://www.theatlantic.com/education/archive/2017/09/why-teachers-need-their-freedom

Wilhelm, J. (2016, March). Working toward conscious competence: The power of inquiry for teachers and learners. *Voices from the Middle, 23*(3), 58–60.

Wilson, D. (2017). 10 strategies to develop teacher agency in 2017. Retrieved from https://learningforward.org/blog-landing/learning-forward-blog/2017/01/06/10-strategies-to-develop-teacher-agency-in-2017

8

FROM TEACHER LEARNER TO TEACHER LEADER

We should pull people forward whenever we can by inspiring them.

Andy Hargreaves (Hargreaves & Boyle, 2015)

A fifth-grade teacher, whom we will call Rachel, recently talked to us about the catchphrase "teacher leader." She was one of those people who played school as a child, rounding up her younger sisters and neighborhood kids in front of her green chalkboard tented on four spindly legs. As an adult, Rachel earned an education degree and began her career teaching second grade, moved up to fourth grade, and now is happily ensconced with her fifth-grade students. "A perfect fit," she said. But for the first time in her life she is having doubts about her chosen profession. "I don't want to be a leader," she said honestly. "I never wanted to be an administrator, and when the grade-level chair position was offered to me, I told my principal that I would do it if she really wanted me to but that I thought someone else might be better at it. I did volunteer to be in charge of the fifth-grade play because then I could work with the kids." In Rachel's school, however, teachers are required to demonstrate leadership ability as part of their annual evaluation. Unfortunately, being the point person for the school play doesn't count as leadership; it is seen as going beyond regular teaching duties, for sure, but is not deemed leadership.

Leadership is simply helping people find meaning.

As we consider the concept of leadership, we look to two people who are among the most transformational thinkers in this area: Michael Fullan and Andy Hargreaves. Fullan's (2017) recent book on leadership is a short but powerful analysis that has clear implications for disciplinary literacy leaders. He writes that the goal of leadership is to cause "breakthroughs by being a part of a process that uplifts large numbers of people. It is to make deep change happen and be meaningful to individuals and the group." Leadership is simply helping people find meaning. If we adopt that view of leadership, then our fifth-grade teacher demonstrates powerful professional leadership. She discusses content and teaching practices with colleagues because she is a voracious reader of professional journals and books that offer new ideas to engage students in her content. Other teachers come to her for help with problems not only because they trust her but also because she has a reputation for being innovative in finding solutions. Her colleagues describe her as passionate but her students *experience* her passion as she offers opportunities for them to realize their own passions. She may not have the designation "leader" beside her name, but there is little doubt that she is a leader in the deepest sense.

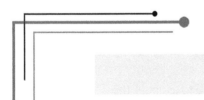

Listening In

Listening in to Carol Ann Tomlinson (2015) as she describes the patterns of effective leaders with whom she has worked:

- They speak and act from deep conviction.
- They always remember the humanity of the people with whom they speak.

- They listen more than they talk and ask more than they tell.

- They cultivate trust through their communications.

- What—and how—they communicate helps others develop a sense of agency and competence.

- They ask a great deal from fellow educators—but always provide support.

- They remember to express gratitude. (pp. 90–91)

Disciplinary Literacy Develops Deep Leadership

One of many benefits of a disciplinary literacy approach is the opportunity for leaders to emerge, even for teachers such as Rachel who might not see themselves as leaders. Such teachers often find they can utilize their content-area expertise in purposeful ways that propels them toward leadership. The library information teacher on our team, Janet, had always performed her job well but it wasn't until she joined the disciplinary literacy cohorts that she was able to exert her influence through leadership practices. Since we first met her, Janet has

- led efforts to create a schoolwide summer reading initiative,

- built a culture of literacy by making digital and print resources widely available to teachers,

- partnered with classroom teachers to plan and teach disciplinary literacy practices within their content areas,

- become a part of a group that approached administration with ideas for how to sustain the disciplinary literacy cohorts, and

- presented with others on her team about the school's literacy initiative at national conferences.

Janet's discipline, library science, acted as a catalyst for leadership activities in ways that her participation in a generic PLC might not have allowed.

Janet meets with library staff to share digital resources for disciplinary literacy instruction.

Not only were leadership opportunities created in our cohorts, but also the type of leadership that surfaced was deeper and more content-driven than what we had typically seen in schools, perhaps because it was based entirely on continuous, collaborative learning and action—the give and take that exemplifies superior leaders. In place of generic teacher-leader roles such as department or grade-level heads, chairs of committees, or even sponsors of clubs, the teachers with whom we worked didn't think in terms of leadership; instead, they *acted* as the leaders Hargreaves describes as "uplifting." They embarked on a journey, "a narrative quest that people pursue together to be part of something greater than themselves" (Hargreaves & Boyle, 2015, p. 45). Like Janet, these leaders assumed additional responsibilities for which they were not paid, continued learning when no in-service or course credits were offered, and made a significant difference in the lives of their students and colleagues because, as true leaders, they could do nothing less.

Disciplinary literacy teams provide a unique fertile ground for leadership training.

We were excited to discover Fullan's (2017) model of leadership for deep work and its associated principles because they seem to describe the behaviors that arose in our disciplinary literacy cohort leaders. Fullan's descriptions include

- Cycles of trying things and making meaning

- Co-learning (among all) dominates

- Leaders listen, learn, ask questions

- Leaders help crystalize, articulate, and feed back what they see

- Leaders act on emerging solutions, including the focus on impact (p. 19)

Disciplinary literacy teams provide a unique fertile ground for leadership training, embodying many of Fullan's descriptors. Members of our cohorts, for example, made meaning of literacy by learning together how it worked to support deeper understandings in content areas. Fullan (2017) describes "deep leaders" as those who disrupt and refine the status quo, and we found that that is exactly what these teacher leaders often did.

Kathleen Duffy, our social studies team member, created electives in her discipline such as a gender studies class that expanded and deepened students' learning in social studies (see pages 29–31 for a description of this class). Nick Yeager's ELA credit make-up course went from a curriculum where students were only required to engage in computer-based work for credits to a vibrant class of reading, discussion, reflection, and goal setting with plans currently in place for a student-led community literacy program. Caroline Milne partnered with other science teachers to move into the national science education scene by presenting at national conferences and becoming mentors in their own department, reimagining science from a subject to be taught to a subject in which students fully engaged in the work of scientists. Caroline has had a major impact on the department through her advocacy for integrating literacy practices as tools for learning science.

Disciplinary Literacy Leadership Roles

In several districts in which we facilitated disciplinary literacy teams, administrators asked us to emphasize the importance of members in the cohorts taking on a leadership role. While we would never agree to a train-the-trainer model, we did understand that teachers were expected to return to their departments or teams and share their new learning in an effort to expand disciplinary literacy. As for becoming teacher leaders, we (and the teachers themselves) often didn't know exactly what this role might look like, especially since teachers were often from various schools with administrators having somewhat different visions of leadership. We sometimes felt that no one had actually thought through how these teachers might lead or what, exactly, was expected of them. One group, for example, was told that its members would have time at each faculty meeting to lead a disciplinary literacy initiative. Unfortunately, their allotted time diminished to the point that they had only a few minutes at a few faculty meetings. This dealt a blow to their collective efficacy, leading to discouragement, frustration, and confusion.

On the other hand, many administrators provided teachers time with their teams or departments to share new learning, offered co-teaching opportunities to deepen content understandings, or made available funding to send teachers to conferences to present or simply learn. Several districts created summer literacy conferences where teachers had opportunities to facilitate sessions on discipline-specific literacy practices.

We tried to create a systematic way of allowing teachers in our cohorts to share more widely what they were learning, but it sometimes seemed as if that aspect of the initiative was beyond our control. Once administrators became members of an administrative disciplinary literacy cohort, however, they began to provide more opportunities for teachers to lead. Unfortunately, there were still some administrators who did not attend the workshops and a few, perhaps unintentionally, who created roadblocks instead of throughways. In spite of those difficulties, leaders did emerge in creative and significant ways.

Following is a closer look at the types of disciplinary literacy leaders that we have identified in our work with teams and cohorts: leading one on one; leading through content knowledge; and leading by reading, writing, speaking, and doing.

LEADING ONE ON ONE

Researchers Beverly Joyce and Bruce Showers (1996) first proposed the idea of peer coaching in 1980 based on their finding that as few as ten percent of teachers implemented in their classroom what they had learned in professional development trainings. Attempting to remedy that problem, Joyce and Showers (2002, as cited in Goodwin, 2014) recommended that teachers form small peer coaching groups that would share learning practices along the way by collaboratively planning and developing curriculum and instruction. The impact was astounding. As we noted in Chapter 7, they found that when a peer coaching component was added to professional learning, the transfer of teachers' knowledge and skills to the classroom could be increased to 95 percent (1996). Peer coaching alone does not account for the increased student learning, however. Teachers also must also have opportunities for study and learning along with demonstrations of how to implement that knowledge with frequent opportunities for practice (2002, as cited in Goodwin, 2014).

Once administrators became members of an administrative disciplinary literacy cohort, they began to provide more opportunities for teachers to lead.

You'll recognize this as the model we employed with our cohorts in Illinois. The workshops provided new learning, demonstrations, and opportunities for practice with time allotted throughout the workshops for peer coaching. Marsha's follow-ups offered further support and resources as teachers met and worked together.

Science teachers meet during their planning period to work on revising a lesson.

We discovered that peer coaching within departments specifically related to disciplinary literacy practices encouraged teachers who were not in cohorts to become curious and ask questions as a way of increasing their own learning. This "curiosity factor" is more prevalent when discussing content-area topics than when engaged in generic professional learning. As an example, Caroline, our science team member, told us that during subject-area team planning meetings, she would often share what she had learned in the cohort workshops, prompting conversations that led some teachers to incorporate new practices into their lessons. At the next science planning meeting, these teachers would describe how they had altered the new practice based on their classroom experience and would then discuss how the practice could be further revised. When Caroline met again with her cohort, she explained how she had shared her learning with her colleagues in ways that specifically met the goals of the science curriculum.

By discussing new learning with teachers who were not cohort members, Caroline acted as an instructional leader to her colleagues. She then furthered that leadership role by passing along her experience to those in her cohort and encouraging them to share disciplinary literacy practices in their own departments. Notice that this was not the result of a canned type of professional learning that was meant to be duplicated but an organic outcome of teachers excited about creating new practices.

We discovered that peer coaching within departments specifically related to disciplinary literacy practices encouraged teachers who were not in cohorts to become curious and ask questions as a way of increasing their own learning.

Listening In

Listening in to Dave Udchik, high school special services language arts teacher, discuss his experience with peer coaching:

Dave Udchik talks with Nick in his classroom about how to implement reading workshop with his students.

"During one of our workshops I heard Nick talk about how he used a reading workshop approach in his class. Afterward I talked with him about how to get started, and I began dropping in during my planning period to observe in his class. Eventually he recommended some of his favorite professional books to me, like Penny Kittle's *Book Love* (2013) and Kelly Gallagher's *Readicide* (2009). We have continued to work together informally this year. My students, many of whom have learning and behavior challenges, are reading more than ever and actually enjoying it—something that was not happening before."

We saw other examples of one-on-one leadership as well: a veteran English teacher mentoring a new teacher who was having difficulty getting his students to give and receive effective peer feedback on their writing; a physics teacher showing others in his cohort how his students had created a picture book to demonstrate their knowledge of physics and then helping his colleagues adapt the activity to their disciplines; and a music teacher working with a colleague on ways to use mentor texts such as concert reviews and articles about musicians in *Rolling Stone* to teach students how to write about music. This cycle of leadership did not require a microphone, a slot on the agenda, or a coronation ceremony at the next school board meeting—but, instead, a knowledgeable teacher collaborating with his or her colleagues.

Listening In

Listening in to a middle school ELL teacher discuss how her learning led to a leadership role with co-teachers:

"As an ELL teacher, I partner with teachers in a variety of subjects. I used to focus only on my students during class, making adaptations and adjustments to fit their needs. Once I joined a DL learning community, my role changed. Teachers in my department became interested in the ideas and strategies I had learned in our workshops. We began to plan lessons together and actually do more team teaching. I had always brought my knowledge of ELL students' learning needs to the table, but now I also had a grasp on how disciplinary literacy instruction could enhance content knowledge. I really felt my ideas and suggestions were respected by my colleagues."

We want to mention here a significant advantage of this type of collaboration: increased trust among teachers. Hargreaves and Fullan (2012) remind us that if trust is invested only in key leaders, instability may result when they leave. Building trust with colleagues, they argue, is foundational for teamwork and change—and, we would add, for developing teacher leaders.

Quoteworthy

"Remember that peer respect is the biggest lever for changing behavior. What you want to do, then, is create opportunities to increase purposeful peer interaction, help establish and consolidate new norms of teachers working together, and build respect for each other. You want to pull or draw people in with the energy and excitement of your own committed practice and also push and nudge them forward with your relentless commitment to being better and doing better for all of your students (Hargreaves & Fullan, 2012, p. 158)."

For the Curious

WHAT TYPE OF FEEDBACK WORKS BEST IN PEER COACHING?

Interestingly, the answer to the above question, according to researchers Joyce and Showers (1996), is *none*. They explain, "We have found it necessary and important to omit verbal feedback as a coaching component" (p. 5). They first make the distinction that in a peer coaching situation when teachers are observing each other, the one teaching is the "coach" and the one observing is the "coached." Observation lessons may be followed by a brief conversation but no feedback. "When teachers try to give one another feedback, collaborative activity tends to disintegrate. Peer coaches told us they found themselves slipping into 'supervisory, evaluative comments' despite their intentions to avoid them" (Joyce & Showers, 2014, p. 9).

Jolene Heinemann and Jennifer Walsh (far left) observe an ELA class taught by Moira Quealy.

LEADING THROUGH CONTENT KNOWLEDGE

A 2017 report on professional development that we discussed in Chapter 6 from the Learning Policy Institute listed "content focus" as the first element of effective professional development (Darling-Hammond, Hyler, Gardener, & Espinoza, 2017). We're not surprised about that—it seems that content is the mortar between the stones. And it is through such content that a different form of teacher leader can also develop, a leader who is truly expert in his or her discipline. Such leaders may have attained advanced degrees in their subject areas, become extremely knowledgeable in a particular aspect of their discipline, or they may have simply been teaching a certain subject for many years and gained extensive experience. We can think of a number of examples: the "science guys," two high school science teachers in Florida who formed an after-school club for students who wanted to delve into complex topics in science such as string theory or quantum physics; the middle school social studies teacher in Indiana who went abroad each summer and infused his lessons with photographs and artifacts from his trips; the ELA teacher in Michigan who had become an expert on Shakespeare and could be counted on to know everything from the square footage of the Globe Theater to the latest speculation that Shakespeare might not have authored the plays attributed to him. It is not unusual to see teachers who are passionate and knowledgeable about their subject become leaders in unexpected ways. Take a look at the following examples from our work:

- Tracy Kalas, a middle school ELA teacher, is a good writer and has a deep knowledge of how to teach writer's craft. Teachers began asking her to write mentor texts to illustrate a particular concept they were addressing in their content area. Tracy worked with teachers in math, chemistry, and history, creating stories for their curriculum to reinforce vocabulary, abstract concepts, or other aspects of the content, often with humor and always with relevancy to the topic under study.

- Before she even joined a cohort, we had heard about Tina Reckamp, a middle school math teacher who had a vast collection of picture books. She eventually joined one of our cohorts and became a resource for other teachers. Teachers soon learned that if they needed a picture book about a particular topic—chemistry, volcanoes, migration, figurative language—they should visit Tina.

- Luci Dvorak, a high school ELA teacher, spoke up during a workshop on inquiry about a professional book she had been using, *Make Just One Change: Teach Students to Ask Their Own Questions* (Rothstein & Santana, 2011). Her cohort was so interested in the ways that Lucy used the book that we had to schedule more time for her to share during the next workshop. She soon became a resource for teachers who wanted to help their students learn to ask better questions.

Quoteworthy

"Adults come to learning with experiences that should be utilized as resources for new learning" (Darling-Hammond et al., 2017, p. 7).

How might knowledge or experience become infused in lesson, practices, or curricula?

Sharing experiences or knowledge isn't always enough, however. The next step, according to the report on Effective Professional Development (Darling-Hammond et al., 2017), is linking "content learning to pedagogies supporting teachers' students and practice" (p. 7). How might knowledge or experience become infused in lessons, practices, or curricula? Imagine how much deeper disciplinary learning could become if we tapped into the knowledge that teachers, as content experts, could bring to the table. What's more, recognizing teachers' achievements increases individual efficacy, a significant component in transferring professional learning to students.

Photo by Janet Anderson.

Colleen Zenner and Michelle Anderson were both members of our literacy cohort. They used their learning to create a new class, Advanced Earth Science, and to present about how to develop science literacy skills at national conferences.

Quoteworthy

When we found out about teacher accomplishments, we began to look for ways to make this information public so they could enjoy a moment in the spotlight, celebrate as a community, and find ways to use each other's talents and experiences as resources. We also realized that taking a few minutes to recognize exemplary practices increased collective efficacy. Following are some ways to get out the word about positive pedagogical happenings.

- At the beginning of workshops or small group follow-up meetings, we asked if anyone had professional news to share. Often other teachers would "tell on" their colleagues—such as when members of a middle school cohort told us about Megan Stass, a math teacher in the group, who had received a "30 Under 30 Literacy Award" that recognizes younger educators who lead efforts to advance literacy.

- We also encouraged teachers to post notes about their own or others' accomplishments in the Google Community.

- Marsha originally included items about literacy cohort members' accomplishments in the "Try Something New" bulletin, but she eventually developed a separate bulletin titled "Resources Among Literacy Leadership Teachers," which she posted and updated periodically in the Google Community. The categories included: conference presentations, bloggers, authors and contributors, honors and scholarships, and other areas of expertise.

While we wanted to celebrate these successes and accomplishments, we were also careful to balance that with our desire not to infuse competition into the cooperative mindset we were trying to nurture. We initially kept teachers apprised of opportunities to present at conferences, write for journals, apply for scholarships, or nominate each other for awards, but gradually teachers took on this responsibility themselves

and shared notices about workshops or posted them in the Google Community folder. We also heard cohort members asking each other for help with their leadership endeavors such as the following:

- "Would you help me with my application to present at the literacy conference?"

- "Will you share your PowerPoint presentation from the science conference?"

- "I want to start a blog and would appreciate any tips you could share since yours has been so successful."

- "Can you tell me a little about your seminar experience in New York, as I'm thinking of applying myself?"

Again, we experienced a sort of organic growth model that grew from inside rather than being imposed from the outside due in large part to the environment of collegiality and sharing that permeated the workshops.

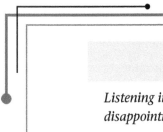

Listening In

Listening in to a middle school ELA teacher from Florida who discusses her disappointment in not being able to share new learning:

"I went to a multi-day workshop on literature circles led by Smokey Daniels, and when I came back to school I was fired up about lit circles. I wanted to share what I had learned, but the other ELA teachers seemed disinterested and my principal didn't offer an opportunity to present what I had learned to the rest of the faculty. I thought other teachers might want to try doing inquiry circles with their students, the topic of one of Smokey's books, or that as a faculty we might do a book study, but I didn't want to push it. Finally, I began looking for a position in another district that seemed to value more innovative teaching practices.

"I have been at a new school for 2 years now and my own learning about literature circles has dramatically increased. The other teachers on my team were eager to know more about collaborative discussions, and now we are using all sorts of informational texts in small groups. Best of all, I have learned from my colleagues how to release control and allow my students to become more independent in their discussions."

This cartoon makes us laugh in part because of the way it stereotypes leadership as only those in charge.

We need leaders at the front of the dogsled, no doubt, but we also need leaders within the disciplines such as those we have been describing in this chapter. Just as disciplinary literacy relies on supporting students in reading, writing, speaking, and doing, so must we support teachers in developing these same skills and then put these skills to work in developing leadership capacity.

"The good news – nearly 100% attendance for the Leadership Seminar. The bad news — now everyone thinks they are in charge."

Cartoon provided by Glasbergen Cartoon Service.

LEADING BY READING

As we made clear in Chapter 3, we know that a foundation of disciplinary literacy is built on students reading texts of all genres in every content area. Often, however, teachers have become so reliant on the textbook that they may not have considered how other texts can supplement their discipline. The voracious teacher readers we discovered in every discipline—*reader leaders*, we like to call them—play an important role in helping others in their cohorts, teams, or departments find supplementary disciplinary-specific texts.

Kathleen, our social studies team member and one of those teachers who reads constantly, offers recommendations of historical fiction and nonfiction to her students as well as suggestions of social studies texts to her colleagues. She, along with Nick and Janet, has encouraged all teachers to create content-area classroom libraries and make reading an important part of every curriculum.

A foundation of disciplinary literacy is built on students reading texts of all genres in every content area.

Book categories in Nick's
classroom library engage students.

A science teacher ReLeah worked with in New York came to life when discussing texts for science topics. Before we left for the day, she had suggested a list of books and articles for various science topics to her colleagues who taught Grades 6 through 12. (See Appendix C and the companion website for some of these recommendations.) A math coach in California, Maria Gutierrez, not only reads texts related to math but she also reads all sorts of books, articles, and websites that might engage middle school students. It became apparent that she was the go-to person if one needed a specific text to round out a content area topic. In Boston, an instructional coach appeared to have read every young adult novel published in the last twenty years. Teachers laughed as they told ReLeah there was nothing she could recommend that this coach hadn't read and passed along to teachers in her school. Such teachers should be acknowledged as leaders and be given opportunities to recommend texts as a way of encouraging wide and frequent reading among students and teachers. See Figure 8.1 for suggestions regarding how to encourage reader leaders to share their gifts.

Figure 8.1

How to Encourage Reader Leaders

- Make content area journals and magazines available to teachers and ask that they share an article a month with colleagues in their disciplines, perhaps as part of their professional learning plan.

- Steal this idea from a high school principal in Georgia. He asked each teacher on his staff to choose and read one book from the "Georgia Peach Book Awards for Teen

Readers" during the summer and discuss the book they read with their students on the first day back at school. The literacy coaches saw teachers checking out additional young adult books and engaging in informal book discussions with students. The library reported an increase in student book check-outs as well.

- Create a faculty book club and include books that aren't just professional reads. Departments or grade levels can also create book clubs to help them keep current on the best books for their disciplines or age groups.

- Ask if a teacher (or several) will sponsor a student book club to help develop student reading leaders.

- Begin every faculty or department meeting by asking "What have you read that you would like to share?"

- Ask teachers to post their own reading outside their doors.

A middle school social studies teacher reader incorporates book talks into his curriculum to promote independent reading for pleasure, then posts pictures of the book jackets on his door.

Listening In

Listening in to Tracy Hendrix and Jennifer Underwood, high school instructional coaches, discuss the formation of a student book club:

"We weren't quite sure how to begin, so we just jumped in. We used the Georgia Peach Book Award titles that our principal had encouraged teachers to read over the summer, especially since they could be connected to so many content areas. We had enough grant money to purchase multiple copies of each title so students would have a wide choice of books from which to choose. At our first meeting, we had so many students that we had to move the following meeting to a larger space! The students decided that they would sponsor a contest with the student body voting on their favorite Georgia Peach book through their English classes. They are now in the process of creating posters, videos, and tweets about the books to encourage students to read the books and then vote. The schoolwide interest in all these books has increased dramatically, but the best part is that students are becoming literacy leaders in their own right."

LEADING BY WRITING

When we first began encouraging members of the cohorts to write articles for professional journals or blogs for educational websites, teachers seemed surprised that we would think their work was of publishable quality.

When we first began encouraging members of the cohorts to write articles for professional journals or blogs for educational websites, teachers seemed surprised that we would think their work was of publishable quality. Marsha provided themes for upcoming journals such as *Educational Leadership* and *Voices from the Middle* and asked teachers to consider contributing something, even a small blog, to appropriate publications. Several teachers experimented with writing and became published authors with widespread influence. Carlynn Ullrich Sherman, middle school special services teacher, published a picture book to supplement her unit on Africa titled *Her Walk*; Karen S. Tischhauser, middle school English language arts teacher, wrote *The Importance of Writing Fiction in the Classroom: Simulation & Thinking*, an article for the *Illinois Reading Council Journal*, fall 2015 issue; and Meg Knapik, middle school math teacher, collaborated with an ELA teacher to create a blog about literacy and math, http://jmliteracy2.blogspot.com.

The library information teacher at West Island College promotes book club selections on a hallway bulletin board.

Listening In

Listening in to Stephanie Hawkins discuss writing for professional science education journals:

"I was asked to write an article titled 'Doppler Dart Demo' after presenting at the National AAPT (American Association of Physics Teachers). I modeled this activity during my talk and it was well received. After my first article, I had the confidence to work in collaboration with other physics teachers to write a second article, 'Physics Take-Outs.' This article highlights ways to get students to make connections between classroom content and everyday life. We describe activities such as paint-pendulum paintings, acceleration with helium balloons, and CD hovercrafts. I'm now working on my third article, which will be published soon! The second article can be found in *The Physics Teacher (54, 189, 2016).*"

Stephanie Hawkins uses ideas for her writing that she has developed in her teaching. These students, from a physics class co-taught with Chris Hawkins (no relation), experiment with the laws of circular motion.

While we might not immediately consider writing as a form of leadership, those who write do, indeed, influence hundreds, sometimes thousands of other educators, helping them "find meaning," Michael Fullan's (2017) succinct definition of leadership. Figure 8.2 lists a number of ways to encourage teachers to write to lead.

Figure 8.2

How to Encourage Writer Leaders

- Foster individual efficacy by reassuring teachers that they have something worthwhile to say and that others are interested in reading about their ideas.

- Make professional journals and blogs available to teachers not only to increase their knowledge but also to provide models of professional writing.

- Ask teachers to consider a coauthored or team piece of writing.

- During team meetings have colleagues from the same discipline read potential submissions from those in their group and offer suggestions if appropriate.

- Help teachers differentiate between good content and good editing. If someone has a great idea or wants to write about an activity, have them approach ELA teachers for help with editing. If that's not feasible, encourage them to send the piece on anyway. Often publishers will accept articles that aren't perfectly written and will edit in-house if the content is relevant and of good quality.

- When articles are published by a teacher, make sure every person on the faculty sees it—and forward a copy to the district office or school board. This practice not only recognizes teacher authors but also shares disciplinary knowledge.

- Have teams create Google accounts where teachers can post disciplinary ideas, research, activities, and content in an accessible format. See a screen shot of a Google Community on page 180.

- Suggest that teachers take photos of innovative projects or activities that support deep learning. A picture with a brief description is often the beginning of a longer piece of writing.

LEADING BY SPEAKING

Marta Constenla is by anyone's measure an exemplary teacher, as evidenced by the description of our visit to her class in Chapter 2. During our cohort meetings, however, she was rather quiet, contributing when she had something to say but certainly not dominating conversations. When we returned the following year and asked members to share what they had been doing over the summer, Marta didn't say much. At the break, however, she showed us a four-page handout she had presented at a regional conference of, the Chicago Area Chapter of American Association of Teachers of Spanish and Portuguese, where she had led a session for world language teachers based on the ideas she had adapted from our workshops. She was not only excited but grateful, expressing how she would have never had the courage to even submit a proposal much less present

There are Ideas for Literacy all around you!!
- Bookstores
- ACS: "Chem Matters" magazine subscription
- Other magazines. (Save hard copies for your classroom)
  - BBC Focus, Discover, National Geographic, Science
- Online News sites
- Websites, social media sites, twitter, facebook

Science teachers Michelle Anderson, Colleen Zenner, and Lauren Pennock presented a session titled "Power of Science Literacy," which began with a slide showing how science is "all around you."

without the encouragement of her cohort. She later e-mailed, "This is a big accomplishment that never would have happened without the cohort. What an honor it was for me to be able to share everything I learned and to witness how well received it was."

Marta's initial experience as a speaker went so well that the next year she presented at the Central States Conference on the Teaching of Foreign Languages. She then went on to become vice president of AATSP, American Association of Teachers of Spanish and Portuguese, Chicago chapter. In her end-of-year cohort reflection, Marta wrote, "This professional development inspired me to take risks inside my classroom and grow professionally outside my classroom. Thank you for being my inspiration and believing in my work."

Many other cohort teachers are now also presenting at regional, state, and national content-area conferences. It's not that the teachers in our cohorts are necessarily any more talented than others; it's that they had the opportunity to utilize their disciplinary literacy skills and, especially important, to develop the efficacy to move into leadership roles.

LEADING BY DOING

Perhaps the most familiar type of leading, leading by doing, occurs when teachers take action, often individually, to influence large groups of people in their schools, districts, or even nationally.

Leading a Schoolwide Disciplinary Literacy Event

One of our cohorts created an event named for their mascot, the bronco: Broncos Read. This team of leaders representing various disciplines set a goal that every student would read a self-selected book from various disciplines over the summer from a list of titles that met the diverse interests of the student population. Through funding provided by the school activity account, each student was given a choice from ten titles and could keep their chosen book with the understanding that they would return to school on National Literacy Day ready to kick off a year of literacy by engaging in discussions and activities related to the book with faculty members who had read the same book. Such an event took a lot of planning and coordination with the library, Literacy Leadership Team, Student Council, National Honor Society, Library Student Board, and the Book Club, as well as a lot of convincing those who were not sure this was such a great idea. It also took a campaign to interest students in the books through their English classes.

"The books were chosen with a wide array of genres and interests in mind. We knew that there simply isn't one perfect book for a community. But within a community, we can develop a culture of reading through choice. We offered nonfiction, fiction, reality fiction, dystopian, and historical fiction," Janet, the team's library information teacher, said. Figure 8.3 shows a list of the books selected for the Broncos Read initiative.

Listening In

Listening in to Alan Sanders, English teacher, as he reflected on the values represented by Broncos Read:

"One of the things I said frequently at that time about our endeavor was that Broncos Read encompasses two complementary values: the power of universal experiences and the richness of personal choice. Awareness of the power and richness of these values is essential to leadership. Leadership is about tapping into those deeply held ideals evidenced by individual choices while channeling energy and resources into collective experiences. It takes much more than one person leading the charge. It takes individual initiative from all corners, collaboration on many platforms, and action across many fields. This is true about leadership in general, but it's especially true about leadership in a literacy initiative because reading in all its forms is both a distinctly personal effort and an impactful collective one. Perhaps the most important lesson that Broncos Read confirms is that a few teachers with a sense of common purpose have power—the power to read books, the power to talk about books, and the power to suggest books to others."

Figure 8.3

Barrington High School
Summer Reading Selections

Nonfiction

Book Title	Disciplinary Literacy Connection
Dead Wake by Erik Larson	Social studies, ELA, science
Shadow Divers by Robert Kurson	History, science, math, health, world language, PE
Drowned City by Don Brown	Social studies, ELA, art

Fiction

Book Title	Disciplinary Literacy Connection
Ready Player One by Ernest Cline	Science, math, technology
Everyday by David Levithan	ELA, health, science
The 5th Wave by Rick Yancey	ELA, health, social studies
The Milk of Birds by Silvia Whitman	Social studies, world language, ELA
The Storied Life of A. J. Fikry by Gabrielle Zevin	ELA
Wonder by R. J. Palacio	ELA, health
The Wild Inside by Christine Carbo	ELA, science, social studies, health
The Perks of Being a Wallflower by Stephen Chbosky	ELA
Salt to the Sea by Ruta Sepetys	Social studies, ELA, health, world language

There were challenges in the implementation, as might be expected from an initiative that encompasses the entire student body and faculty, but the team learned quite a bit about what to do and not do the following year. That's not the point of this story, however. This team of teachers, acting as impact leaders, utilized the expertise of members of the cohorts to offer books that spanned the disciplines and expanded content area reading.

Leading an Interdisciplinary Event

Kamaria Shauri-Webb, an ELA teacher at Peachtree Charter Middle School in DeKalb County, also found herself in a leadership role when her students read *A Long Walk to Water: Based on a True Story* (Park, 2010), a story about two Sudanese children, a boy who was a "lost child of Sudan" and a girl who had to walk four hours, twice a day, to obtain water for her family. Through her participation in a disciplinary cohort where the group was studying ways to incorporate project-based learning, she reached out to a social studies teacher, Ingrid Gero, to create an interdisciplinary unit for the grade-level content area teachers to implement based on the following questions:

- Science: Why is water important for survival?

- Social studies: How does water impact health?

- ELA: What is the story of water worldwide?

- Math: How can we chart water usage in the school and at home?

She then worked with parents to extend the experience by having students carry two

Students at Peachtree Middle School carried two one-gallon jugs of water two miles after reading *A Long Walk to Water* as a way of understanding the events in the book.

one-gallon jugs of water for two miles to understand what women must do each day to have clean water in many countries. The students also created a PSA video on the water crisis in various countries.

To cap off the project, students held a special fundraising day in which students paid $3 to dress down for the day. They raised over $3,000 and made a donation to water.org for UN World Water Day.

One reason we love Michael Fullan's approach to leadership is because he understands that educational leaders' only profit is students' deep learning. As Fullan (2017) puts it, "The building block of transformation involves unleashing the role of students as change agents" (p. 63). That means that when students engage in deep, content area learning they are not only "protégés" who need teachers as mentors, but they also become change agents for their teachers. This reciprocity completes the cycle of leadership in ways that will ultimately benefit society as a whole.

Figure 8.4

How to Grow Strong Disciplinary Literacy Leaders

- Be open to a broad definition of leadership to include those who lead, as Fullan (2017) suggests, by uplifting others, making change happen, and affecting people in a meaningful way.

- Celebrate even small teacher accomplishments and awards.

- Allow potential leaders to learn how to lead by giving them opportunities to do what they do best, especially in the areas of disciplinary reading, writing, and speaking.

- Recognize and encourage differentiated leadership.

- Find opportunities for co-teaching and peer coaching.

- Make clear that when teachers help students become leaders, they themselves are leading.

- Release accountability into the hands of disciplinary leaders or a disciplinary literacy leadership team.

- View learning as a key component of leading.

- Listen to teacher leader ideas and provide space for their implementation.

- Engage in distributed disciplinary literacy leadership.

- Be open to projects suggested by your disciplinary literacy leadership teams, and provide available resources to help them carry out their plans.

- Be careful when conducting walk-throughs or evaluations that inadvertent negative comments don't shut down leadership potential.

The Power of Disciplinary Literacy Leadership

We end this chapter by offering the story of Tim Kramer, a middle school social studies and ELA teacher, who exemplifies how willingness to take a leadership risk in his own discipline ended up having impact on countless students and teachers.

At the start of Tim's first cohort meeting, we asked if anyone had read a good book lately. We recall that Tim had to be practically pushed by a teacher on his team to share one of the many books he had read over the summer. We were all amazed as Tim fluently talked about book after book from many genres that he had read and recommended to his students. We soon asked him to contribute book recommendations at every cohort meeting, and we shared those with the other cohorts as well. With a little encouragement, he became a regular presenter at the Illinois Reading Conference, and within a year he was asked to be on the board of the Abraham Lincoln Book Award committee, sponsored by the Illinois School Media Association. He is now using his voice to interview authors for his popular blog, and that's not all. Listen to Tim as he describes how he embraced leadership as a part of his role as teacher.

Listening In

Listening in to Tim Kramer as he discusses his path to leadership:

"When ReLeah Lent came to consult with District 220 in Barrington, Illinois, I was eager to participate in the cohort. I still remember my principal approaching me with a printed list of names of people he wanted to join; my name was written on the bottom of his list in scribbled pencil. I later learned one of my colleagues suggested that I would benefit from being a part of the cohort. It turns out, years later, that that colleague was right.

"The cohort was focused on content-area literacy in the classroom. We always began the workshops with simple book talks on what we are currently reading. I have always been an avid reader so my cohort quickly found me dominating these book talks, listing book after book that I had finished since our last meeting. I was surprised that everyone seemed so interested in my recommendations.

"During one meeting later in the cohort, one of my colleagues suggested I begin a book blog to spread my love of reading to an even larger pool of people. So I started a blog (http://mrkramersbookblog. blogspot.com/) with the first entry titled, 'So they said I should start a blog. . . .' And since then, I have published over 300 blog posts! Each post I also tweet out via Twitter and I add to Goodreads in the hope of getting more great titles into the hands of adults and youngsters alike.

"After the blog really started to garner some praise within my district, ReLeah and Marsha suggested I present my blog at reading conferences. I was hesitant at first; I mean, who am I to present at conferences? But I submitted a proposal and was accepted to present at the Illinois Reading Conference—and I have now presented 4 years in a row. At the 2016 Illinois reading conference, I approached a handful of authors, including Jason Reynolds, Jordan Sonnenblick, Tim Green, and Laurie Halse Anderson, and asked if they would be willing to participate in Q & A sessions for my blog. After hearing that Steve Sheinkin and Andrew Smith had previously participated, and because I had blogged on each of their books before, they all agreed! Let me tell you, my students almost died when they saw those Q & As posted live for the world to see.

"My favorite part of writing this blog is the fact that students and parents alike, from across the entire K–12 district, asked me or e-mailed me for book recommendations. I grew as a leader of literacy in my district as a result of this work.

"The incredible impact of my blog made me want to venture further into sharing what I was doing in my classroom. In the 2015–2016 school year, I collaborated with a seventh-grade history teacher, Anne Schmitt, who was doing a personal learning project with her history class. I took much of what she was doing with her class, modified it to fit my sixth-grade ancient history curriculum on Egypt, and then added on to it with a feedback component. During this process I reached out and connected with schools around the country ranging from Illinois to Texas to Massachusetts. Once my students' projects were finished, we sent their projects out to the partner schools for feedback on the strengths of the projects, what areas could be improved upon, and general feedback. It was exhilarating to see my students come in eager for the newest feedback (which we then used to reflect and plan for future lessons). After this experience, I decided to try to share again. I typed up a summary article that was published on the great resource Middleweb.com ('Using Global Feedback to Build Growth Mindset,' Middleweb.com). Through this site, our learning and the process of creating the lesson was shared with literally thousands of people around the world! How cool is that? I then went on to present this idea at the Illinois Reading Conference in back-to-back sessions along with my book blog talk. Talk about going from a teacher who was content with reaching his own students to having a broader impact.

"I am always eager to connect and to collaborate. I can be reached via e-mail at tkramer@barrington220.org and can be found on Twitter @ BMSPKramer. Please reach out to me if you have ideas, questions, or any other reactions to my blog or my tweets. It is my strong belief that the more of us who collaborate, the better our teaching and learning will be."

Tim Kramer in action with his students.

We have not addressed in this chapter the critical importance of "official" leaders such as district and school administrators as well as instructional coaches, for without their endorsement and encouragement, potential teacher leaders may, in effect, wither on the vine. In referring back to the Model of Disciplinary Literacy graphic on page 156, you'll see that continuous administrative and coaching support are vital elements of sustaining a culture of disciplinary literacy. Chapter 9 goes deeper into those roles.

Fostering Disciplinary Literacy Dialogue

1. What does leadership mean to you? Who in your professional life has exemplified the qualities of a good leader? What were those qualities? Compare your list to the deep leadership model developed by Michael Fullan on page 216.

2. In what ways can administrators support teacher leaders in your school? If there is a culture of "top-down" leadership, how can this be shifted to include distributed disciplinary leadership? Is anything happening at your school that discourages teacher leadership from emerging?

3. Read over the list in Figure 8.4 detailing how to grow strong disciplinary literacy leaders. Which of these elements are in place in your grade level, department, school, or district? In what ways could the others be strengthened?

4. The members of the disciplinary literacy cohorts in Illinois embraced peer coaching by establishing relationships and being willing to mentor others in every way possible. A more formal view of peer coaching (see *How to Plan and Implement a Peer Coaching Program* by Pam Robbins, 1991) involves colleagues working together around a shared observation of teaching, which might include a preconference, an observation, and a post-conference. A lesson-study format is also a type of peer coaching.

   - Does any form of peer coaching exist in your grade level, department, school, or district?

   - If not, what might it look like?

   - How could be implemented?

Resources for Continued Learning

Baum, K., & Krulwich, D. (2017). A new approach to PD—and growing leaders. *Educational Leadership, 74*(8), 62–66.

Fullan, M. (2017). *Indelible leadership: Always leave them learning.* Thousand Oaks, CA: Corwin.

Hall, P., & Simeral, A. (2008). *Building teachers' capacity for success: A collaborative approach for coaches and school leaders.* Alexandria, VA: ASCD.

Sterrett, W. (2016). *Igniting teacher leadership: How do I empower my teachers to lead and learn?* Alexandria, VA: ASCD.

Toll, C. A. (2017). 5 Perspectives for leadership success. *Educational Leadership, 74*(8), 28–31.

9

LEADING THE DISCIPLINARY LITERACY CHARGE

Leadership is the capacity to transform vision into reality.

Warren G. Bennis, founding chairman of the Leadership
Institute at the University of Southern California (Booher, 1992)

Ana Gutierrez and Jack Sokoloff, principals of two middle schools in
Little Lake School District near Los Angeles, arrived early to ReLeah's
workshop. This was the first of several days of professional learning about
disciplinary literacy with the entire staffs of both schools. Each principal
sat at a table with a group of teachers and actively participated in the
workshop, obviously at ease with such learning. From speaking out about

favorite books to brainstorming with small groups of teachers about skills needed to read in various subject areas, they were in the middle of everything. "Change isn't easy," Ana said, "and we can't lead the change if we don't share in the learning."

We could begin and end this chapter with that one quote.

Administrative Leaders as Learners

Shelly Cloke, principal of Frank Maddock High School in Alberta, Canada, also sat with a group of her teachers during a similar workshop. Shelly's reflection shows the importance of participation in professional learning alongside her teachers:

Principal Jack Sokoloff works alongside math teachers at a disciplinary literacy workshop.

"I joined the table with teachers on my staff who teach mechanics, construction, welding, and foods and was able to see a unique perspective on the importance of literacy in those subjects. Being part of this group reinforced the idea that each discipline has its own language, so to speak, and we had a great discussion about what it means to be literate in the language of each discipline.

"One thing that stood out was that in the vocational subjects, the language is that of the whole, the function of the parts and the interconnection between them. They start with the whole, an engine or a birdhouse for example, and the language is developed by examining the parts of the whole and how each fits and functions within it.

"Added to the language of vocational disciplines is that of communication, teamwork, and safety. These are integral components, more so than they are in other disciplines. Their language also relies on more of the senses than others. Learning to interpret the sound of an engine uses sight, sound, and touch.

"Delving further into this idea, I started to wonder if, by viewing each vocational discipline as having its own language lends a stronger 'legitimacy' to the discipline. If we examine what it means to be mechanically literate or literate in the food sciences, do we not raise awareness of the complexity of the discipline and bring it to the academic level of other disciplines such as math and English?

"Our next step as a staff is to define the language of our disciplines. What does it mean to be mechanically literate or to 'speak' the language of math? Our hope is that by examining the different languages of each discipline, we will come to see the similarities as well, such as how each discipline relies on the learning of vocabulary and interconnection."

Shelly said that she often sat with teachers in major content areas during workshops but that she wanted to show teachers of other disciplines that their work was valued as well. At the conclusion of the session, she remarked that she had learned so much while being a part of their community. Her learning led her to reflect on how she might take the work they had begun at the workshop to the next level—the mark of a true instructional leader.

For the Curious

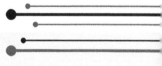

HOW IMPORTANT IS IT FOR PRINCIPALS TO LEARN WITH TEACHERS?

"Robinson, Lloyd, and Rowe (2008) conducted research on the impact of school principals on student achievement and found that the most significant factor—twice as powerful as any other—was the degree to which the principal participated as a learner with staff in helping to move the school forward." (Fullan & Quinn, 2016, p. 84)

Conversely, absentee administrators set the stage for all sorts of problems, beginning with a perception on the part of many teachers that leaders aren't supportive of what is being learned or for others a sense that administrators feel that they are somehow too busy or too important to share in a day of professional growth with their staff. We could relate countless stories of quality professional learning that never met its potential because administrators were, in effect, left behind. In those cases, teachers' learning expanded, along with their practices, but school leaders who were not part of that learning didn't know what they didn't know. In schools where teacher leaders involved in professional learning are given authority to make decisions, the outcomes may be better, but at some point administrators must deeply understand what instructional direction teachers are taking (or being asked to take) and why, especially if they are in the role of evaluating teacher performance.

Listening In

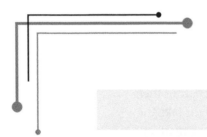

Ty Gorman, associate principal, leads a book discussion with students in ELA class. Classroom teachers invite administrators and staff once a month to discuss books around a common theme.

Photo by Janet Anderson

Listening in to Ty Gorman, an administrator at Barrington High School, who joined our first cohort of teachers as a participant:

"If you want teachers to buy into something, you're going to need to experience it as teachers do. Sometimes that learning is difficult for all of us. You have to become vulnerable and show that you are struggling to learn something new just as they are."

At one school, the assistant principal "in charge" of the team embarking on a disciplinary literacy journey "popped" in and out of the workshop, trying to show support and learn what she could but she was clearly and, perhaps justifiably, distracted. "Could you just tell me what I should look for during evaluations?" she asked us hurriedly. We didn't know how to begin to answer her question and didn't feel comfortable even trying. How could a day of active learning with thoughtful input from educators be reduced to a summary of "look fors" for the purpose of a standardized evaluation? It wasn't possible, and, what's more, it wasn't fair to the teachers who were trying to modify their practice in ways that were challenging for many of them. It's somewhat similar to a teacher who evaluates students on their learning when he doesn't fully understand the information himself. As we've said many times in this book, disciplinary literacy isn't a product; it is a process that ebbs and flows, as all learning does, and participation in that process is necessary for a true understanding of it.

Leading a school where literacy is infused in all disciplines requires a strong understanding of disciplinary literacy and how it should permeate every part of instruction. Since most principals, like most instructional coaches, haven't taught all subjects, they must trust their teachers' expertise while bolstering their continuing development in various areas: content knowledge, literacy understandings, effective discipline-specific instructional practices, teacher efficacy, and peer coaching.

Disciplinary literacy isn't a product; it is a process that ebbs and flows, as all learning does, and participation in that process is necessary for a true understanding of it.

VALUING TRUST

Not surprising, virtually every exemplary administrator we interviewed for this book listed trust as a key factor in teachers' professional learning. Heath McFaul, associate high school principal, said, "We should stay out of good people's way." He tells a story of an administrator who asked a teacher on her staff, "What can I do to help you?" Her simple answer: "Believe in me." He points to that experience as one that molded his own philosophy as an administrator and reminds him to always value the teachers with whom he works. When we were at his school, several teachers told us to make sure we made time to talk with Heath, with one saying, "He may not always be able to get us what we need, but he tries—and tells us honestly why he can't if it isn't possible. He treats us as professionals."

Quoteworthy

"If trust breaks down among any constituency, it can spread like a cancer by eroding academic performance and ultimately undermining the tenure of the instructional leader. In this day and age, no leader can long survive the demise of trust" (Tschannen-Moran, 2004, p. 173).

Caroline (left) and her department head, Julie, collaborate on how to help students best learn about a new computer program related to space science.

Trust goes both ways, as Caroline, the science teacher on our team, noted. Administrators must "believe in" teachers, but teachers also must be able to trust school leaders. "Our department chair, Julie, models trust, both professionally and personally. When she conducts an evaluation, it is a learning experience for both of us, and she encourages us to take risks, even during evaluations. She also opens up her classroom for us to observe her," Caroline said.

As we talked with Caroline and Julie, we were struck with the parity of the relationship, despite the fact that Julie was Caroline's immediate supervisor. It is no coincidence that the teachers in this particular department took greater risks than those in other departments, with one teacher even trying out a new practice during an evaluation. In addition, Julie encourages trust through peer mentorship rather than competition—and sees mistakes as opportunities for deepening learning. As a result, science teachers have exhibited strong literacy leadership and student achievement has soared. We remarked that this department was in actuality a community of learners with Julie as facilitator of that community. In fact, Caroline said she felt safe enough with Julie to pointedly tell her that she felt Julie was resisting doing a seminar with her own students and she should just "jump in and try it."

"Caroline is so used to taking pedagogical risks herself that she recognized that I was holding back," Julie said. "And she was right."

Simply put, for a disciplinary literacy approach to work, trust is a foundational building block. Unlike other initiatives where compliance or the ability to follow steps in a program or curriculum determines success, this model relies on teachers connecting content knowledge with literacy understandings and developing the efficacy, autonomy, and ability to make significant changes, often in differentiated ways. It is a form of deep recursive learning that is immediately applied, revised, shared, and reflected on. Such shifts require profound interpersonal trust or what Greg Anig (2013) calls "relational" trust. If the trust fails to develop or is violated, apprehension inhibits progress, risk taking shuts down, and teachers return to "safe" practices that can hinder student learning as well as teacher growth.

Megan Tschannen-Moran, author of *Trust Matters: Leadership for Successful Schools* (2004), reminds us that "teachers will be more willing to take the risk to try new instructional strategies when a culture of trust pervades the school" and that "trustworthy principals can move their schools to higher levels of productivity and success" (p. 180). We discovered her research to be accurate with our cohorts as well. In departments or grade levels where administrators trusted teachers to "try something new" from our workshops or book studies, they were more innovative and willing to transfer new learning back to the classroom. On the other hand, in departments where administrators showed distrust through "helicopter leadership" or made disparaging comments that indicated a lack of trust, individual efficacy waned and collective efficacy virtually ceased to exist.

For administrators who want to engage in a bit of reflection about their own trust quotient, they can take our survey in Figure 9.1.

Unlike other initiatives where compliance or the ability to follow steps in a program or curriculum determines success, this model relies on teachers connecting content knowledge with literacy understandings.

Figure 9.1

Administrators' Trust Survey

To what extent do you

- Listen more than talk?

- Avoid disagreements or hard discussions because you don't trust the outcome?

(Continued)

(Continued)

- Observe that teachers act more out of compliance than real commitment to new learning or practices?

- See teachers sharing ideas (as opposed to engaging in competition) in teacher meetings or professional learning settings?

- Communicate that you know change takes time and are willing to support deep learning rather than quick fixes?

- Ask for teachers' input before taking action on important disciplinary literacy decisions?

- Acknowledge teachers' strengths, viewing challenges as opportunities to learn rather than as failures?

- Admit what you don't know?

- Hear teachers asking you to drop in to observe lessons?

- Observe teachers taking risks or trying out new practices?

- Sense that teachers are comfortable when you join professional learning communities, book studies, or coaching sessions?

- Perceive that teachers feel comfortable coming to you with new ideas or challenges?

- Reassure teachers that you are there to remove barriers?

- Voice your understanding that too many new initiatives diffuse energy and attention?

- Believe in the power of collaborative professional learning and collective efficacy?

- Release some administrative control in favor of teacher autonomy?

RETHINKING ACCOUNTABILITY

While *trust* has been bounced around a lot in educational circles, it may be considered "soft" by some since it doesn't have the word "accountability" strapped to its hip. Kanter (2004) created a capacity-building framework around three "connected cornerstones" of accountability, collaboration, and initiative. We see these components as the building blocks of trust and view accountability as a function of trust, not the other way around. Kantor explains that in the most effective schools, people want to share information and take responsibility for their actions—not because they are being held to a preset standard of accountability but because they desire and are committed to improvement.

Janet, our team's library information teacher, mentioned that in all her years in education she had never seen teachers so willing to meet during lunch or their planning periods for the purpose of pedagogical discussions as she had seen with those who participated in the cohorts. Marsha noticed teachers meeting before and after school or even in the halls during change of class. Accountability was not a part of the equation, but trust, autonomy, and individual and collective efficacy were.

Traditional accountability may actually interfere with improvement as individuals strive to meet levels determined by state or district evaluations.

Interestingly, traditional accountability may actually interfere with improvement as individuals strive to meet levels determined by state or district evaluations. Teachers who attempt to show they are "excellent" in asking questions during a lesson, for example, may focus on that singular skill instead of the underlying concept of inquiry. Our cohort teachers, for the most part, began to surpass "behaviors" on an evaluation as they deepened their practice in ways that were often difficult to quantify.

Figure 9.2 offers ideas for making accountability visible and also serves to increase teacher efficacy, intrinsic motivation, and performance instead of relying solely on traditional evaluation measures or checklists.

Figure 9.2

Nontraditional Ways to Make Accountability Visible

- Ask teachers to write a reflection of their most effective disciplinary literacy practices prior to any type of standard evaluation. Point out innovative ideas in faculty meetings.

- During formal evaluations, engage teachers in a discussion of why they are doing what they are doing. This is especially important when evaluators don't have a background in the content area of the teachers they are evaluating.

- Ask teachers to keep a chart of disciplinary literacy topics in professional learning community meetings such as ideas, new research, or inquiries and send a photo of it to

(Continued)

(Continued)

you after their meetings. Such charts could also be posted in a professional learning area and utilized during the next meeting to increase follow-through.

- Begin each faculty meeting with sharing "what works" in disciplinary literacy. Ask teachers who rarely share to contribute.

- Create a "living document" teachers can add to and revise as they explore and become more aware of their disciplinary thinking. See Appendix items for reading, writing, and thinking in the disciplines 271–374, available for download from the companion website.

- Look for evidence of disciplinary literacy on hallway or classroom walls.

- Instead of evaluations that focus on teacher "performance" in front of the class, observe how students participate in the discipline and discuss with the teacher how student participation exemplifies learning in his or her subject.

- Ask teachers how mistakes may have led to increased professional learning or better lessons.

- Have teachers bring a lesson to their evaluation and ask them how they would improve it the next time they teach it.

- Be on the lookout for ways to pair teachers so that each can learn from the other's strengths. Ask for an honest reflection on the part of teachers.

- Keep a chart of teachers' goals and refer to these when evaluating to foster intrinsic accountability. If teachers' goals change because of new learning, ask them to update their goal statements.

- Discuss with other administrators or school leaders how capacity building can be seen as a type of accountability. How could it be evaluated, for example?

BUILDING CAPACITY

We said from the outset that we wanted to work ourselves out of a job in Barrington District 220 as we shifted the joys and responsibilities of literacy learning to teachers in the building. We also know that most administrators, while not wanting to be out of a job, do want content area teachers to take ownership of disciplinary literacy learning as, in fact, they should.

For that to happen, however, administrators must be committed to capacity building, defined as "the capability of the individual or organization to make the changes required" regarding "the development of knowledge, skills, and commitments" (Fullan & Quinn, 2016, pp. 56–57). The shift to a disciplinary literacy model pivots on the ability of the staff to engage in capacity building, specifically through collaboration, collective efficacy, and content-based literacy learning. The rather rapid cycle of new learning, experimentation, sharing, feedback, adaptation, and trying again—much like a lesson study approach—rests in the hands of teachers who are committed to the process and who are empowered to make the necessary changes for sustainability. See the Graph of Disciplinary Literacy Participatory Learning (Figure 7.2) for how such a cycle might work.

The shift to a disciplinary literacy model pivots on the ability of the staff to engage in capacity building, specifically through collaboration, collective efficacy, and content-based literacy learning.

Quoteworthy

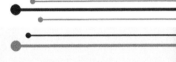

"The key to a capacity building approach lies in developing a common knowledge and skill base across all leaders and educators in the system, focusing on a few goals, and sustaining an intense effort over multiple years. A capacity building approach creates a foundation for sustainable improvement. The leader who helps develop focused collective capacity will make the greatest contribution to student learning" (Fullan & Quinn, 2016, p. 57).

If teachers begin to feel that the work they are doing can be quickly overturned by someone in a higher position, especially if that someone has not spent hours immersed in learning, the commitment to change diminishes and can turn into full-scale resistance or, at best, indifference. While other school-related decisions may be left solely to administrators, disciplinary literacy leadership should be grown from within as we discussed in Chapter 8.

In each of our cohorts, many teachers stepped up to the challenge of building capacity, but one very active literacy leadership team emerged from Barrington High School, which consisted of the four teachers you met in Chapter 2. As time went on, they found their roles changing as they sought to make disciplinary literacy shifts systemic and long-lasting. Their principal, Steve McWilliams, relied on them to sustain the culture of literacy and provided the requested resources as they were available. The team went to conferences together not only to present what they had learned but also to continue their own learning, and they brought new knowledge back to their departments and the school as a whole. Their roles expanded not only as a team but as individual capacity-builders as well, specifically in the following ways:

While other school-related decisions may be left solely to administrators, disciplinary literacy leadership should be grown from within.

- Janet, the library information teacher, began going more frequently into classes to offer digital literacy instruction.

- Nick, the English teacher who was now heading up a program to reach at-risk students, was able to procure a large classroom library. Teachers came into his classroom while he was teaching to check out books for their students or find a book to use in their discipline.

- Caroline, the science teacher, began taking on a more visible role in her department, opening up her classroom for observation, mentoring new science teachers in scientific literacy, and encouraging colleagues to infuse literacy into their lessons.

- Kathleen, the social studies teacher, became a model to other teachers of how to incorporate inquiry-based literacy learning, the "doing" of social studies through study and action.

The literacy leadership team leads a session on disciplinary literacy at a national conference.

While we continue to suggest to administrators that capacity can optimally be built when literacy leadership teams are allotted extra time to sustain disciplinary literacy learning, we know that the logistical or financial means to make this happen can be tricky. Nevertheless, we keep pushing because we know the importance of sustainability. We suggest, for example, an additional planning period for key members, perhaps on a rotating basis each grading period, or stipends for planning after school. With our four-year disciplinary literacy initiative in Illinois, we know, without a doubt, that school leaders alone would not have been able to sustain the innovations created by teachers without a literacy leadership team. As we write this chapter, for example, a member of one of the cohorts is working with the literacy leadership team and principal to write a substantial grant that will support ELL students' literacy skills in all disciplines. This type of capacity building is one that will continue to grow long after a consultant is gone. Here are some other ways that schools have found to build capacity, specifically in sustaining a disciplinary literacy approach:

1. Provide ongoing, embedded literacy professional learning for the entire staff, with support and follow-up by a coach or consultant. Beware of reducing this learning to "strategy" acquisition in place of literacy learning that can be adapted to various disciplines.

2. Form a literacy leadership team made up of members of various departments. (See Figure 9.3 for tips regarding how to create a literacy leadership team.)

3. Make sure professional learning communities or disciplinary literacy cohorts are grounded in continuous disciplinary literacy leaning and collaborative inquiry. This may require the help of a literacy consultant, coach, book study, or even professional learning off site. (See Figure 9.4 for more information about how to create an effective book study.)

4. Provide the resources, especially time and space, so teachers will have the capacity to grow.

5. Ensure that teachers, especially those in cohorts or teams, experience encouragement, support, and opportunities to stretch their skills and knowledge. Remember that individual and collective efficacy are the most important components for increased student learning—as well as for building capacity.

6. Encourage cross-curricular or cross-team collaboration to encourage stronger relationships and deeper understandings across contents.

7. Foster leadership in all areas and look for leaders who shine in nontraditional ways (see Chapter 8).

8. Utilize summer as a time for reflection, learning, and planning collaboratively.

9. Find opportunities for co-teaching and peer coaching within disciplines.

Figure 9.3

How to Create a Literacy Leadership Team

- Invite teachers from various content areas, the instructional or literacy coach if you have one, and the library information teacher if appropriate to make up this team. Note that this team is in addition to interdisciplinary cohorts or DL learning communities. Consider inviting one member from each DL learning community, cohort, grade level, or department to be a part of the literacy leadership team.

- Keep the group size between six and eight, if possible. Depending on the size of the school, this number might need to be revised.

- The team should meet regularly—with the principal or a designated administrator.

- Provide a specific time for the group to meet as well as a budget. If at all possible, allot an extra planning period that rotates among members, one that might change each grading period or semester. This is especially important if the school does not have a literacy or instructional coach.

- The team's responsibilities may include

  o Planning ongoing disciplinary literacy professional learning

  o Keeping track of both formal and informal data (such as teacher and student surveys or library check-out records). The team should not become a testing data team, however

  o Creating a physical space to house resources and an online location for sharing documents and ideas

  o Creating opportunities to build capacity among all teachers by showcasing innovative disciplinary literacy instruction or events such as workshops that teachers lead

As we mentioned earlier, book studies are a valuable way of increasing content knowledge as well as building capacity. When done well, they also create strong collegial bonds and allow teachers a space for analyzing student work and revising lessons based on discipline-specific literacy practices. Within our cohorts, teachers decided how they would engage in their book study. Some met before or after school on designated days, others met over lunch, and a few groups decided to conduct their meetings electronically with fewer face-to-face sessions. Marsha met with the groups if they wanted her to facilitate or sit in, but all groups used the book studies as opportunities to try out suggestions in their classrooms

Prairie Middle School principal Travis Lobbins (third from left) learned about disciplinary literacy along with his teachers by participating in this small book study group. Teachers told us that he supported their efforts and provided a safe environment for risk taking.

and return to the next meeting with their observations. While our groups used ReLeah's books as their text since we were building disciplinary literacy background and they could "question the author," we most often suggest that groups choose their area of interest or need and find a book that fits their requirements. In fact, we generally have found that requiring one book for the entire faculty to read undermines autonomy, efficacy, and differentiated professional learning.

Listening In

Mary Stec, instructional coach at a middle school, discusses how book study has built capacity within the staff:

"Over the past 5 years, our middle school staff members have participated in a variety of book studies. Each has proven to be an effective way to grow professionally, build a common understanding among staff, and test out new strategies and ideas with the support of colleagues. The feedback from teachers highlighted that the mix of grade levels and content teachers in the book study groups created an opportunity for sustained reflection and rich discussion.

"One year our teachers were given eight learning team options based on their goals for professional learning. Two of these options were book studies. Twenty-four teachers opted to engage in a book study of Daniels and Ahmed's book *Upstanders: How to Engage Middle School Hearts and Minds With Inquiry* (2015). After reading the book, this group planned and implemented inquiry within their own disciplines. The learning team meeting dates were scheduled to give teachers a chance to read, reflect, and try out some strategies or new ideas prior to the next book study meeting. At the start of second semester, all book study participants developed a product that demonstrated their learning.

"Ten other staff members elected to participate in a book study on Troy Hicks and Kristen Hawley Turner's *Argument in the Real World: Teaching Adolescents to Read and Write Digital Texts* (2017). Our main goal was to investigate as a group how argument can be represented in video, blogs, infographics, and social media and how students can be producers of this type of content in our classrooms. As we move to integrate digital literacy in all content areas, this book study gave a core group of teachers a common understanding of how we can help students share their thoughts with the world in a medium that will be most effective for reaching the intended audience."

Figure 9.4

Guide for Implementing a Professional Book Study

Topic:

Date:

Text & Chapter:

Facilitator:

Members Present:

Five-Minute Rewind: Facilitator and recorder review major points of discussion from last meeting.

Five-minute Fast Forward: Facilitator reminds group of goals of study.

Sample Group Actions:

- Begin the meeting with members sharing best quotes from their reading (or something with which they disagree).

- Have members bring observations from a lesson or student work to share. Provide time for sharing.

- Have a few members take sections of the text to summarize.

- List questions that members have and chart them for future meetings.

- List other resources that might be needed to further learning (professional materials, classroom resources, or something else, like notes from classroom observations).

- Before leaving, have members reflect on new learning that occurred as a result of the meeting (not only from the book itself). What will members do with this new learning?

Disciplinary Literacy Coaching: The Glue That Holds It All Together

Coaching is a leadership role unto itself, but coaching for disciplinary literacy can look different than literacy or instructional coaching. The changes we have described in this book are complex and sometimes daunting for teachers, especially those who may be deeply entrenched in "the way things have always been done" or those who feel a reluctance to make changes that they sometimes see as inefficient, such as decreasing the practice of PowerPoint lectures.

The role of a disciplinary literacy coach requires knowledge about literacy but not comprehensive knowledge about each content area.

Helping teachers internalize shifts that position disciplinary literacy as a tool for teaching students to analyze, evaluate, and construct texts or view and speak as an expert in the field often takes nuanced yet specific support. The role of a disciplinary literacy coach requires knowledge about literacy but *not* comprehensive knowledge about each content area. The coach will, instead, rely on content area teachers to bring to the table disciplinary knowledge and then utilize that knowledge as teachers collaborate to identify and put into practice the discipline-specific literacy skills students need in their subjects to read, write, speak, reason, and do.

Unfortunately, literacy or instructional coaches may face scrutiny or even criticism from content area teachers who feel they don't know enough about their disciplines to effectively coach them. We recommend that administrators take care in the tasks they assign coaches. In one district, for example, the coach was expected to guide teachers in creating a science scope and sequence as well as specific lesson plans for content the coach had never taught. As you might expect, there was resentment from the teachers in the department and the coach began to feel inept—even though she had studied the science textbooks before the meeting as if preparing for an exam. She could not possibly have learned enough about the content, however, to lead teachers in such a monumental task. Her time and expertise would have been more effectively put to use helping teachers learn how to use literacy as a valuable tool for teaching the content they knew so well.

Quoteworthy

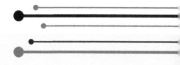

"Effective coaches . . . take on a co-learner stance. By this we mean the coach learns about teaching with teachers rather than being a person who claims to 'know and tell' teachers what to do" (Rodgers & Rodgers, 2007, p. 17).

The disciplinary literacy coach's job is to support teachers in their disciplinary processes, that is, in their understanding of how students will construct knowledge and communicate that knowledge using literacy tools in content-specific ways. We have found the book *Collaborative Coaching for Disciplinary Literacy: Strategies to Support Teachers in Grades 6–12* (Elish-Piper, L'Allier, Manderino, & Di Domenico, 2016) helpful and offer the authors' eight guidelines for instructional coaches in Figure 9.5, with our notation directly below each italicized guideline. Figure 9.6 shows specific responsibilities for a disciplinary literacy coach.

Figure 9.5

Effective Disciplinary Literacy Coaching: Eight Guidelines

1. *Build capacity*

The authors recommend a strong literacy leadership team, which we agree is essential for building capacity.

2. *Consider teacher knowledge*

Be prepared to work individually with some teachers who may not yet have as strong a knowledge base as others.

(Continued)

(Continued)

3. *Create sustainability*

See the graphic that represents our model for Creating a Schoolwide Culture of Disciplinary Literacy on page 60.

4. *Spend as much time as possible working directly with teachers and teacher leaders*

This guideline is a difficult one for all coaches to achieve, but as much as possible try to avoid administrative meetings, being turned into a data or testing coordinator, or taking on non-coaching duties. Teachers need your support in professional learning settings as well as in classrooms.

5. *Situate the coach as a collaborator, not an expert*

Make this guideline clear from the beginning and tread carefully on that slippery slope from collaborator to expert. This will be a shift for both the teachers and the coach as they combine teachers' knowledge of content with the coach's knowledge of literacy to create classroom approaches that build content knowledge *through* reading, writing, thinking, and doing in the disciplines.

6. *Let collaboration develop*

Facilitate collaboration among teachers by stepping out of the way and listening more than talking. Don't be afraid to set aside a topic you had in mind and follow the teachers' lead, all within the framework of disciplinary literacy.

7. *Leverage coaching strategies*

Be mindful that as a disciplinary literacy coach your coaching strategies involve helping content teachers utilize their expertise. Ask questions that prompt teachers to reflect on the practices unique to their discipline so that activities or strategies can be customized to their subject areas.

8. *Focus on student learning*

Enough said.

Adapted from Elish-Piper, L., L'Allier, S. K., Manderino, M., & Di Domenico, P. (2016). *Collaborative coaching for disciplinary literacy: Strategies to support teachers in grades 6–12* (pp. 17–18). New York, NY: Guilford Press.

Because disciplinary literacy coaching differs from traditional literacy coaching, it might be helpful to bring coaches together from a region or district to explore fully the challenges inherent in such coaching. (See Figure 9.6 for a clear list of responsibilities of a disciplinary literacy coach.) When ReLeah facilitated such a day of learning for coaches in a district where disciplinary literacy was the primary focus, she offered scenarios

Figure 9.6

Responsibilities of a Disciplinary Literacy Coach

As a Disciplinary Literacy Coach

You are responsible for	You are not responsible for
Helping teachers reflect on their practice and learning goals	Telling teachers what to think about their practice and learning goals
Providing support and resources as teachers create lessons that incorporate discipline-specific literacy skills (reading, writing, speaking, viewing, reasoning, and doing)	Creating lessons for teachers
Showing teachers how reading strategies specific to their discipline can support content learning	Teaching generic reading strategies to large groups of teachers
Guiding teachers in identifying discipline-specific literacy skills and habits	Identifying discipline-specific literacy skills and habits for teachers
Helping teachers understand the domains of literacy in their disciplines (vocabulary, comprehension, multi-modal texts, speaking, writing, participating)	Creating domains of literacy for all disciplines
Helping teachers shift into 21st-century teaching (including the use of collaboration, inquiry, problem solving, wide reading, writing to learn, digital literacy)	Evaluating teachers on their ability to shift into 21st-century teaching
Demonstrating through model lessons by collaborating with teachers on their content	Assuming teaching responsibilities for teachers
Utilizing one-on-one cognitive coaching practices after observational lessons	Assessing teachers' strengths or challenges after observational lessons
Supporting peer coaching	Mandating peer coaching
Facilitating teams, grade levels, or cohorts as they engage in the work of disciplinary literacy	Administrating teams, grade levels, or cohorts

Disciplinary literacy coach Jennifer Underwood (upper right) works with ELA teachers as they analyze student writing samples.

such as the following for discussion and role playing. More sample scenarios can be found in the online companion website, http://resources/corwin .com/lent-voigtDLinAction

- You have been working closely with a science teacher on having students *do* more science rather than simply reading about it. You feel you are making progress but suddenly he says he feels this "approach" is taking too much time and he needs to revert to a more traditional approach.

- The PE teacher wants to incorporate disciplinary literacy but has no idea how to begin.

- Most of the ELA teachers want to engage in a reading workshop approach rather than using whole-class novels but there are a few teachers who are resistant.

One coach took the role of teacher and the other took the role of coach, with each pair being given a scenario such as those provided earlier in which to engage. Several pairs volunteered to re-create their discussion in front of the entire group. After a bit of hamming it up and much laughter on the part of the "coach" and "teacher," the group provided valuable feedback to the actors.

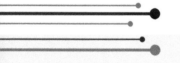

Quoteworthy

"Effective and efficient literacy coaches are not experts; they have expertise" (Puig & Froelich, 2011, p. 62).

Administrators and coaches have enormous responsibilities that sometimes seem impossible. They must be effective listeners, facilitators, teachers, and learners as they build capacity, develop trust, spur inquiry, encourage autonomy, and cultivate efficacy. Their job description is as nebulous as a new parent's, yet they are tasked with helping seasoned and novice teachers make some of the most difficult shifts in their teaching lives. Our advice? Tap into the expertise of content area teachers while providing continuous professional learning, build capacity through disciplinary literacy learning communities, and then try to relax as teachers use their collective efficacy to improve student learning.

Fostering Disciplinary Literacy Dialogue

1. What obstacles prevent administrators from becoming fully involved in professional learning? How can these be overcome in your school or district?

2. Use the questions in Figure 9.1, "Administrators' Trust Survey," to engage in an honest dialogue with other administrators about trust in your school or district.

3. Accountability can be a sticky wicket under the best of circumstances. Is it possible to rethink accountability and evaluation so that it becomes more formative and instructive than evaluative? If so, how?

4. It is no secret that building capacity is a very challenging endeavor that often seems to be more a crab walk than forward momentum. What challenges have you experienced in the past when trying to build capacity? What have you learned? What can you do differently?

5. To what extent are coaches empowered to do their jobs in your school or district? What other "tasks" might take them away from the important work of supporting teachers' understanding and practice of disciplinary literacy? How can they be better supported in their jobs?

Notes:

Resources for Continued Learning

Combs, J. P., Harris, S., & Edmonson, S. (2017). Four essential practices for building trust. *Educational Leadership, 72*(7), 18–22.

Danielson, C. (2016). Creating communities of practice: If not teacher evaluation, what should drive teacher improvement? *Educational Leadership, 73*(8), 18–23.

Dean, T. R. (2018, May). What is a high school literacy specialist? *Journal of Adolescent & Adult Literacy, 59*(6), 652–652.

Elish-Piper, L., L'Allier, S. K., Manderino, M., & Di Domenico, P. (2016). *Collaborative coaching for disciplinary literacy: Strategies to support teachers in grades 6–12.* New York, NY: Guilford Press.

Hall, P., & Simeral, A. (2008). *Building teachers' capacity for success: A collaborative approach for coaches and school leaders.* Alexandria, VA: ASCD.

Puig, E. A., & Froelich, K. S. (2011). *The literacy coach: Guiding in the right direction.* Saddle River, NJ: Pearson Education.

Reilly, M. (2015). Getting genuine commitment for change: Strategies to turn resistance into willingness, complaints into commitment. *Educational Leadership, 72*(7), 42–46.

Tomlinson, C. A. (2017). Shining a light on leadership: Transformative teachers and principals follow three practices. *Educational Leadership, 74*(8), 91–92.

CODA

Be patient toward all that is unsolved. Try to love the questions themselves.

Maria Rilke Rainer (1934/2013)

One of the questions we are often asked about disciplinary literacy instruction is, "How do you know when it's successful?" Our answer always comes back to this: There *is* no certain way of knowing. And what may be even more disconcerting is that, like all good teaching and learning, success is rarely static. One day a PLC, grade level, department, or content area may seem to have it all figured out, shining like stars . . . and the next day? The sky turns cloudy. An interdisciplinary project might bring together various disciplines where kids utilize literacy in ways that make them look like they have been experts in the field forever. And the following week the same students may struggle with reading a straightforward text.

Success in disciplinary literacy is not easily measured because what counts are often the intangibles—synergy, authentic communities of learning, inquiry, intrinsic motivation, innovation, curiosity, creativity, problem solving, and efficacy. What *can*

A moment of success in the classroom.

be more easily measured is the visible: multi-modal text sets in classrooms, students reading on their own and asking questions, collaborative problem solving, evidence of real-world learning, disciplinary speaking, content-specific writing, and active engagement on the part of students *and* teachers. Success might well be measured in what we observe and, yes, even in what we feel when we walk into classrooms such as the ones we've described in this book.

Or maybe it's not in the classroom where success is always demonstrated. In listening to students such as those who spoke so eloquently to lawmakers and the president after the horrific shooting in Parkland, Florida, we knew their teachers had taught them how to harness the power of literacy for its rightful purpose—and no standardized test could adequately measure their achievement. They took their education into the real world and put disciplinary literacy to work: constructing understandings, engaging in civic debate, and communicating clearly what matters for their future. Ultimately, this is what we want from disciplinary literacy teaching and learning—and why it's worthwhile to commit to this process and all the work necessary to create and sustain a schoolwide culture of deep reading, writing, and thinking.

APPENDIX A

DISCIPLINARY LITERACY IN ENGLISH LANGUAGE ARTS

Note. Amazon, Goodreads, and teacher and student readers were valuable resources in helping us with summaries of recommended titles.

When students of English read, they

- Find meaning through literary techniques
- Identify underlying messages that evolve as theme
- Recognize bias
- Use context to learn new vocabulary or words used in new ways

- Summarize, synthesize, analyze, and evaluate
- Comprehend how devices such as tone, foreshadowing, or irony affect the text
- Question through critical lenses
- Make connections
- Pay attention to the craft of writing
- Recognize elements of stories, poems, or novels
- Understand perspective

When students of English write, they

- Utilize a process: drafting, revising, and editing
- Understand how to flexibly utilize organization, details, elaboration, and voice to enhance meaning
- Ask for and appropriately utilize feedback
- Avoid formulaic writing
- Employ literacy techniques and devices appropriately
- Use credible evidence
- Avoid bias when appropriate
- Employ various perspectives
- Utilize mentor texts
- Adapt communication for various audiences
- Employ effective techniques for argumentation

When students of English think, they

- Use reflection as a tool for understanding
- Ask questions of the text
- Compare texts or themes
- Communicate as a way of clarifying

- Make connections among texts, themes, or the real world
- Respect multiple viewpoints
- Listen to others
- Compare texts, sources, and perspectives

Websites for Teaching ELA

http://www.nytimes.com/section/learning

The Learning Network is an excellent resource for teachers with activities, articles, and contests for students.

http://www.goodreads.com

Free website for book lovers. See reviews, ratings, recommendations, and awards lists. Designed to help students find good books, join a discussion group, or contact authors.

http://www.poets.org

Produced by the Academy of American Poets, this online source contains poems, poets' biographies, essays about poetry, and resources for K–12 teachers.

http://www.makeuseof.com

This site describes ten websites for reading short stories and flash fiction.

https://newsela.com

This popular site contains news articles that can be used in every subject.

https://www.readworks.org/

Teachers can access thousands of high-quality, free K–12 articles, and create online assignments with them.

https://www.commonlit.org/

A rich collection of free and accessible texts enables students to explore unique resources that support literacy and critical thinking.

https://www.vocabulary.com/

Vocabulary.com helps readers learn new words, play games that improve vocabulary, and explore language.

http://www.adlit.org/

Access a range of resources for teachers, students, and parents including award winning book lists, video interviews with top young adult (YA) authors, themed book lists for teen readers, historical fiction book lists, blogs, research, and multi-media resources centered on YA literature.

https://www.nwp.org/

This is a valuable resource devoted to improving writing and learning in all classes.

Websites for Award Winning Young Adult Literature

http://guysread.com

A web-based program to help boys become self-motivated, life-long readers.

http://www.ala.org/yalsa/alex-awards

The Alex Awards are given to ten books written for adults that have special appeal to young adults, ages 12 through 18.

http://www.ala.org/yalsa/printz-award

The Michael L. Printz Award is an award for a book that exemplifies literary excellence in young adult literature.

http://www.nationalbook.org/aboutus_history.html#.WiHBH0xFxRQ

Find lists of the latest National Book Award winners, including those written for students. Books listed on this site are reliably good, often future classics.

http://www.npr.org

This National Public Radio site includes news articles on a variety of topics including science, health, politics, technology, world, business, race, and culture.

http://www.ala.org/rt/emiert/cskbookawards

The Coretta Scott King Book Awards are given to outstanding African American authors and illustrators of books for children and young adults that demonstrate an appreciation of African American culture and universal human values.

https://www.literacyworldwide.org/get-resources/reading-lists

Young Adults' Choices highlights thirty books selected by teenage reviewers. A popular site for engaging student readers.

http://www.ala.org/yalsa/teenstopten#nominees

The Teens' Top Ten is a "teen choice" list, where teens nominate and choose their favorite books of the previous year. Nominators are members of teen book groups in fifteen school and public libraries around the country.

http://www2.ncte.org/awards/orbis-pictus-award-nonfiction-for-children/

The NCTE Orbis Pictus Award is given to nonfiction books for children and teens.

https://www.booklistonline.com/Booklist-s-50-Best-YA-Books-of-All-Time-Kraus-Daniel/pid=8945051

Fifty best young adult novels of all time based on literary quality as well as significant influence.

Visit the companion website at
resources.corwin.com/lent-voigtDLinAction
to download this appendix.

APPENDIX B

DISCIPLINARY LITERACY IN MATH

When mathematicians read, they

- Isolate information they have been given and look for information they need
- Identify patterns and relationships
- Decipher symbols and abstract ideas
- Apply mathematical reasoning and number sense
- Seek accuracy
- Analyze, formulate, and interpret
- Evaluate data
- Ask questions
- Consider the unique vocabulary, language, and word parts specific to math

When mathematicians write, they

- Explain, justify, describe, estimate, or analyze
- Use representations
- Seek precision
- Utilize real-world situations
- Communicate ideas clearly
- Draw conclusions
- Use symbols and abstractions
- Include reasons and examples

When mathematicians think, they

- Use all available information to solve problems
- Consider generalizations, exceptions, and patterns
- Bring forth previous understandings
- Know when to estimate and generalize
- Create a plan for solving problems
- Determine relevance of given information

Websites for Teaching Math

http://www.nytimes.com/section/learning

This Learning Network site is an excellent resource for teachers and has activities, articles, and contests for students.

http://www.educationworld.com/acurr/mathchat/mathchat019.shtml

Once on this website, click on professional development, then Math Chat, which will connect math to real-life uses.

http://www.mathalicioius.com

Great site that provides real-world problems and more.

http://www.RealWorldMath.org

This site uses Google Earth to showcase math activities in real-life situations.

Book Recommendations for Starting a Classroom Library

The Boy Who Reversed Himself by William Sleator. Laura's weird neighbor has the ability to travel to the fourth dimension. This science-fiction thriller keeps the reader involved.

Do the Math: Secrets, Lies and Algebra by Wendy Lichtman. An easy-to-read novel about an eighth-grade girl who finds new meanings for algebra. This book can spark interest in students who don't see themselves as mathematicians. If you like this one, look at Lichtman's second book, *Do the Math #2: The Writing on the Wall*.

The Great Divide: A Mathematical Marathon by Dayle A. Dodds, illustrated by Tracy Mitchell. In this crafty story of a cross-country race, numerical division accounts for the narrowing of the field. Students say they enjoy math presented in this way.

The Magic of Math by Arthur Benjamin. Solving for *x* and figuring out why. The author uses examples from ice-cream scoops and poker hands to measuring mountains. Arithmetic, algebra, geometry, and calculus, plus Fibonacci numbers and infinity are explained in interesting, real-life situations.

The Man Who Counted: A Collection of Mathematical Adventures by Malba Tahan. A fun read for younger students, this classic helps readers engage in mathematical thinking. A gifted resource teacher in North Carolina created a unit for fifth-grade students around this book that she will share. Contact Kristy Cossett at kcossett@chccs.k12.nc.us.

Math Talk: Mathematical Ideas in Poems for Two Voices by Theoni Pappas. This readers' theater script for math students allows them to explore mathematical concepts while having a bit of fun in the process. Check out another of this author's books: *The Joy of Mathematics: Discovering Mathematics All Around You.*

Mathematical Curiosities: A Treasure Trove of Unexpected Entertainments by Alfred Posamentier. The authors explore the unusual in math while making it fun for readers. Their examples are both engaging and thought provoking. Older readers will embrace the challenges while also being entertained by in this text.

Mathematics, an Illustrated History of Numbers: 100 Ponderables by Tom Jackson. Quick summaries of 100 math ideas from integers to chaos, all explained in one- or two-page essays and diagrams. The wonderful illustrations add to the appeal of this book.

The Mathematics Lover's Companion: Masterpieces for Everyone by Edward Scheinerman. This book includes ideas from number theory to geometry to probability.

Math Talk: Mathematical Ideas in Poems for Two Voices by Theoni Pappas. This readers' theater script for math students allows them to explore mathematical concepts while having a bit of fun in the process. Check out another of this author's books: *The Joy of Mathematics: Discovering Mathematics All Around You.*

Multiplying Menace: The Revenge of Rumpelstiltskin (A Math Adventure) by Pam Calvert, illustrated by Wayne Geehan. The story is based on Rumpelstiltskin with a magic stick. Whimsical illustrations make multiplying whole numbers and fractions entertaining for younger students.

The Number Devil: A Mathematical Adventure by Hans Magnus. A whimsical read that explores numbers of all types: infinite, prime, Fibonacci, and more. This book would make a great read-aloud for younger students.

Secrets of Mental Math by Arthur Benjamin and Michael Sherman. The mathemagician's guide to speedy calculation and amazing math tricks.

Sir Cumference and the Dragon of Pi by Cindy Neuschwander, illustrated by Wayne Geehan. This book plays with math and language. Join Radius on his quest to solve a riddle and discover the magic number. Be sure and look up other titles by this author and illustrator.

A Slice of Pi: All the Math You Forgot to Remember from School by Liz Strachan. This book includes interesting math stories, quirky calculations, and funny anecdotes about algebra, geometry, and trigonometry. Will appeal to anyone with an inquiring mind.

Visit the companion website at
resources.corwin.com/lent-voigtDLinAction
to download this appendix.

APPENDIX C

DISCIPLINARY LITERACY IN SCIENCE

When scientists read, they

- Assume an objective stance
- Ask "why" and "how" more than "what"
- Rely on data, sketches, charts, and illustrations
- Make connections from known concepts to new concepts
- Determine validity of sources and quality of evidence
- Pay attention to patterns
- Make predictions
- Review and reflect

- Recognize importance of precise scientific vocabulary
- Search for answers
- Look for details and evidence

When scientists write, they

- Use precise wording
- Compose in phrases, bullets, graphs, or sketches
- Favor passive voice
- Seek exactness over craft
- Communicate in a systematic format
- Distinguish facts from opinions
- Generate questions
- Provide details, narratives, and causal effects
- Use technical language

When scientists think, they

- Allow curiosity to drive learning
- Look for connections
- Understand when they need more data
- Rely on prior knowledge or research
- Consider new hypotheses or evidence
- Propose explanations
- Create solutions
- Question
- Pay attention to ethical concerns and stewardship
- Consider how to present knowledge
- Visualize or create models as a way of understanding and representing

Websites for Teaching Science

http://www.npr.org

The National Public Radio site includes news articles on a variety of topics including science, health, politics, technology, world, business, race, and culture.

http://www.sciencedaily.com

This popular science news website covers all sorts of science topics, from health and medicine to matter and energy.

http://www.nbc.com

The NBC site offers current science news with sections also on health, business, and more.

http://www.sciencenews.org

An award-winning biweekly news magazine, this site covers important research in all fields of science, publishing concise, accurate, and current articles that appeal to both general readers and scientists.

https://www.livescience.com/topics/youtube-science-channels

This is the source for YouTube's most intriguing and entertaining science videos.

http://www.sciencenewsforstudents.org

A great source for psychology, health, and science articles that are current and of high interest.

https://biomimicry.org/history/

Biomimicry is an approach to finding nature-inspired solutions for a healthy planet. This site includes a variety of fields such as energy, architecture, transportation, agriculture, medicine, and communication.

https://docs.google.com/document/d/1P6ByKHS-pLLxq-487WfgWp3B6MZyItO3dl6ZfR9mcZc/edit?usp=sharing

Use this website for interactive sites that are useful as a review for biology topics.

https://askabiologist.asu.edu/venom/what-are-proteins

This site has visually appealing information on an assortment of biology topics.

http://www.ebizmba.com/articles/science-websites

Check out the most popular science websites all in one place.

http://www.ala.org/aboutala/offices/resources/sciencenovels

This site offers a list of scientifically themed novels for students, elementary through middle school.

Book Recommendations for Starting a Classroom Library

The Break of the Finch by Jonathan Weiner. In this story of groundbreaking scientific research, readers learn from scientists as they watch Darwin's finches and come up with a new understanding of life itself. This talented author uses elegant language to explain scientific theory.

Chicken, Pig, Cow On the Move by R. Ohi & M. Kusugak. Students can analyze the motion of the animals by creating motion maps, position versus time graphs, and velocity versus time graphs. A good book for a kinematics and/or acceleration unit.

Climbing Mount Improbable by Richard Dawkins. The author offers careful explanations and beautiful illustrations in this discussion of evolutionary adaptation. The author explores amazing adaptations, from spiders to figs to the evolution of wings.

The Disappearing Spoon by Sam Kean. Read aloud the chapter titled "Geography Is Destiny" as an introduction to the periodic table.

Enlightenment Now: The Case for Reason, Science, Humanism, and Progress by Steven Pinker. Cognitive scientist Steven Pinker uses seventy-five graphs that will stun the reader and illustrate the good that is happening in the world. He addresses such topics as peace, happiness, health, and prosperity.

Four Fish: The Future of the Last Wild Food by Paul Greenberg. Readers will learn about the four fish that dominate our menus—salmon, sea bass, cod, and tuna—and the process that gets them to our table. Greenberg also explores the impact humans have had on the ocean.

Headstrong: 52 Women Who Changed Science and the World by Rachel Swaby. Students will enjoy reading about famous scientists and Nobel Prize winners as well as lesser known innovators who changed our lives.

The Immortal Life of Henrietta Lacks by Rebecca Skloot. Twenty years after Henrietta Lacks dies of cancer, her family finds out that her cells had been taken without permission and were being used in biological research. The intersection of socioeconomic factors with science and medicine will fascinate readers.

Lives of the Scientists: Experiments, Explosions (and What the Neighbors Thought) by Kathleen Krull, illustrated by Kathryn Hewitt. Students will love reading about famous scientists while also learning about unusual facts, quirky personality traits, and funny stories.

Mr. Archimedes' Bath by Pamela Allen. This picture book is an excellent way to teach the data collection method of determining the volume of a solid. It delights readers with animal characters and funny illustrations.

One Minute Mysteries: 65 Short Mysteries by Eric Yoder and Natalie Yoder. This book makes science fun. Each 1-minute mystery (solutions included) exercises critical thinking skills while covering Earth, space, life, physical, chemical, and general science.

The Periodic Table: Elements With Style by Adrian Dingle, illustrated by S. Basher. Designed to resemble popular social media websites, the pages of this book feature "homepages" for each of the chemical elements. Profiles, supposedly written by the elements themselves, are informative and entertaining.

Rosalind Franklin: The Dark Lady of DNA by Brenda Maddox. In 1962, Wilkins, Crick, and Watson received the Nobel Prize, however, Rosalind Franklin, a girl of fifteen, provided the data and photographs of DNA that were crucial to their discovery. Find out more about the story behind the story.

Science Verse by Jon Scieszka, illustrated by Lane Smith. Science concepts become sing-along songs or poems that make science lively.

The Sixth Extinction by Elizabeth Colbert. The author delves into man-made extinctions occurring during our present time, a phenomenon the author calls the 6th extinction. She explores the threat of human behavior in a compelling account.

Soonish: Ten Emerging Technologies That'll Improve and/or Ruin Everything by Kelly and Zach Weinersmith. These authors investigate future technologies through interviews of scientists, exploring topics such as nuclear fusion, powered toasters, and 3D organ printing. Students love this book.

Sports Science for Young People by George Barr. Barr explores the scientific principles underlying sports. Topics include inertia versus motion, gravity, speed, trajectory, and action versus reaction.

Stiff: The Curious Lives of Human Cadavers by Mary Roach. This author has a series of books about science topics. Students love these books, which are weird, gross, funny, and informative.

Superbug: The Fatal Menace of MRSA by Maryn McKenna. McKenna, a science journalist, pulls readers into her fascinating research about this pathogen and the shocking truth about its impact.

> Visit the companion website at
> **resources.corwin.com/lent-voigtDLinAction**
> to download this appendix.

APPENDIX D

DISCIPLINARY LITERACY IN SOCIAL STUDIES

When social scientists read, they

- Identify bias
- Untangle conflicting perspectives and claims
- Corroborate information and sources
- Contextualize sources
- Examine text structure
- Compare and contrast events, accounts, perspectives, documents, and visuals
- Infer what is not explicit

- Analyze and interpret
- Determine meaning of words, often within context
- Understand how to deconstruct maps, charts, infographics, and photographs

When social scientists write, they

- Create timelines with accompanying narratives
- Utilize information and/or evidence from multiple sources
- Organize conflicting ideas or perspectives into a whole
- Systemize large quantities of information
- Use the past as a mirror to the present
- Summarize social or political consequences of an event
- Rely on primary and secondary sources

When social scientists think, they

- Sift through fragments of information
- Consider big ideas across long periods of time
- Compare and contrast varying accounts, time periods, and events
- Connect causes with effects
- Synthesize events or ideas across long periods of time
- Recognize bias
- Think critically
- Synthesize information
- Consider belief systems of the time periods and cultures

Websites for Teaching Social Studies

New York Times Learning Network: http://www.nytimes.com/section/learning

An excellent resource for teachers with activities, articles, vocabulary, visuals, and even contests for students.

http://www.ccsoh.us/socialStudiesLiteracy.aspx

Go to bottom of this site for the middle and high school modules. Click on commonlit. This site provides a free collection of news articles, poems, short stories, and documents.

http://dcmoboces.libguides.com/c.php?g=249752&p=2259875

This is a social studies and literacy Libguide. Each tab has a list of resources.

http://www.zoomin.edc.org

American Association of School Librarians voted this site as one of the best content resources for 2016. It provides access to historical essays and documents.

American Rhetoric: http://www.americanrhetoric.com/

This great resource offers text, audio, and video clips of past and current speeches.

Teaching Tolerance: https://www.tolerance.org/

This invaluable resource offers lesson plans, activities, texts, films, and texts on social justice and critical thinking. It also includes tips on how teachers can engage students in current events, especially those of a sensitive nature.

National Museum of American Indians: http://nmai.si.edu/nk360/

This site is an initiative to promote and inspire improvement of teaching and learning by the National Museum of American Indians. It provides new perspectives on Native American history, cultures, and contemporary lives.

Library of Congress: https://loc.gov/

This far-reaching site offers primary documents, activities, and discussion starters for virtually any topic in American history. The search bar will take you to a trove of resources.

https://www.weareteachers.com/social-studies-websites/

This best social studies websites are offered in one place.

Book Recommendations for Starting a Classroom Library

All We Have Left by Wendy Mills. Two stories interweave in this heartbreaking yet hopeful story that explores the pivotal events of September 11, 2001.

Beneath a Scarlet Sky by Mark Sullivan. In 1940s Italy, teenager Pino Lella joins an underground railroad helping Jews escape over the Alps and falls for a beautiful widow. Find out how Pino becomes the personal driver of one of the Third Reich's most powerful commanders.

Eleven by Tom Rogers. Moving and powerful read aloud focusing on a boy whose birthday falls on 9/11/2001.

Eyes of the World: Robert Capa, Gerda Taro, and the Invention of Modern Photojournalism by Marc Aronson and Marina Budhos. Capa and Taro were photographers in the 1930s who brought a human face to war. It includes a cast ranging from Langston Hughes and George Orwell to Pablo Picasso and Ernest Hemingway.

The 57 Bus by Dashka Slater. Read about two teenagers whose lives cross paths during a bus ride home. One is a white teen from a middle class neighborhood and the other is a black teen in a rough, poor neighborhood. One is charged with two hate crimes.

Getting Away With Murder: The True Story of the Emmett Till Case by Chris Crowe. An event that many regard as the catalyst for the Civil Rights movement, the details of the murder of Emmett Till, a black teenager from Chicago, are revealed in this true narrative with new details and insights about Emmett, his family, and the trial.

A Good Country by Laleh Khadivi. Reze Courdee, a 16-year-old, straight-A student and chemistry whiz, tries to assimilate into American culture, but life takes a drastic turn when Reze returns to Syria as part of the Muslim nation.

Hillbilly Elegy: A Memoir of a Family by J. D. Vance. This is a memoir of a Yale-educated lawyer who grew up in rural Kentucky to poor, drug-addicted parents and was raised by his grandmother. He discusses how cyclical poverty and drug addiction are killing the culture of this demographic.

I Am Malala by Malala Yousafzal. A young girl who loved to learn in Pakistan was considered a blasphemous troublemaker by the Taliban. She continued her quest to learn and eventually was the youngest Nobel Peace Prize winner.

The Invention of Wings: A Novel by Sue Monk Kidd. A historical novel that will appeal to older readers about abolitionism, feminism, and racism, with wonderful citations at the end.

Just Mercy: A Story of Justice and Redemption by Bryan Stevenson. Engaging nonfiction story of how an African American Harvard-educated lawyer goes back to his home state of Alabama to help death-row inmates receive justice under present-day Jim Crow practices. Eye-opening account of systemic injustice in our present-day judicial system.

The Librarian of Auschwitz by Antonio Iturbe; Lilit Thwaites, translator. Based on the experience of real-life 14-year-old prisoner of Auschwitz, Dita Kraus, this is the incredible story of a girl who risked her life to keep the magic of books alive during the Holocaust.

Long Way Down by Jason Reynolds. This novel takes place in 60 potent seconds—the time it takes a kid to decide whether or not he's going to murder the guy who killed his brother—and is written in short, fierce staccato narrative verse. This book will prompt thoughtful discussion about teenage gun violence.

Loving vs. Virginia: *A Documentary Novel of the Landmark Civil Rights Case* by Patricia Hruby Powell. Alternating first-person narratives written in free verse address the differences between the "intent" of the law and the application of the law as well as federal versus state laws and human rights.

Nightingale by Kristin Hannah. A tale of two sisters where bolder Isabelle enjoys her life in Paris and older Viann lives peacefully in the country with husband Antoine. Hannah writes beautifully about love, freedom, the bond between two sisters, and the strength of women.

Notorious RBG: The Life & Times of Ruth Bader Ginsburg by Irin Carmon and Shana Knizhnik. A fascinating account of a most spectacular woman rising to the top of the American judicial system with her brain, skills, and perseverance to overcome the obstacles facing females in 20th-century law careers.

#NotYourPrincess: Voices of Native American Women edited by Lisa Charleyboy and Mary Beth Leatherdale. An eclectic collection of poems, essays, interviews, and art that combine to express the experience of being a Native American woman. The women in this book give teen readers insight into the lives of women who, for so long, have been invisible and powerless.

The Pact by Amanda West Lewis. Lewis takes us on a journey into World War II through the perspective of Peter Gruber, a 10-year-old German boy. Peter, a sensitive and intelligent youth, struggles with the cruelty of the war, the propaganda of the Nazis, and the morality of World War II's Hitler Youth.

Salt to the Sea by Ruta Sepetys. Near the end of World War II, four refugees band together, desperate to make their way towards a ship, the *Wilhelm Gustloff*, with hopes of safety and freedom. This is their tale of lies, war, tragedy, and struggle. Look for

Sepetys's award-winning *Shades of Gray* for another historical novel set during World War II.

That's Not in My American History Book by Thomas Aires and Jeff Riggenbach. A compilation of quirky, little-known stories from U.S. history that are great for reading aloud to introduce new topics or for enrichment.

The Whydah: *A Pirate Ship Feared, Wrecked, and Found* by Martin W. Sandler. The 1650s to the 1730s marked the golden age of piracy, and the *Whydah* was one of those ships, commanded by Black Sam Bellamy. Following a storm in 1717, the ship went down with its treasures and was finally found 200 years later by archaeologists. Based on the recovered artifacts, readers will learn about that much-mythologized era of pirates.

X: A Novel by Ilyasah Shabazz, and Kekla Magoon. This fictionalized account of Malcolm X's teen years poignantly presents the young man's struggles with identity, racism, and crime.

Add these nonfiction books with strong visual primary documents to your library as well:

- *Beyond Courage: The Untold Story of Jewish Resistance During the Holocaust* by Doreen Rappaport
- *Bomb: The Race to Build—and Steal—The World's Most Dangerous Weapon* by Steve Sheinkin
- *Claudette Colvin: Twice Toward Justice* by Phillip Hoose
- *Courage Has Not Color: The True Story of the Triple Nickles, America's First Black Paratroopers* by Tanya Lee Stone
- *Hitler Youth: Growing Up in Hitler's Shadow* by Susan Campbell Bartoletti
- *Written in Bone: Buried Lives of Jamestown and Colonial Maryland* by Sally M. Walker

Visit the companion website at
resources.corwin.com/lent-voigtDLinAction
to download this appendix.

APPENDIX E

DISCIPLINARY LITERACY IN ART

When artists read, they

- Synthesize knowledge and personal experience
- Connect artistic ideas and works with societal, cultural, and historical context
- Understand specialized vocabulary such as harmony, rhythm, and timbre
- Consider others' perspectives by reading reviews of concerts, musicals, and albums
- Compare their experiences to others by reading biographies, articles, blogs, and books
- Apply theories of creativity to their own artistic processes
- Note specific, technical details when reading instructions to duplicate a process
- Find ideas and inspiration from reading to apply to their art work

- Attend to details and descriptions to illustrate an author's ideas
- Are curious and responsive to new and varied perspectives

When artists write, they

- Translate visual input to verbal output
- Use knowledge of artistic elements and genres to analyze artistic work
- Interpret intent, meaning, and ideas conveyed in artistic work
- Evaluate artistic work by applying criteria
- Synthesize influences that have impacted artistic work including culture and setting
- React personally to artistic work including emotional and aesthetic responses
- Compare different genres, styles, performances, and techniques
- Articulate their ideas, explain the evolution of their ideas, and/or explain their process

When artists participate in their discipline, they

- Generate artistic ideas and work
- Draw from a variety of sources to develop creative ideas
- Apply problem-solving skills to determine composition, fitting together various elements
- Develop artistic skills in craft and technique through experimentation and repetition
- Refine and complete artistic work
- Seek, evaluate, and apply feedback about their artistic work
- Make decisions about how to convey meaning through artistic work

Websites for Teaching Art

https://www.metmuseum.org/

All the big museums have excellent art education websites: Metropolitan Museum of Art, Art Institute of Chicago, Museum of Contemporary Art in Chicago, Getty Museum, Smithsonian Art Museum, and so on.

http://www.carolhurst.com/subjects/art.html

Find resources such as novels, picture books, and nonfiction with ides about literacy activities to incorporate into art classes. Some ideas are for younger students (K–9) but can be adapted for higher grades.

http://www.nytimes.com/section/learning

This Learning Network site is an excellent resource for teachers that offers activities, articles, and contests for students.

http://www.pbslearningmedia.org

This is a national and international news site for students that contains articles in the areas of science, economics, health, and arts, and media. It can be searched by topic categories, grade level, or subject area.

http://www.askart.com/art/Styles/1550/n/Funk%20Art

This site is an online database containing close to 300,000 artists. The content features painters, sculptors, and illustrators ranging from early artists to modern urban expressionists. Digital images, biographical information, books, and periodical references are available.

http://www.creativebloq.com/web-design/artist-websites-10135048

This site presents ideas about creating a website that will showcase an artist's portfolio online. It features five very different websites each with its own way of furthering the artist's work and representing unique personalities.

Book Recommendations for Starting a Classroom Library

The Art of Eric Carle by Eric Carle. This autobiography includes photographs and sketches with a section about the way Carle creates his work. Read writings by Carle and some of his colleagues as well as an editor's experiences with Carle.

The Art of Harry Potter by Marc Sumerak. The book contains artwork from the *Harry Potter* books, including paintings, drawings, computer-generated models, costume sketches, and set designs.

The Art of Spray Paint by Lori Zimmer offers inspirations and techniques from Masters of Aerosol.

Art That Changed the World with chief consultant Ian Chilvers. This book tells the story of every major art style, movement by movement, giving art lovers a visual timeline showing key paintings that sparked each transition and explaining major events that shaped their evolution.

Artists and Their Cats by Alison Nastasi has pictures and stories about famous artists like Pablo Picasso, Andy Warhol, and Georgia O'Keeffe. This is a great read aloud.

Artist's Journal Workshop by Kathy Johnson. This journal features rich visual examples on every page with guidance and inspiration. Includes twenty-seven international artists who share pages and advice from their own art journals as well as twenty-five hands-on exercises to spark students' creativity.

The Bird King: An Artist's Notebook by Shaun Tan. Looking through these pages offers a glimpse into the workings of Tan's genius and insights.

The Creative Habit: Learn It and Use It for Life by Twyla Tharp. Tharp is a modern choreographer, but her book applies to any creative process. The author offers accessible advice about creative work and habits while dispelling the myth of the "creative genius" who just spontaneously creates masterpieces.

Drawing on the Right Side of the Brain: The Definitive (4th ed.) by Betty Edwards. Translated into more than ten languages, this book provides drawing exercises as well as explanations of how the brain works while drawing.

Endangered by Tim Flach. Cinematic photographs of threatened and endangered species including polar bears, elephants, pandas, Monarch butterflies, and Siamese crocodiles. Readers will appreciate the artistry while connecting on an emotional level.

50 Contemporary Photographers You Should Know by Floriane Fine and Brad Finger. Part of the "50 . . . You Should Know" series, these authors offer the perfect introduction to the best contemporary photographers and their most iconic works.

Frida and Diego: Art, Love, Life by Catherine Reef. The two most famous Mexican artists are featured in this book with insights into their artistic development, politics, and complex relationship. The book is illustrated with old photos and examples of their inspiring art.

Manga for the Beginner Chibis by Christopher Hart. This book contains everything you need to start drawing the characters of Japanese comics.

Mapping Inner space (2nd ed.) by Nancy Margulies and Nusa Maal. This book helps readers learn about visual mapping, a form of notetaking that improves understanding and retention.

Maya Lin: Thinking With Her Hands by Susan Rubin. Maya Lin is the college student who won the design competition to build the Vietnam Veterans Memorial in Washington, D.C. This book crosses multiple interests—American history, civic activism, art history, and cultural diversity.

Pop Painting by Camilla d'Erric offers inspiration and techniques from the pop surrealist art phenom.

Scholastic Art Magazine: *Classic and Contemporary Artists, Art History* includes hands-on workshops and student artist profiles. Each issue has a different focus.

The Secret Lives of Color by Kassia St. Clair contains one-page stories about the unknown history of colors and the vivid stories behind them.

Vincent and Theo: The Van Gogh Brothers by Deborah Heiligman is a meticulously researched biography drawing on the 658 letters Vincent wrote to Theo during his lifetime.

Be on the lookout for picture books about artists that offer stunning art such as

- *Frida* by Jonah Winter and Ana Juan
- *The Fantastic Jungles of Henri Rousseau* by Michelle Markel
- *Radiant Child: The Story of a Young Artist, Jean-Michel Basquiat* by Javaka Steptoe

Visit the companion website at
resources.corwin.com/lent-voigtDLinAction
to download this appendix.

APPENDIX F

DISCIPLINARY LITERACY IN A WORLD LANGUAGE

When students of a world language listen and speak, they

- Segment words and sentences into parts then blend the sounds together

- Imitate speech tone, rhythm, and prosody

- Exercise working memory by holding and manipulating language

- Employ flexible problem solving when they don't have exact vocabulary, finding creative ways to express thoughts

When students of a world language read, they

- Use cognates, words that are related in origin to another word, to determine meaning (e.g., brother in English and *bruder* in German)
- Infer vocabulary meaning from context
- Reread with a decoding focus on first reading and a comprehension focus during second reading
- Read aloud in groups so they can "hear" the language
- Rely on predictions and guesses to aid understanding
- Consider to cultural practices and perspectives

When students of a world language write, they

- Don't think in or translate from English
- Apply rules of the world language: syntax (word order) and orthography (spelling)
- Assume a mindset that focuses on approximations and practice
- Analyze then imitate patterns, structures, and organization of mentor texts
- Prioritize communication of ideas over correctness in syntax and spelling

When students of a world language reason, they

- Transfer skills from their native language
- Use the three modes of communication (interpersonal, interpretive, and presentational)
- Assume an open mind and curiosity about different points of view
- Look for similarities and differences in cultures

Websites for Teaching World Languages

Tip: A Google search for "best authentic resources for world language teachers" will also yield many lists that others have compiled, sorted, and categorized.

All Languages

Link	Description
http://www.audio-lingua.eu/?lang=en	Audio
http://newsmap.jp/	Text, current events
http://www.miscositas.com/authenticmaterials.html	Variety
http://blog.calicospanish.com/2012/11/30/authentic-language-listening-resources.html	Audio/Video
https://www.thepaperboy.com/index.cfm	Online newspapers worldwide
https://newsela.com/text-sets/#/featured	Database of current events
https://bebrainfit.com/brain-benefits-learning-second-language/	Articles about brain benefits of learning a world language
https://www.1jour1actu.com	French from France website. Video-clips and articles about sports, culture, the environment, and current events. Also contains pages for teachers

French

Link	Description
http://www.thefrenchcorner.net/2013/07/where-to-find-authentic-resources-for.html?m=1	Variety of sources by proficiency level
http://www.pinterest.com/csctfl/french-teacher-favorites/	Variety of sources, shared by CSCTFL
https://www.facebook.com/AATFrench?ref=br_tf https://twitter.com/AATFrench	Links shared by AATF
https://www.utm.edu/staff/bobp/french/french.html	Tennessee Bob's Famous French Links

Link	Description
http://fr.ver-taal.com/culture.htm	Audio
https://www.TV5Monde.com	Teacher resource page with ways to use their videos and activities
https://savoirs.rfi.fr/fr/apprendre-enseigner/langue-francaise/journal-en-francais	Authentic news broadcasts in simplified but authentic French along with transcripts
http://nrj.com/	Streaming popular music with one for France
https://www.mycanal.fr/	Clips of TV shows available online
https://www.youtube.com/user/cestpassorcierftv	A program exploring science topics for young adolescents available on YouTube

German

Link	Description
http://www.goethe.de/ins/us/saf/prj/sig/enindex.htm?wt_sc=stepintogerman.com	Audio, video, music, and soccer focus
http://www.kino.de/	Film trailers and movies Kid-centered videos, articles, games, and news

Spanish

Link	Description
http://audiria.com/	Audio, prepared activities, and podcasts
http://zachary-jones.com/zambombazo/	Audio, video, text, music, and prepared activities
http://infografias.org/	Infographs
http://www.laits.utexas.edu/spe/index.html	Native speakers talking about various topics
http://www.ver-taal.com/	Audio
http://www.wordreference.com/	Online translation dictionary
http://dle.rae.es/?id=DglqVCc	Dictionary of the Spanish language by the RAE (Real Academia Española)

Visit the companion website at
resources.corwin.com/lent-voigtDLinAction
for downloadable resources.

APPENDIX G

DISCIPLINARY LITERACY IN HEALTH

When health professionals read, they

- Assume an objective stance when reading for information (see empathy item below)
- Read for What (facts), then Why (cause effect relationships), then How (applications)
- Rely on data, sketches, and charts
- Determine validity of sources and quality of evidence
- Seek to understand specialized vocabulary
- Seek to understand science behind information
- Read for details and precise interpretation of concepts

- Look for answers related to relevant questions

- Note new discoveries, findings, and treatments

- Seek to deepen understanding of individuals with physical, emotional, and/or social challenges

- Assume perspective of others when reading to understand social, emotional, and physical challenges

- Make connections to own personal, mental, or physical health

When health professionals write, they

- Use precise wording

- Compose in phrases, bullets, graphs, or sketches

- Favor passive voice

- Seek exactness over craft

- Distinguish facts from opinions

- Communicate in a systematic, precise, and objective format

- Consider science and chemistry behind symptoms, feelings, and behavior

When health professionals think, they

- Allow curiosity and personal interests to drive learning

- Seek evidence to form theories

- Look for connections and cause-effect relationships

- Understand when they need more data

- Consider new hypotheses or evidence

- Translate data to inform understanding

- Consider interplay of physical, mental, social, and emotional factors

- Apply new information to actions and decisions

Websites for Teaching Health

http://www.nytimes.com/learning/issues_in_depth/teenhealth.html

Part of the Learning Network, this site will take you to articles and lesson plans directly related to teen health issues.

http://www.pbslearningmedia.org

This site offers national and international news for students as well as articles in the areas of science and health.

http://www.npr.org

The National Public Radio site includes news articles on a variety of topics including science and health.

http://www.sciencedaily.com

This popular science news website covers health and medicine.

http://www.sciencenewsforstudents.org

This is a great source for psychology, health, and science articles that are current and of high interest.

https://www.sciencedaily.com/news/health_medicine/teen_health/

A resource for high interest articles on health, technology, environment, society, and quirky topics that will be sure to grab the interest of your students.

https://consumer.healthday.com/espanol/

This resource for current health news including information on diabetes, mental health, AIDS information, and discussion of clinical trials.

http://www.healthday.com/lifestyle-news.html

This website (available in Spanish and English) has one-page articles and videos about current topics such as cyberbullying, sports and adolescent brains, and high-nicotine E Cigs.

https://www.nutrition.gov/subject/life-stages/teens/tweens-and-teens

Nutrition.gov is a USDA-sponsored website that offers credible information for healthful eating choices. It serves as a gateway to reliable information on nutrition, healthy eating, physical activity, and food safety for consumers.

https://www.girlshealth.gov/

Created to help girls (ages 10–16) learn about health, growing up, and issues they may face such as drugs, alcohol, feelings, relationships, and fitness.

Book Recommendations for Starting a Classroom Library

Chew On This: Everything You Don't Want to Know About Fast Food by Charles Wilson and Eric Schlosser. Schlosser's best-selling book, *Fast Food Nation*, was published for adults in 2001. Now he and his coauthor have written a book for young people.

David and Goliath by Malcolm Gladwell. This book challenges how we think about obstacles and disadvantages, offering a new interpretation of what it means to be discriminated against, suffer from a disability, lose a parent, or endure any number of other apparent setbacks. Draws on history, psychology, and powerful story-telling.

Drums, Girls, and Dangerous Pie by Jordan Sonnenblick. Steven plays drums in the All-City Jazz Band and has a crush on the hottest girl in school, who doesn't even know he's alive. Suddenly Steven's world is turned upside down when he is forced to deal with his brother's illness and his parents' attempts to keep the family in one piece.

Falling Over Sideways by Jordan Sonnenblick. Claire's eighth-grade year is not going as she hoped. She is faced with mean girls, boys, and changing friendships. Then her father suffers a stroke, and everything changes. Now Claire must find the strength to handle both the pressures of middle school and an uncertain future.

The Fault in Our Stars by John Green. Despite the tumor-shrinking medical miracle that has bought her a few years, Hazel's condition is still terminal. When a new boy suddenly appears at Cancer Kid Support Group, things change.

The Impossible Knife of Memory by Laurie Halse Anderson. Anderson takes a look at post-traumatic stress syndrome, specifically regarding soldiers who return home to their families. How will they and their loved ones deal with this phenomenon that impacts so many families?

It's Not Yet Dark by Simon Fitzmaurice. In this powerful true story, Simon was diagnosed with ALS, or Lou Gehrig's disease, and given four years to live. He begins to write using an eye-gaze computer and allows us to see life through his perspective.

This is an unforgettable book about the power of love, what connects us, and what it means to live life fully.

Out of My Mind by Sharon Draper. Eleven-year-old Melody can't walk, talk, or write, because she has cerebral palsy. But she also has a photographic memory; she can remember every detail of everything she has ever experienced. Although most people dismiss her as mentally challenged, Melody refuses to be defined by her disability. This book will change how readers look at people with a disability.

The Pregnancy Project: A Memoir by Gaby Rodriguez & Jenna Glatzer. Author details how she was able to fake her own pregnancy and reveals all that she learned from the experience. Gaby's story is about fighting stereotypes, overcoming others' low expectations, and creating the life she wants.

Skinny by Donna Cooner. A 300-pound, 15-year-old girl can't shed the image she has of herself so she opts for gastric bypass surgery. Questions about self-acceptance, body image, and the underlying reasons for obesity make this a compelling read for all ages.

Smashed by Lisa Luedeke. Katie Martin wants to leave her small-town loneliness behind forever. She is a field hockey star on the fast track to a college scholarship, but her relationship with alcohol has always been a little questionable. Then trouble finds her. This fast-paced novel is about addiction, accountability, and the impact of low self-esteem.

Speak by Laurie Halse Anderson. Melinda is an outcast because she busted an end-of-summer party by calling the cops, so now nobody will talk to her. It is through her work on an art project that she is finally able to face what really happened at that terrible party. Themes include dealing with peer pressure and learning how to speak up for oneself.

Superbug: The Fatal Menace of MRSA by Maryn McKenna. Medicine disregards it, antibiotics can't control it. MRSA-drug-resistant staph may be the most frightening epidemic since AIDS.

Turtles All the Way Down by John Green. This novel goes deeply into issues of obsessive-compulsive disorder told from the point of view of a high school girl.

The Wild Life of Our Bodies by Rob Dunn. Read about predators, parasites, and partners that shape who we are today.

 Visit the companion website at
resources.corwin.com/lent-voigtDLinAction
to download this appendix.

APPENDIX H

DISCIPLINARY LITERACY IN MUSIC

When musicians read, they

- Synthesize knowledge and personal experience
- Connect artistic ideas and works with societal, cultural, and historical context
- Understand specialized vocabulary such as harmony, rhythm, and timbre
- Consider others' perspectives by reading reviews and critiques of concerts, musicals, and albums
- Determine validity of sources and quality of evidence in critiques
- Search for innovative processes
- Compare their experiences to others by reading biographies, articles, blogs, and books
- Apply theories of creativity to their own artistic processes

- Find inspiration that fuels creativity
- Learn the sonic properties and structural elements of musical instruments

When musicians write, they

- Analyze artistic work
- Interpret intent and meaning in artistic work
- Evaluate artistic work by applying criteria
- Synthesize influences that have impacted artistic work including culture and setting
- React personally to artistic work including emotional and aesthetic responses
- Compare different genres, styles, performances, and techniques
- Share their practice routines, techniques, and personal disciplines
- Seek to educate and inspire other musicians
- Explore ethnomusicology and the music of other cultures
- Share personal stories and experiences of their relationship to their craft

When musicians participate in their discipline, they

- Generate artistic ideas and work
- Develop artistic skills through repetition and practice
- Experiment, refine, and solve problems in technique
- Seek, evaluate, and apply feedback about their artistic work
- Refine and complete artistic work
- Convey meaning through presentation of artistic work
- Exhibit artistic skills in craft and technique during presentation
- Interact with others to realize a common vision
- Seek to respond and react to the present moment through improvisation

(Adapted from National Core Art Standards. Retrieved from http://www.nationalcorearts standards.org)

Websites for Teaching Music

https://www.nytimes.com/section/arts/music

This is a source for articles, reviews, events, and critiques of all kinds of music.

http://www.nytimes.com/section/learning

This Learning Network site is an excellent resource for teachers and has activities, articles, and contests for students.

https://www.nammfoundation.org/articles/music-in-the-news

Find music in the news, articles, research, and discussions of issues related to music at this site.

https://www.npr.org/music/

National Public Radio's music section has it all: interviews, sessions, lists, reviews, All Songs Considered, and well-crafted articles; it's a veritable feast of music discovery that is diverse in its content.

http://tetw.org/Music

Interesting short articles and essays about music abound at this site such as the positive influence of music, music psychology, and pop music.

https://www.intunemonthly.com/about-in-tune-2/

This magazine is written for teen-aged music students, but the readership stretches from middle school into college and from students to teachers. This website provides content that supplements but does not duplicate the magazine.

https://sites.google.com/a/dpi.wi.gov/disciplinary-literacy-in-music/home

This site, from the Wisconsin Department of Public Education, provides ideas and tools to develop disciplinary literacy in the arts.

https://www.museumofmakingmusic.org

A celebration and exploration of musical instruments and the role they have played in society through the 20th century and beyond.

Book Recommendations
for Starting a Classroom Library

Arts With the Brain in Mind by Eric Jensen. This book for teachers explains how to use musical, visual, and kinesthetic activities to enhance brain development, develop thinking skills, and make classrooms positive and inclusive. It presents separate theories for musical, visual, and kinesthetic arts.

A Band of Angels by Deborah Hopkinson. This book is fiction but is based on real events and people. In 1868, at the age of fifteen, Ella is sent with other former slaves to Fisk School. With the guidance of her music teacher, she joins a group of students who become famous for introducing spirituals to the world. This book is an inspiring story with beautiful illustrations. Good read aloud.

Bob Dylan: The Nobel Lecture. Bob Dylan became the first American musician in history to be awarded the Nobel Prize in Literature. In his Nobel lecture, Dylan reflects on his life and literary influences, providing both an eloquent artistic statement and an intimate look at one of the world's most fascinating cultural figures.

Classic Rock: The Stories Behind the Greatest Songs of All Time by Tim Morse. Artists like John Lennon, Stevie Nicks, Elton John, and Keith Richards reveal the process of creating the songs that became hits.

Deep Blues: A Musical and Cultural History of the Mississippi Delta by Robert Palmer. Palmer traces the journey of the blues from its rural beginnings, to the bars of Chicago's South Side, and on to international popularity. Included in this musical history are stories about great blues musicians such as Muddy Waters, Sonny Boy Williamson, John Lee Hooker, B. B. King, Ike Turner, and more.

DownBeat—The Great Jazz Interviews edited by Frank Alkyer. Culled from the *DownBeat* archives, this book includes in-depth interviews with literally every great jazz artist and personality who ever lived. Features classic photos and magazine covers.

Lives of the Musicians: Good Times, Bad Times (and What the Neighbors Thought) by Kathleen Krull. Here are the life stories of such diverse figures as Vivaldi, Mozart, Scott Joplin, Nadia Boulanger, and Woody Guthrie. Readers will learn about both their musical natures and the personal characteristics that make their lives so fascinating.

Solo: When the Heart Gets Lost Let the Music Find You by Kwame Alexander with Mary Rand Hess. The only thing Blade and his father (a washed-up rock star and drug addict) have in common is the music that lives inside them. The book, written in verse, touches on family, identity, and the history of rock and roll.

Sound Man by Glyn Johns. Johns helped create some of rock's most iconic albums, including those by the Beatles, the Rolling Stones, Eric Clapton, the Eagles, and the Who. In this memoir Johns shares incredible stories about the musicians with whom he's worked.

StickMan: The Story of Emmett Chapman and the Instrument He Created by Jim Reilly. This is a biography of Emmett Chapman who discovered, developed, and refined a new way for musicians to interact with stringed and fretted musical instruments.

This is Your Brain on Music: The Science of a Human Obsession by Daniel J. Levitin. Levitin shares research about how music and the brain interact. He explores such topics as why we are so attached to the music we listened to as teenagers, whether practice or talent is the driving force behind musical expertise, and why jingles get stuck in our head.

 Visit the companion website at **resources.corwin.com/lent-voigtDLinAction** to download this appendix.

APPENDIX I

TECHNOLOGY OR DIGITAL LITERACY

Digital literacy is the ability to use information and communication technologies to find, evaluate, create, and communicate information, requiring both cognitive and technical skills. The American Library Association's digital-literacy task force

When students use digital literacy skills to build new knowledge, they

- Discern strengths and weaknesses of different search engines

- Navigate and evaluate multiple sources on the Internet

- Evaluate reliability and relevance of content from different websites, authors, and sources

- Exchange ideas within and across communities
- Synthesize input from multiple sources

When students use digital literacy skills to create and communicate content, they

- Consider digital media options such as PowerPoint, podcasts, online discussions, blogs, videos, and Twitter
- Determine the most effective platform to convey information by evaluating strengths and weaknesses
- Apply knowledge about appropriate and safe Internet behavior
- Develop fluency with features of the digital technology being used
- Experiment and take risks in an effort to determine the most effective way to convey content
- Make design decisions based on purpose and point of view of potential audience
- Represent ideas symbolically, including color, sound, and images to communicate or persuade
- Collaborate with others (online or in person) to exchange ideas and create a product
- Edit work and seek feedback about clarity, message, and impact

Websites for Teaching Digital Literacy

http://fcit.usf.edu/matrix/digitaltools.php

This website provides ideas for using various digital tools. It includes professional learning, evaluation tools, resources, and research. From The Technology Integration Matrix: A project of the Florida Center for Instructional Technology.

http://reader.mediawiremobile.com/Corwin/issues/109391/viewer?page=1
Corwin Connect provides videos, downloadable forms, books, and articles.

http://www.learning.com/solutions/digital-literacy

This website addresses how and what to teach this generation of digital natives to be successful in the classroom and afterwards. It includes apps, coding, online safety, and more.

https://techboomers.com

This resource supports teachers who feel overwhelmed by the influx of technology into schools and society. Resources, articles, tutorials, courses, and lessons are available for those who want to learn on their own.

https://www.edutopia.org/article/digital-citizenship-resources
Find articles, videos, and other resources on media and digital literacy.

Professional Books for Teaching Digital Literacy Skills

Apps for Learning, Middle School: iPad, iPod Touch, iPhone by Harry J. Dickens and Andrew Chinches. Learn about some of the best apps for middle school classrooms, such as powerful language skill builders like Play2Learn and SpellBoard; NASA HD and Solar Walk, which take you on a trip across the galaxy; Book Creator to make your own unique digital books; and Drawing Pad to produce a work of art.

Argument in the Real World: Teaching Adolescents to Read and Write Digital Texts by Troy Hicks and Kristen Hawley Turner. Hicks and Turner share strategies on how to teach students the logic of argument using digital texts such as Twitter, Facebook, viral videos, Internet memes, blogs, and so forth.

Creating Innovators: The Making of Young People Who Will Change the World by Tony Wagner. Wagner explores how parents, teachers, and employers can help young people become innovative. He suggests we nurture creativity, spark imaginations, and teach students to learn from failure and persevere. Schools, colleges, and work places with innovative cultures are described.

Creative Schools: The Grassroots Revolution That's Transforming Education by Ken Robinson and Lou Aronica. These authors challenge us to rethink the nature and purpose of education. Robinson suggests we draw on technological and professional resources to face the challenges of the 21st century. Anecdotes, observations, and research are included to prompt thinking and possibly inspiration.

Digital Storytelling in the Classroom: New Media Pathways to Literacy, Learning, and Creativity (2nd ed.) by Jason Ohler. Teachers learn how to teach students to read, write, speak, and create art within the context of digital storytelling while reaching deeper understandings in all areas of the curriculum.

Five Skills for the Global Learner: What Everyone Needs to Navigate the Digital World by Mark Barnes. Readers learn about creating and sharing digital information, using social media, digital publishing, building a personal learning network, and using aggregators to create, maintain, and share content. This book includes tips and examples for using PLNs, Facebook, Twitter, Skype, YouTube, Jing, and other essential tools.

Teaching in the Digital Age: Using the Internet to Increase Student Engagement and Understanding by Kristen J. Nelson. Nelson helps teachers encourage active student involvement through Internet-based projects that focus on individual learning styles and problem solving. The author includes lesson plans, curriculum standards, and assessment rubrics.

Worlds of Making: Best Practices for Establishing Makerspace for Your School by Laura Fleming. Readers will find invaluable guidance for creating a vibrant Makerspace on any budget. Practical strategies and anecdotal examples help create an action plan.

Visit the companion website at
resources.corwin.com/lent-voigtDLinAction
to download this appendix.

APPENDIX J

DISCIPLINARY LITERACY IN PHYSICAL EDUCATION

When students of physical education read, they

- "Read" video clips, paying attention to minute details such as body positions, team formation, individual mistakes, and pivotal moments

- Interpret specialized vocabulary and phrases related to motor skills, sports, and fitness

- Visualize movements from verbal and written descriptions

- "Read" a sports performance and evaluate strengths and weaknesses of individuals and teams

- Notice author's perspective when reading blogs and articles or listening to commentary
- Translate symbols, diagrams, illustrations, and charts to concepts
- Interpret and analyze numerical data related to sporting events and individual performances
- "Read" meaning of body positions and gestures from coaches, teammates, and referees
- Interpret fitness readings gathered from technology (e.g., personal fitness monitors like FitBit, heart monitor, body fat ratio)
- Notice themes of perseverance, overcoming obstacles, and learning from mistakes in novels, sportscasts, articles, and sports movies
- Attend to cause-effect relationships between nutrition, exercise routines, and mindset on fitness and performance
- Evaluate written or oral feedback from coaches and teammates
- Analyze details related to game rules and regulations, noting similarities and differences pertaining to different athletic competitions

When students of physical education write and discuss, they

- Use short, succinct sentences or phrases to describe details
- Compose and defend arguments based on evidence and expert sources
- Communicate with charts, diagrams, sketches, and symbols
- Employ precise vocabulary and technical jargon when describing movement
- Express analysis of athletic competitions in terms of strategies, team tactics, and player moves
- Analyze problems and propose solutions related to physical fitness, team performance, or pace of progress
- Apply knowledge of physical fitness to articulate goals for personal improvement
- Provide feedback that is specific and detailed
- Note similarities and differences between sports
- Make connections between specific conditioning practices to strength and agility

- Persuasively communicate priority of cooperation and selflessness in team sports over individual performance
- Articulate cause-and-effect relationship between physical activity and health, mood, self-discipline, and social interaction

Resources for Teachers and Coaches

https://www.weareteachers.com/social-studies-websites/

Those Who Can Coach Can Teach: Collaborating with Athletic Coaches by Mary Ehrenworth and colleagues. Excellent article about including coaches to raise the level of students' close reading, argumentation skills, and academic agency. Describes how English, science, and history teachers collaborate with athletic coaches to intensify close reading, argumentation, and overall academic engagement.

Writing on the Bus: Using Athletic Team Notebooks and Journals to Advance Learning and Performance in Sports by Richard Kent. Good resource for coaches to promote reflection, goal-setting, and analysis through writing.

Websites

http://www.writingathletes.com
The author shares ways of using writing activities with athletes through journals and team notebooks.

https://www.physical-literacy.org.uk/resources/
This website by the International Physical Literacy Association contains blogs, research, and articles about physical literacy.

https://www.nutrition.gov/subject/life-stages/teens/tweens-and-teens
This USDA-sponsored website offers credible information to help make healthful eating choices. It serves as a gateway to reliable information on nutrition, healthy eating, physical activity, and food safety for consumers.

http://www.sciencedaily.com
Students can research topics related to sports, fitness, and nutrition such as articles about sports injuries, research on muscles, and impact of exercise on the heart.

http://www.carolhurst.com/subjects/sports.html

This website contains recommended books and lesson ideas for middle school readers.

http://kassandcorn.com/teachercoach/

Two teachers create units, classes, and programs that support movement and student growth in reading and writing that can be adapted for older students.

https://www.shapeamerica.org//standards/upload/National-Standards-Flyer.pdf

A website by Shape America lists standards for K–12 physical education.

https://dpi.wi.gov/sspw/physical-education/disciplinary-literacy

Wisconsin's website provides a definition of physical literacy along with teaching ideas.

http://www.healthday.com/lifestyle-news.html

This website (available in Spanish and English) has one-page articles and videos about current topics such as cyberbullying, sports and adolescent brains, and high-nicotine E Cigs.

http://www.nytimes.com/section/learning

This Learning Network site is an excellent resource for teachers and has articles about sports, health, and nutrition.

Book Recommendations for Starting a Classroom Library

Athletic Shorts: Six Short Stories by Chris Crutcher. Although each of these six stories has something to do with sports, growing up is a more prominent theme.

Beartown: A Novel by Fredrik Backman. The author of *A Man Called Ove* writes about a small, hockey-mad town whose hopes and loyalties are torn apart by a crime no one wants to believe happened.

The Best American Sports Writing edited by Glenn Stout and Howard Bryant. These stories prompt readers to ask difficult questions about who we are, as individuals and as a nation: What does it mean when a football player takes a knee during the national anthem, who decides where the remains of an American legend should rest, and how far will people go to reclaim dreams that seem out of reach.

The Boys in the Boat: The True Story of an American Team's Epic Journey to Win Gold at the 1936 Olympics by Daniel James Brown. The inspiration for the PBS *American Experience* Documentary. Following the Great Depression comes the astonishing tale of nine working-class boys who at the 1936 Olympics showed the world what courage and resolve really meant. (A Young Readers Adaptation is available for fourth to seventh grade.)

The Crossover by Kwame Alexander. Josh tells his family's story in verse, in this fast-paced middle grade novel of basketball, family, and brotherhood. Recommended for Grades 5 through 7, but older students will also enjoy reading it.

Friday Night Lights: A Town, a Team, and a Dream by H. G. Bissingation. Excellently written and reported, this book investigates all the positive and negative nuances that accompany the football culture in a small Texas town in the late 1980s. It deals frankly with racism, sexism, homophobia, underage drinking, and the glorification of sports and masculinity and will spark reflection and discussion among older students.

Ghost by Jason Reynolds. This story about overcoming tragedy and finding where you belong is the first of Reynolds's middle grade track series. Set on the track field, it includes themes of bullying, controlling anger, escaping your past, and pursuing things you're passionate about.

Gutless by Carl Deuker. Brock, a talented athlete, doesn't like to take hits on the football field. When he is cut from the team, he and his friend Richie experience cruel bullying by the quarterback. Find out how Brock reacts when the bullying goes too far, and he must confront his fears. Plenty of football action and realistic dilemmas faced by teens make this a winner.

Hit Count by Chris Lynch. Arlo is committed to becoming a football star, despite his mother's growing concern about concussions and their effects. Eventually Arlo must sit out because of his high "hit count," yet he is still driven by his desire to play. Lynch tells a story that will make readers think about the American love affair with contact sports, the passion and football mentality of players, along with the very real dangers caused by head trauma.

Miss Mary Reporting: The True Story of Sportswriter Mary Garber by Sue Macy, illustrated by C. F. Payne. This illustrated biography of Mary Garber, one of the first female sports journalists in American history, is fascinating for readers of all ages. In a time when African American sports were not routinely covered, Mary led the way. Today the Mary Garber Pioneer Award is presented every year in Mary's honor.

101 Questions About Muscles: To Stretch Your Mind and Flex Your Brain by F. Hickman Brynie. This author answers various questions about muscles, including "How much of human body weight is muscle?," "How does weightlifting build muscle?," and "Why do men have bigger muscles than women?"

The Playbook: 52 Rules to Aim, Shoot, and Score in This Game Called Life by Kwame Alexander. This book is illustrated with photographs by Thai Neave and is intended to provide inspiration on the court of life. Each rule contains wisdom from well-known athletes and role models such as Nelson Mandela, LeBron James, and Serena Williams. It is written for grades 5 through 7, but older students will also appreciate its themes.

Scorecasting: The Hidden Influences Behind How Sports Are Played and Games Are Won by Tobias J. Moskowitz and L. Jon Wertheim. University of Chicago behavioral economist Tobias Moskowitz teams up with veteran *Sports Illustrated* writer L. Jon Wertheim to debunk some of the most cherished truisms of sports—Does defense really win basketball games? Is there really a home field advantage? These authors reveal the hidden forces and true statistics that shape how basketball, baseball, football, and hockey games are played, won, and lost.

17 Indisputable Laws of Teamwork by John C. Maxwell. This book is about the vital principles of team building. It is written for coaches, players, teachers, students, CEOs, and volunteers. Interesting stories about others who have been empowered by these principles demonstrate attitudes for building a successful team.

Summer Ball by Mike Lupica. When 13-year-old Danny attends one of the top basketball camps with his team, he meets some surprises. For one thing, being at the top just means the competition tries that much harder to knock him off. This author has written several young adult best sellers about sports as well as columns, novels, and nonfiction books for adults.

Twelve Rounds to Glory by Charles R. Smith Jr. This is an in-depth look at Muhammad Ali's life through twelve rhyming poems with unique artwork that combines collage and water color. Readers will journey with "The Greatest" through his struggles and victories—in the ring and in life. From his fights with Sonny Liston and Joe Frazier to his battles against societal prejudice and war, Ali believed in standing up for his beliefs.

Women in Sports: 50 Fearless Athletes Who Played to Win by Rachel Ignotofsky. A richly illustrated book highlights the achievements and stories of fifty notable women athletes from the 1800s to today such as skateboarder Patti McGee and gymnast Simone Biles. The book also contains infographics on topics that women athletes will want to read: muscle anatomy, a timeline of women's participation in sports, pay and media statistics for female athletes, and influential women's teams.

Visit the companion website at
resources.corwin.com/lent-voigtDLinAction
to download this appendix.

REFERENCES

Abbott, E. (2017). *Flatland: A romance of many dimensions*. Overland Park, KS: Digireads Publishing. (Originally published 1884)

Allington, R., & Johnson, P. (2002). *Reading to learn: Lessons from exemplary fourth-grade classrooms*. New York, NY: Guilford Press.

Allington, R. L., & McGill-Franzen, A. (2003). The impact of summer reading setback on the reading achievement gap. *Phi Delta Kappa, 85*(1), 68–75.

Anderson, R. C., Wilson, P. T., & Fielding, L. G. (1988). Growth in reading and how children spend their time outside of school. *Reading Research Quarterly, 23*, 285–303: as cited in Cited in Scientific Learning. (2008, March). *Educator's briefing: Adding ten minutes of reading time dramatically changes levels of print exposure*. Oakland, CA: Author.

Applebee, A., & Langer, J. (2013). *Writing instruction that works: Proven methods for middle and high school classrooms*. New York, NY: Teachers College Press.

Armstrong, T. (2016). *The power of the adolescent brain: Strategies for teaching middle and high school students*. Alexandria, VA: ASCD.

Ashton, P. T., & Webb, R. B. (1986). *Making a difference: Teachers' sense of efficacy and student achievement*: as cited in Donohoo, J. (2017). *Collective efficacy: How educators' beliefs impact student learning*. Thousand Oaks, CA: Corwin.

Bain, R. (2006). Rounding up unusual suspects: Facing the authority hidden in history textbooks and teachers. *Teachers College Record, 108*(10), 2080–2114.

Barlin, D. (2016). Trust is missing from school-improvement efforts. *Education Week*. Retrieved from https://www.edweek.org/ew/articles/2016/10/05/trust-is-missing-from-school-improvement-efforts.html?r=1811323899&mkey=479A6068-64F7-11E8-A5E9-E518B9682667

Beghetto, R. A. (2016). *Big wins, small steps: How to lead for and with creativity*. Thousand Oaks, CA: Corwin.

Benjamin, A. (2015). *The thing about jellyfish*. Boston, MA: Little, Brown.

Berger, W. (2014). *A more beautiful question: The power of inquiry to spark breakthrough ideas*. New York, NY: Bloomsbury.

Boaler, J. (2016). *Mathematical mindsets: Unleashing students' potential through creative math, inspiring messages and innovative teaching*. San Francisco, CA: Jossey-Bass.

Booher, D. (1992). *Executive's portfolio of model speeches for all occasions*. Englewood Cliffs, NJ: Prentice Hall.

Bransford, J. D., Brown, A. L., & Cocking, R. R. (Eds.). (2000). How people learn: Brain, mind, experience, and school: as cited in Chick, N. (n.d.). *Metagognition*. Nashville, TN: Vanderbilt University. Retrieved from https://cft.vanderbilt.edu/guides-sub-pages/metacognition/

Brookhart, S. (2017). *How to give effective feedback to your students* (2nd ed.). Alexandria: VA: ASCD.

Brozo, W. G., Moorman, G., Meyer, C., & Stewart, T. (2013). Content area reading and disciplinary literacy: A case for the radical center. *Journal of Adolescent & Adult Literacy, 56*(5), 353–357.

Butler, D. L., & Winne, P. H. (1995). Feedback and self-regulated learning: A theoretical synthesis. *Review of Educational Research, 65*(3), 245–281.

Callaway, E. (2018, February 6). Geneticists unravel secrets of super-invasive crayfish. *Nature*. Retrieved from https://www.scientificamerican.com/article/geneticists-unravel-secrets-of-super-invasive-crayfish/

Cambourne, B. (1998). *The whole story: Natural learning and the acquisition of literacy in the classroom*. New York, NY: Scholastic.

Cambridge International Education Teaching and Learning Team. (n.d.). What is metacognition? Oxford, UK: Cambridge Assessment International Education. Retrieved from https://cambridge-community.org.uk/professional-development/gswmeta/index.html

Chaffee, S. (2017). "Rejecting the myth of the 'super teacher.'" Retrieved from http://www.wbur.org/cognoscenti/2017/05/02/no-perfect-teacher-sydney-chaffee

Chappuis, J. (2012, September). How am I doing? *Educational Leadership, 70*(1), 36–40.

Chick, N. (n.d.). *Metagognition*. Nashville, TN: Vanderbilt University. Retrieved from https://cft.vanderbilt.edu/guides-sub-pages/metacognition/

Cobb, C., & Blachowicz, C. (2014). *No more "look up the list" vocabulary instruction.* Portsmouth, NH: Heinemann.

Collins, A., Holum, A., & Brown, J. S. (1991). Cognitive apprenticeship: Making thinking visible. *American Educator, 15*(3), 6–11. Bath, Somerset, England: The 21st Century Learning Initiative. Retrieved from http://www.21learn.org/archive/cognitive-apprenticeship-making-thinking-visible/

Cross, D. I. (2009). Creating optimal mathematics learning environments: Combining argumentation and writing to enhance achievement. *International Journal of Science and Mathematics Education, 7*(5), 905–930.

Csikszentmihalyi, M. (1996). *Creativity: The psychology of discovery and invention.* New York, NY: HarperCollins.

Cullinan, B. E. (2000). Independent reading and school achievement. *Journal of the American Association of School Librarians, 3*. Retrieved from http://www.ala.org/aasl/sites/ala.org.aasl/files/content/aaslpubsandjournals/slr/vol3/SLMR_IndependentReading_V3.pdf

Daniels, H., & Ahmed, S. R. (2015). *Upstanders: How to engage middle school hearts and minds with inquiry.* Portsmouth, NH: Heinemann.

Darling-Hammond, L., Hyler, M. E., Gardener, M., & Espinoza, D. (2017). *Effective teacher professional development.* Washington, DC: Learning Policy Institute. Retrieved from https://learningpolicyinstitute.org/sites/default/files/product-files/Effective_Teacher_Professional_Development_REPORT.pdf

Darling-Hammond, L., Wei, R. C., Andree, A., Richardson, N., & Orphanos, S. (2009). State of the profession: Study measures status of professional development. *Journal of Staff Development, 30*, 42–44.

Datnow, A., & Hubbard, L. (2016). Teacher capacity for and beliefs about data-driven decision making: A literature review of international research. *Journal of Educational Change, 17*(1), 7–28. Retrieved from https://link.springer.com/article/10.1007/s10833-015-9264-2

Dobbs, C., Ippolito, J., Charner-Laird, M. (2016, September/October). Layering intermediate and disciplinary work: Lessons learned from a secondary social studies teacher team. *Journal of Adolescent & Adult Literacy, 60*(2), 131–139.

Donohoo, J. (2017). *Collective efficacy: How educators' beliefs impact student learning.* Thousand Oaks, CA: Corwin.

Dozier, C., Johnston, P., & Rogers, R. (2006). *Critical literacy/critical teaching.* New York, NY: Teachers College Press.

Draper, R. J. (Ed.), Broomhead, P., Jensen, A. P., Nokes, J. D., Siebert, D. (Co-Eds.). (2010). *(Re)imagining content-area literacy instruction.* New York, NY: Teachers College Press.

Draper, S. M. (2010). *Out of my mind*. New York, NY: Simon & Schuster.

DuFour, R. (2004). What is a "professional learning community"? [Electronic version]. *Educational Leadership, 61*(8), 6–11.

DuFour, R., & Reeves, D. (2015). Professional learning communities still at work (if done right). *Education Week*. Retrieved from https://www.edweek.org/tm/articles/2015/10/02/professional-learning-communities-still-work-if-done.html

Ehrenworth, M., Minor, C., Federman, M., Jennings, J., Messer, K., & McCloud, C. (2015). Those who can coach can teach. *Journal of Adolescent & Adult Literacy, 59*(1), 15–20. Retrieved from https://ila.onlinelibrary.wiley.com/doi/abs/10.1002/jaal.430

Elish-Piper, L., L'Allier, S. K., Manderino, M., & Di Domenico, P. (2016). *Collaborative coaching for disciplinary literacy: Strategies to support teachers in grades 6–12*. New York, NY: Guilford Press.

Eurydice Network. (2011).*Teaching reading in Europe: Contexts, policies and practices*. Brussels, Belgium: Education, Audiovisual and Culture Executive Agency. Retrieved from http://eacea.ec.europa.eu/education/eurydice/documents/thematic_reports/130EN_HI.pdf

Fisher, D., & Frey, N. (2017). Show & tell: A video column / modeling disciplinary thinking. *Educational Leadership: Literacy in Every Classroom, 74*(5), 82–83.

Fisher, D., Frey, N., & Hattie, J. (2016). *Visible learning for literacy*. Thousand Oaks, CA: Corwin.

Freire, P. (1998). *Teachers as cultural workers: Letters to those who dare teach*. Cambridge, MA: Westview Press.

Fullan, M. (2017). *Indelible leadership: Always leave them learning*. Thousand Oaks, CA: Corwin.

Fullan, M., & Quinn, J. (2016). *Coherence: The right drivers in action for schools, districts, and systems*. Thousand Oaks, CA: Corwin.

Gallagher, K. (2009). *Readicide: How schools are killing reading and what you can do about it*. Portsmouth, NH: Stenhouse.

Gallagher, K. (2014, April). Making the most of mentor texts. *Educational Leadership, 71*(7), 28–33. Retrieved from http://www.ascd.org/publications/educational-leadership/apr14/vol71/num07/Making-the-Most-of-Mentor-Texts.aspx

Goble, P., & Goble, R. R. (2015). *Making curriculum pop: Developing literacies in all content areas*. Golden Valley, MN: Free Spirit.

Goodwin, B. (2014, May). Keep professional learning groups small, but connected. *Educational Leadership, 71*(8), 80–82.

Goodwin, B. (2014, September). Curiosity is fleeting, but teachable. *Educational Leadership, 72*(1), 74–75.

Goodwin, B., & Hein, H. (2016, December/2017, January). What skills do students really need for a global economy? *Educational Leadership*, *74*(4), 83–84.

Gormley, W. T., Jr. (2017). *The critical advantage*. Cambridge, MA: Harvard Educational Press.

Gottfredson, L. S. (2010, Spring). Pursuing patterns, puzzles, and paradoxes. *General Psychologist*, *45*(1), 26–32.

Graves, M. F. (2006). *The vocabulary book: Learning and instruction*. New York, NY: Teachers College Press.

Graves, M. F. (2009). Vocabulary instruction in the middle grades. *Voices from the Middle*, *15*(1), 13–19.

Greenleaf, C., Cribb, G., Howlett, H., & Moore, D. W. (2010, December/2011, January). Inviting outsiders inside disciplinary literacy: An interview with Cynthia Greenleaf, Gayle Cribb, and Heather Howlett. *Journal of Adolescent & Adult Literacy*, *54*(4), 291–293.

Gruber, M. J., Gelman, B. D., & Ranganath, C. (2014). States of curiosity modulate hippocampus-dependent learning via the dopaminergic circuit. *Neuron*, *84*(2), 486–496.

Gunel, M., Hand, B., & Prain, V. (2007). Writing for learning in science: A secondary analysis of six studies. *International Journal of Science and Mathematics Education*, *5*(4), 615–637. doi:10.1007/s10763-007-9082-y

Hargreaves, A., & Boyle, A. (2015, February). Uplifting leadership. *Educational Leadership*, *72*(5), 42–47.

Hargreaves, A., Earl, L., & Ryan, J. (2003). *Schooling for change: Reinventing education for early adolescents*. London, UK: Taylor & Francis.

Hargreaves, A., & Fullan, M. (2012). *Professional capital: Transforming teaching in every school*. New York, NY: Teachers College Press.

Hart, J. (2017, August 9). The big lesson from the world's best school system? Trust your teachers. *The Guardian*. Retrieved from https://www.theguardian.com/teacher-network/2017/aug/09/worlds-best-school-system-trust-teachers-education-finland

Hattie, J. (2012, September). Know thy impact. *Educational Leadership: Feedback for Learning*, *70*(1), 18–23.

Hattie, J. (2016). 3rd Annual Visible Learning Conference (subtitled Mindframes and Maximizers) held in Washington, DC on Monday, July 11th 2016: as cited in Donohoo, J. (2017). *Collective efficacy: How educators' beliefs impact student learning*. Thousand Oaks, CA: Corwin.

Hattie, J. (2017). Hattie ranking: 252 influences and effect sizes related to student achievement. Retrieved from https://visible-learning.org/hattie-ranking-influences-effect-sizes-learning-achievement/

Hicks, T., & Turner, K. H. (2017). *Argument in the real world: Teaching adolescents to read and write digital texts*. Portsmouth, NH: Heinemann.

Hiebert, E. H. (2014). The forgotten reading proficiency: Stamina in silent reading. In E. H. Hiebert (Ed.), Stamina, silent reading, & the Common Core State Standards: as cited in Springer, T., Wilson, T., & Dole, J. (Dec. 2014, Jan. 2015). Ready or not: Recognizing and preparing college-ready students. *Journal of Adolescent & Adult Literacy*, *58*(4), 299–307.

Houston, K. (2010). 10 ways to think like a mathematician [Booklet]. Retrieved from http://www.kevinhouston.net/pdf/10ways.pdf

International Literacy Association. (2017). *Content area and disciplinary literacy: Strategies and frameworks* [Literacy Leadership Brief]. Newark, DE: Author.

International Reading Association. (2014). Leisure reading: A joint position statement of the International Reading Association, the Canadian Children's Book Center, and the National Council of Teachers of English. Newark, DE: Author. Retrieved from http://www.literacyworldwide.org/docs/default-source/where-we-stand/leisure-reading-position-statement.pdf

Irwin, N. (2007, June 2). We may be closer to full employment than it seemed. That's bad news. *New York Times*. Retrieved from https://www.nytimes.com/2017/06/02/upshot/we-may-be-closer-to-full-employment-than-it-seemed-thats-bad-news.html

Ivey, G., & Fisher, D. (2006). *Creating literacy-rich schools for adolescents*. Alexandria, VA: ASCD.

Jacobs, V. A. (2008). Adolescent literacy: Putting the crisis in context. *Harvard Educational Review*, *78*(1), 7–39.

Joyce, B., & Showers, B. (1980). Improving inservice training: The message of research. *Educational Leadership*, *37*(5), 379–385: as cited in Joyce, B., & Showers, B. (1996). The evolution of peer coaching. *Educational Leadership*, *53*(6), 12–16.

Joyce, B., & Showers, B. (2002). Student achievement through staff development (3rd ed.): cited in Goodwin, B. (2014, May). Keep professional learning groups small, but connected. *Educational Leadership*, *71*(8), 80–82.

Kame'enui, E., & Baumann, J. (2012). *Vocabulary instruction research to practice* (2nd ed.). New York, NY: Guilford Press.

Kanter, R. M. (2004). *Confidence*. New York, NY: Three Rivers Press.

Kashdan, T., & Steger. M. (2007). Curiosity and pathways to well-being and meaning in life: Traits, states, and everyday behaviors. *Motivation and Emotion*, *31*(3), 159–173.

Kittle, P. (2013). *Book love: Developing depth, stamina, and passion in adolescent reading*. Portsmouth, NH: Heinemann.

Kolodner, J. L. (2002). Facilitating the learning of design practices: Lessons learned from an inquiry into science education. *Journal of Industrial Teacher Education*, *39*(3), 9–40.

Krashen, S. (2004). *The power of reading: Insights from research* (2nd ed.). Portsmouth, NH: Heinemann.

Lee, V., Smith, J., & Croninger, R. (1995, Fall). Another look at high school restricting. More evidence that it improves student achievement and more insight into why. *Issues in Restructuring Schools, 9*, 1–10.

Lent, R. (2007). *Literacy learning communities: A guide for creating sustainable change in secondary schools.* Portsmouth, NH: Heinemann.

Lent, R. C. (2016). *This is disciplinary literacy: Reading, writing, thinking, and doing . . . content area by content area.* Thousand Oaks, CA: Corwin.

Lent, R. C., & Gilmore, B. (2013). *Common core CPR: What about the adolescents who struggle . . . or just don't care?* Thousand Oaks, CA: Corwin.

Luke, A. (2001). Foreword. In E. B. Moje & D. G. O'Brien (Eds.), Constructions of literacy: Studies of teaching and learning in and out of secondary schools (pp. ix–xii): as cited in Moje, E. (2008). Foregrounding the disciplines in secondary literacy teaching and learning: A call for change. *Journal of Adolescent & Adult Literacy, 52*(2), 96–107.

Marzano, R. J. (2004). *Building background knowledge for academic achievement: Research on what works in schools.* Alexandria, VA: ASCD.

McAllum, R. (2014). Reciprocal teaching: Critical reflection on practice. *Kairaranga, 15*(1), 26–35.

McKenna, M. C., Conradi, K., Lawrence, C., Jang, B. G., & Meyer, J. P. (2012). Reading attitudes of middle school students: Results of a U.S. survey. *Reading Research Quarterly, 47*(3), 283–306. doi:10.1002/rrq.021

Meek, A. (1991). On thinking about teaching: A conversation with Eleanor Duckworth. *Educational Leadership, 48*(6), 30–34.

Metsisto, D. (2005). Reading in the mathematics classroom. In J. M. Kenney (Ed.), *Literacy strategies for improving mathematical instruction.* Alexandria, VA: ASCD.

Michalko, M. (2001). *Cracking creativity: The secrets of creative genius.* Berkeley, CA: Ten Speed Press.

Moje, E. (2008). Foregrounding the disciplines in secondary literacy teaching and learning: A call for change. *Journal of Adolescent & Adult Literacy, 52*(2), 96–107.

Moje, E. B., & Sutherland, L. M. (2003). The future of middle school literacy education. *English Education, 35*(2), 149–164.

Monte-Sano, C., & Miles, D. (2014). Toward disciplinary reading and writing in history. In P. Smagorinsky (Ed.), *Teaching dilemmas & solutions in content literacy* (pp. 29–52). Thousand Oaks, CA: Corwin.

Moore, D. W., Bean, T. W., Birdyshaw, D., & Rycik, J. A. (1999). *Adolescent literacy: A position statement for the Commission on Adolescent Literacy of the International Reading Association.* Newark, DE: International Reading Association.

Morgan, J. (2013). "12 habits of highly collaborative organizations." *Forbes.* Retrieved from https://www.forbes.com/sites/jacobmorgan/2013/07/30/the-12-habits-of-highly-collaborative-organizations/

Nagy, W., Anderson, R., & Herman, P. (1987). Learning word meanings from context during normal reading. *American Educational Research Journal, 24,* 237–270.

Nagy, W., Herman, P., & Anderson, R. (1985). Learning words from context. *Reading Research Quarterly, 17,* 233–255.

National Assessment of Educational Progress. (n.d.). *Average reading score for fourth-grade students not significantly different in comparison to 2013; eighth-grade students score lower than 2013.* Washington, DC: Author. Retrieved from https://www.nationsreportcard.gov/reading_math_2015/#reading?grade= 4

National Center for Education Statistics. (n.d.). *Reading literacy: Average scores.* Washington, DC: Author. Retrieved from https://nces.ed.gov/surveys/pisa/pisa2015/pisa2015highlights_4.asp

The National Commission on Writing in America's Schools and Colleges. (2003). *The neglected "R": The need for a writing revolution.* Berkeley, CA: Author. Retrieved from https://www.nwp.org/cs/public/print/resource/2523

The National Commission on Writing in America's Schools and Colleges. (2005). *Writing: A powerful message from state government.* Berkeley, CA: Author. Retrieved from https://www.nwp.org/cs/public/print/resource/2541

National Council for the Social Studies. (2016). Media literacy. *Social Education, 80*(3), 183–185.

Newman, F., & Associates. (1996). Authentic achievement: Restructuring of schools for intellectual quality: as cited in Wilhelm, J. (2016, March). Working toward conscious competence: The power of inquiry for teachers and learners. *Voices from the Middle, 23*(3), 58–60.

Newman, F., & Wehlage, G. (1995). Successful school restructuring: A report to the public and educators by the Center on Organization and Restructuring of Schools: as cited in Wilhelm, J. (2016, March). Working toward conscious competence: The power of inquiry for teachers and learners. *Voices from the Middle, 23*(3), 58–60.

O'Brien, D. G., Moje, E. B., & Stewart, R. A. (2001). Exploring the context of secondary literacy: Literacy in people's everyday school lives. In E. B. Moje & D. G. O'Brien (Eds.), Constructions of literacy: Studies of teaching and learning in and out of secondary classrooms (pp. 27–48): as cited in Moje, E. (2008). Foregrounding the disciplines in secondary literacy teaching and learning: A call for change. *Journal of Adolescent & Adult Literacy, 52*(2), 96–107.

OECD. (2010). *PISA 2009 results: Learning to learn—Student engagement, strategies and practices* (Vol. 3). Paris, France: Author. Retrieved from doi:10.1787/9789264083943-en

OECD. (2011, October). *PISA in focus*. Paris, France: Author. Retrieved from http://www.oecd.org/pisa/pisaproducts/pisainfocus/48910490.pdf

Ostroff, W. L. (2016). *Cultivating curiosity in K–12 classrooms: How to promote and sustain deep learning*. Alexandria, VA: ASCD.

Palincsar, A. S., & Brown, A. L. (1984). Reciprocal teaching of comprehension-fostering and comprehension-monitoring activities. *Cognition and Instruction, 1*(2), 117–175. Retrieved from https://www.scribd.com/document/243849260/Reciprocal-Teaching-of-Comprehension-Brown

Palmisano, M. J. (2013). *Taking inquiry to scale: An alternative to traditional approaches to education reform*. Washington, DC: National Council of Teachers of English.

Park, L. S. (2010). *A long walk to water*. Boston, MA: Houghton Mifflin.

Paul, A. M. (2013, March 18). Four ways to give good feedback. *Time*. Retrieved from http://ideas.time.com/2013/03/18/four-ways-to-give-good-feedback/

Perle, M., Grigg, W., & Donahue, P. (2005). *The nation's report card: Reading 2005 (NCES-2006-451)*. Washington, DC: U.S. Department of Education, National Center for Education Statistics.

Pink, D. H. (2012). *Drive: The surprising truth about what motivates us*. New York, NY: Riverhead Books.

Porter, M. K., & Masingila, J. O. (2000). Examining the Effects on Conceptual and Procedural Knowledge in Calculus. *Educational Studies in Mathematics, 42*(2), 165–177. Retrieved from http://www.jstor.org/stable/3483283

Puig, E. A., & Froelich, K. S. (2011). *The literacy coach: Guiding in the right direction*. Saddle River, NJ: Pearson Education.

Rainer, M. R. (1993). *Letters to a young poet*. New York, NY: W. W. Norton & Company. (Originally published 1934)

Rainey, E., & Moje, E. B. (2012). Building insider knowledge: Teaching students to read, write, and think within ELA and across the disciplines. *English Education, 45*(1), 71–90.

Reeves, D. (2010). *Transforming professional development into student results*. Alexandria, VA: ASCD.

Reilly, J. (2015). *Stick man: The story of Emmett Chapman and the instrument he created.* Calgary, Alberta, Canada: Two Handed Press.

Reio, T. G., & Wiswell, A. (2000). Field investigation of the relationship among adult curiosity, workplace learning, and job performance. *Human Resource Development Quarterly, 11*(1), 5–30.

Richardson, W. (2016, December / 2017, January). Getting schools ready for the world. *Educational Leadership, 74*(4), 25–29.

Ritchhart, R. (2015). *Creating cultures of thinking: The 8 forces we must master to truly transform our schools.* New York, NY: John Wiley & Sons.

Rivero, V. (2010, December 10). Interview: Doing the math with Conrad Wolfram. Retrieved from https://edtechdigest.com/2010/12/10/interview-doing-the-math-with-conrad-wolfram/

Robbins, P. (1991). *How to plan and implement a peer coaching program.* Alexandria, VA: ASCD.

Roberts, T., & Billings, L. (2012). *Teaching critical thinking: Using seminars for 21st century literacy.* New York, NY: Routledge.

Robinson, V. M. J., Lloyd, C. A., & Rowe, K. J. (2008). The impact of leadership on student outcomes: An analysis of the different effects of leadership types: as cited in Fullan, M., & Quinn, J. (2016). *Coherence: The right drivers in action for schools, districts, and systems.* Thousand Oaks, CA: Corwin.

Rodgers, A., & Rodgers, E. M. (2007). *The effective literacy coach: Using inquiry to support teaching & learning.* New York, NY: Teachers College Press.

Rosenberg, E. (2017, November 28). Andrew Jackson was called "Indian killer." Trump honored Navajos in front of his portrait. *The Washington Post.* Retrieved from https://www.washingtonpost.com/news/retropolis/wp/2017/11/28/andrew-jackson-was-called-indian-killer-trump-honored-navajos-in-front-of-his-portrait/?utm_term=.163a41fc8863

Rothstein, D., & Santana, L. (2011). *Make just one change: Teach students to ask their own questions.* Cambridge, MA: Harvard Education Press.

Salen, K. (2008). Toward an ecology of gaming. In K. Salen (Ed.), *The ecology of games: Connecting youth, games, and learning* (pp. 1–20). The John D. and Catherine T. MacArthur Foundation Series on Digital Media and Learning. Cambridge, MA: MIT Press. doi:10.1162/dmal.9780262693646.001

Sawyer, K. (2017). *Group genius: The creative power of collaboration.* New York, NY: Basic Books.

Scarborough, H. S. (2001). Connecting early language and literacy to later reading (dis)abilities: Evidence, theory and practice. In S. B. Neuman & D. K. Dickinson (Eds.), *Handbook of early literacy research* (Vol. 1, pp. 97–110). New York, NY: Guilford Press.

Scardamalia, M., Bereiter, C., & Steinbach. R. (1984). Teachability of reflective processes in written composition. *Cognitive Science, 8,* 173–190.

Schoenfeld, A. H. (1983). Problem solving in the mathematics curriculum: A report, recommendation and an annotated bibliography. *Mathematical Association of America Notes*, No. 1.

Schoenfeld, A. H. (1985). *Mathematical problem solving*. Orlando, FL: Academic Press.

Schoenfeld, A. H. (1991). On mathematics as sense-making: An informal attack on the unfortunate divorce of formal and informal mathematics. In J. F. Voss, D. N. Perkins, & J. W. Segal (Eds.), *Informal reasoning and education* (pp. 311–343). Hillsdale, NJ: Erlbaum.

Scieszka, J., & Smith, L. (1995). *Math curse*. New York, NY: Viking.

Shanahan, T., & Shanahan, C. (2008). Teaching disciplinary literacy to adolescents: Rethinking content area literacy. *Harvard Educational Review: Adolescent Literacy, 78*(1), 40–59.

Shanahan, T., & Shanahan, C. (2012). What is disciplinary literacy and why does it matter? *Topics in Language Disorders, 32*(1), 7–18.

Shanahan, T., & Shanahan, C. (2015). Disciplinary literacy comes to middle school. *Voices from the Middle, 22*(3), 10–13.

Shanahan, T., & Shanahan, C. (2017). Disciplinary literacy: Just the FAQs. *Educational Leadership: Literacy in Every Classroom, 74*(5), 18–22.

Shaw, G. (2000). *Keeping Mozart in mind*. San Diego, CA: Academic Press.

Sherman, C. U. (2015). *Her walk*. Bloomington, IN: Authorhouse.

Showers, B., & Joyce, B. (1996). The evolution of peer coaching. *Educational Leadership, 53*(6), 12–16.

Simmons, D. C., & Kameenui, E. J. (Eds.). (1998). *What reading research tells us about children with diverse learning needs: Bases and basics*. Mahwah, NJ: Erlbaum.

Simon, H. A. (1996). Observations on the sciences of science learning. *Journal of Applied Developmental Psychology, 21*(1), 115–121: as cited in Salen, K. (2008). Toward an ecology of gaming. In K. Salen (Ed.), *The ecology of games: Connecting youth, games, and learning* (pp. 1–20). The John D. and Catherine T. MacArthur Foundation Series on Digital Media and Learning. Cambridge, MA: MIT Press. doi:10.1162/ dmal.9780262693646.001

Sizer, T. (1984). *Horace's compromise: The dilemma of the American high school*. New York, NY: Houghton Mifflin.

Sparks, D. (2002). *Designing powerful professional development for teachers and principals*. Oxford, OH: National Staff Development Council.

Springer, S. E., Wilson, T. J., & Dole, J. A. (2014, December/2015, January). Ready or not: Recognizing and preparing college-ready students. *Journal of Adolescent & Adult Literacy, 53*(4), 299–307.

Stanford History Education Group. (n.d.). *Historical thinking chart*. Stanford, CA: Authors.

Swan, G. E., & Carmelli, D. (1996). Curiosity and mortality in aging adults: A 5-year follow-up of the Western Collaborative Group Study. *Psychology and Aging, 11*, 449–454.

Tischhauser, K. S. (2015, Fall). The importance of writing fiction in the classroom: Simulation and thinking. *Illinois Reading Council Journal, 43*(4), 20–31.

Tjan, A. (2017). *Good people: The only leadership decision that really matters.* New York, NY: Penguin.

Tomlinson, C. A. (2015, April). One to grow on: Communication that powers leadership. *Educational Leadership, 72*(7), 90–91.

Towles, A. (2016). *A gentleman in Moscow.* New York, NY: Viking.

Tschannen-Moran, M. (2004). *Trust matters: Leadership for successful schools.* San Francisco, CA: Jossey-Bass.

Tschannen-Moran, M., & Barr, M. (2004). Fostering student learning: The relationship of collective teacher efficacy and student achievement. *Leadership and Policy in Schools, 3*(3), 189–209.

Vescio, V., Ross, D., & Adams, A. (2008). A review of research on the impact of professional learning communities on teaching practice and student learning. *Teaching and Teacher Education, 24*(1), 80–91. doi:10.1016/j.tate.2007.01.004

Von Stumm, S., Hell, B., & Chamorro-Premuzic, T. (2011). The hungry mind: Intellectual curiosity is the third pillar of academic performance. *Perspectives on Psychological Science, 6*(6), 574–588: as cited in Goodwin, B. (2014, September). Curiosity is fleeting, but teachable. *Educational Leadership, 72*(1), 74–75.

Wagner, T., & Dintersmith, T. (2015). *Most likely to succeed: Preparing our kids for the innovation era.* New York, NY: Scribner.

Wai, J. (2013). How to think like a scientist: Learn these techniques to make a scientific discovery. *Psychology Today.* Retrieved from https://www.psychologytoday.com/blog/finding-the-next-einstein/201307/how-think-scientist

Wein, E. (2012). *Code name Verity.* New York, NY: Hyperion.

Wiggins, G. (2012, September). Seven keys to effective feedback. *Educational Leadership, 70*(1), 10–16.

Wilder, P., & Herro, D. (2016). Collaborative symbiosis and responsive disciplinary literacy teaching. *Journal of Adolescent & Adult Literacy, 59*(5), 539–549.

Wilhelm, J. (2016, March). Working toward conscious competence: The power of inquiry for teachers and learners. *Voices from the Middle, 23*(3), 58–60.

Wilhelm, J. D., & Smith, M. W. (2016). The power of pleasure reading: What we can learn from the secret reading lives of teens. *English Journal, 105*(6), 25–30. Retrieved from http://www.ncte.org/library/NCTEFiles/Resources/Journals/EJ/1056-jul2016/EJ1056Power.pdf

Wilhelm, J. D., & Smith, M. W. (2017). *Diving deep into nonfiction: Transferable tools for reading any nonfiction text*. Thousand Oaks, CA: Corwin.

William, D. (2012). Feedback: Part of a system. *Educational Leadership, 70*(1), 30–34.

Willis, J. (2008). *Teaching the brain to read: Strategies for improving fluency, vocabulary, and comprehension*. Alexandria, VA: ASCD.

Wisconsin Department of Public Instruction. (n.d.). *Literacy in all subjects*. Madison, WI: Author. Retrieved from https://dpi.wi.gov/standards/literacy-all-subjects

Wolf, P. (2001). *Brain matters: Translating research into classroom practice*. Alexandria, VA: ASCD.

INDEX

A SAGE Publishing Company

CORWIN HAS ONE MISSION: to enhance education through intentional professional learning.

We build long-term relationships with our authors, educators, clients, and associations who partner with us to develop and continuously improve the best evidence-based practices that establish and support lifelong learning.

Because...
ALL TEACHERS ARE LEADERS

Do you have a minute? Of course not. That's why at Corwin Literacy we have put together a collection of just-in-time, classroom-tested, practical resources from trusted experts that allow you to quickly find the information you need when you need it.

RELEAH COSSETT LENT

This Is Disciplinary Literacy helps content-area teachers put into action the key literacies of their specialties—taking students from superficial understanding to deep content expertise.

JEFFREY D. WILHELM AND MICHAEL W. SMITH

Through classroom-tested lessons and compelling short excerpts, *Diving Deep Into Nonfiction* helps students read well by noticing the rules and conventions of nonfiction texts.

LAURA ROBB

In *Read, Talk, Write*, Laura Robb brings her trademark practicality with 35 lessons and reproducibles that ensure your students succeed as well as love what they do.

GRETCHEN BERNABEI AND JENNIFER KOPPE

With 50 short texts written by famous individuals driven by "an itch" to say something, this book provides students with mentor texts to express their own thoughts.

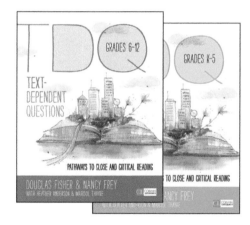

DOUGLAS FISHER, NANCY FREY, HEATHER ANDERSON, AND MARISOL THAYRE

Learn the best ways to use text-dependent questions as scaffolds during close reading and discover the big understandings they yield. Includes illustrative video, texts and questions, cross-curricular examples, and online facilitator's guides.

MICHAEL W. SMITH AND JON-PHILIP IMBRENDA

Forming effective arguments is essential to students' success in academics and life. This book's engaging lessons offer an innovative approach to teaching this critical, transferable skill.

To order your copies, visit corwin.com/literacy

CORWIN Literacy